Communications in Computer and Information Science 2636

Series Editors

Rationale

The CCIS series is devoted to the publication of proceedings of computer science conferences. Its aim is to efficiently disseminate original research results in informatics in printed and electronic form. While the focus is on publication of peer-reviewed full papers presenting mature work, inclusion of reviewed short papers reporting on work in progress is welcome, too. Besides globally relevant meetings with internationally representative program committees guaranteeing a strict peer-reviewing and paper selection process, conferences run by societies or of high regional or national relevance are also considered for publication.

Topics

The topical scope of CCIS spans the entire spectrum of informatics ranging from foundational topics in the theory of computing to information and communications science and technology and a broad variety of interdisciplinary application fields.

Information for Volume Editors and Authors

Publication in CCIS is free of charge. No royalties are paid, however, we offer registered conference participants temporary free access to the online version of the conference proceedings on SpringerLink (http://link.springer.com) by means of an http referrer from the conference website and/or a number of complimentary printed copies, as specified in the official acceptance email of the event.

CCIS proceedings can be published in time for distribution at conferences or as post-proceedings, and delivered in the form of printed books and/or electronically as USBs and/or e-content licenses for accessing proceedings at SpringerLink. Furthermore, CCIS proceedings are included in the CCIS electronic book series hosted in the SpringerLink digital library at http://link.springer.com/bookseries/7899. Conferences publishing in CCIS are allowed to use our online conference service (Meteor) for managing the whole proceedings lifecycle (from submission and reviewing to preparing for publication) free of charge.

Publication process

The language of publication is exclusively English. Authors publishing in CCIS have to sign the Springer CCIS copyright transfer form, however, they are free to use their material published in CCIS for substantially changed, more elaborate subsequent publications elsewhere. For the preparation of the camera-ready papers/files, authors have to strictly adhere to the Springer CCIS Authors' Instructions and are strongly encouraged to use the CCIS LaTeX style files or templates.

Abstracting/Indexing

CCIS is abstracted/indexed in DBLP, Google Scholar, EI-Compendex, Mathematical Reviews, SCImago, Scopus. CCIS volumes are also submitted for the inclusion in ISI Proceedings.

How to start

To start the evaluation of your proposal for inclusion in the CCIS series, please send an e-mail to ccis@springer.com

Sanju Tiwari · Tasneem Bano · M. A. Jabbar ·
Fernando Ortiz-Rodriguez · Azanzi Jiomekong
Editors

Applied Machine Learning and Data Analytics

7th International Conference, AMLDA 2024
Shamshabad, India, December 20–21, 2024
Revised Selected Papers

Editors
Sanju Tiwari
Sharda University
Greater Noida, Uttar Pradesh, India

M. A. Jabbar
Vardhaman College of Engineering
Hyderabad, Telangana, India

Azanzi Jiomekong
University of Yaounde
Cameroon, South Africa

Tasneem Bano
Muffakham Jah College of Engineering
and Technology
Telangana, Telangana, India

Fernando Ortiz-Rodriguez
Universidad Autonoma de Tamaulipas
Tamaulipas, Mexico

ISSN 1865-0929 ISSN 1865-0937 (electronic)
Communications in Computer and Information Science
ISBN 978-3-032-18292-0 ISBN 978-3-032-18293-7 (eBook)
https://doi.org/10.1007/978-3-032-18293-7

This Springer imprint is published by the registered company Springer Nature Switzerland AG
The registered company address is: Gewerbestrasse 11, 6330 Cham, Switzerland

Preface

This volume comprises the principal proceedings of the 7th International Conference on Applied Machine Learning and Data Analytics (AMLDA 2024). AMLDA serves as an annual forum for the discussion of the latest scientific findings and technological advancements in the field of Machine Learning.

The International Conference on Applied Machine Learning and Data Analytics is a leading forum in the field of artificial intelligence. AMLDA 2024 showcased pioneering research across all dimensions of machine learning, as well as in significant application domains such as healthcare and medical imaging informatics, biometrics, forensics, precision agriculture, risk management, robotics, and satellite imaging.

The AMLDA 2024 conference was attended by a diverse group of participants, including academic and industrial researchers and engineers, as well as graduate students and postdoctoral researchers. This annual event serves as a forum for the exchange of knowledge regarding the latest scientific and technological developments in the domain of applied machine learning and data analytics.

The primary scientific agenda of the conference included 11 papers: 10 comprehensive research papers and one brief research paper, selected from a total of 44 reviewed submissions. This selection corresponds to an acceptance rate of 25% for the submitted research papers. The review process was double-blind, and submissions received three reviews each, on average.

The General and Program Committee chairs extend their gratitude to all individuals who contributed to the success of AMLDA 2024. We express our appreciation to the co-chairs of the main event and the more than 50 reviewers who ensured a rigorous review process, resulting in an exemplary scientific program.

We express our gratitude for the generous support provided by the local chairs and individuals from Vardhaman College of Engineering, India, as well as from Springer for their ongoing assistance. Additionally, we extend our appreciation to our sponsors, the community, and the webmaster for their indispensable contributions to this edition of AMLDA 2024. The editors wish to conclude the preface by warmly acknowledging our supporting keynote speakers, the program committee for their diligent commitment to conducting reviews, and, finally, our dedicated authors who contributed to making this event truly international.

November 2024

Sanju Tiwari
Tasneem Bano Rehman
M. A. Jabbar
Fernando Ortiz-Rodriguez
Fidel Jiomekong

Preface

Organization

General Chairs

Sanju Tiwari	Sharda University, Greater Noida, India
Tasneem Bano Rehman	Muffakham Jah College of Engineering and Technology, India
M. A. Jabbar	Vardhaman College of Engineering, India
Fernando Ortiz Rodriguez	Universidad Autónoma de Tamaulipas, Mexico
Fidel Jiomekong	University of Yaoundé, Cameroon

Program Chairs

Sven Groppe	Universität zu Lübeck, Germany
Shishir Kumar Shandilya	VIT Bhopal University, India
José Melchor Medina-Quintero	Universidad Autónoma de Tamaulipas, Mexico
Andries Engelbrecht	University of Stellenbosch, South Africa

Publicity Chairs

P. Sivakumara	University of Malaya, Malaysia
Vania V. Estrela	Universidade Federal Fluminense, Brazil
Patience Usoro Usip	University of Uyo, Nigeria

Workshop Chairs

Yusniel Hidalgo Delgado	Universidad de las Ciencias Informáticas, Cuba
Shikha Mehta	JIIT Noida, India
C. A. Dhawale	P. R. Pote Patil College of Engineering and Management, India

Special Session Chairs

Tanima Datta	IIT BHU, India
David Hicks	Texas A & M University Kingsville, USA

Antonio De Nicola	ENEA, Italy
Patrice Boursier	International Medical University, Malaysia

Tutorial Chairs

Hari Prabhat Gupta	IIT BHU, India
Ayush Goyal	Texas A & M University Kingsville, USA

Program Committee

Abhishek Hazra	NUS, Singapore
Anand Panchbhai	Logy.AI, India
Ajit Kumar	Soongsil University, South Korea
Beyzanur Cayir	Necmettin Erbakan University, Turkey
Bidush Kumar Sahoo	G.I.E.T. University, India
Carlos Pereira	ISEC, Portugal
Debajyoty Banik	Anurag University, India
Deepak Dharrao	Symbiosis Institute of Technology, Pune, India
Fatima Zahra Amara	University of Khenchela, Algeria
Fernando Ortiz-Rodriguez	Universidad Autónoma de Tamaulipas, Mexico
František Zbořil	Brno University of Technology, Czech Republic
Gloria Cerasela Crisan	Vasile Alecsandri University of Bacău, Romania
Gourav Shrivastava	SAGE University, India
Ifiok James Udo	University of Uyo, Nigeria
Jolanta Mizera-Pietraszko	Military University of Land Forces, Poland
José Everardo B. Maia	Universidade Estadual do Ceará, Brazil
Joseph A. Brown	Innopolis University, Russia
Jude Hemanth	Karunya University, India
Karima Saidi	Batna University, Algeria
Khushbu Doulani	IIIT Lucknow, India
Kusum Lata	Sharda University, India
Manoj Kumar	Directorate of Technical Education & Training, Odisha, India
M. A. Jabbar	Vardhaman College of Engineering, India
Meenakshi Srivastava	Amity University, Lucknow, India
Meriem Djezzar	University of Khenchela, Algeria
Mounir Hemam	University of Khenchela, Algeria
Müge Oluçoğlu	Dokuz Eylül University, Turkey
Namrata Nagpal	Amity University, Lucknow, India
N. D. Patel	VIT Bhopal, India

Neeranjan Chitare	Northumbria University, UK
Onur Dogan	İzmir Bakırçay University, Turkey
Patience U. Usip	University of Uyo, Nigeria
Radu-Emil Precup	Politehnica University of Timisoara, Romania
Ritu Tanwar	NIT Uttarakhand, India
Ronald O. Ojino	Co-operative University of Kenya, Kenya
Sachinandan Mohanty	KIIT University, India
Sashikala Mishra	Symbiosis International University, India
Shankru Guggari	KLE Technological University, India
Shishir Kumar Shandilya	VIT Bhopal University, India
Sven Groppe	Universität zu Lübeck, Germany
Tasneem Bano Rehman	Muffakham Jah College of Engineering and Technology, India
Sanju Tiwari	Sharda University, India
Sourav Banerjee	Kalyani Government Engineering College, India
Tanusree Dutta	Vardhaman College of Engineering, India
Udit Chawla	University of Engineering & Management, Kolkata, India
Youssef Mourdi	Cadi Ayyad University, Morocco
Yusniel Hidalgo Delgado	Universidad de las Ciencias Informáticas, Cuba

Contents

Analyzing COVID-19 Discourse on Twitter in Argentina: Trends, Sentiments, and Key Themes

Anabel Pineda-Briseño[1(✉)], Josimar Chire-Saire[2], and Jimy Frank Oblitas[3]

[1] TecNM/Instituto Tecnológico de Matamoros, Matamoros, Tamaulipas, Mexico
anabel.pb@matamoros.tecnm.mx
[2] University of São Paulo (USP), São Carlos, Brazil
jecs89@usp.br
[3] Universidad Privada del Norte, Trujillo, Peru
jimy.oblitas@upn.edu.pe

Abstract. In the era of the COVID-19 pandemic, social media platforms have become essential conduits for disseminating information. Twitter, with its real-time nature and global reach, has played a pivotal role in facilitating this dynamic. This research paper delves into the multi-faceted landscape of Twitter conversations surrounding the pandemic in Argentina from its onset in 2020 through 2023. Utilizing advanced Natural Language Processing (NLP) and sentiment analysis techniques, we examine the emotional tone and evolving topics of discussion among the Argentine Twitter community. Our findings reveal significant trends in public sentiment and highlight key moments that influenced the discourse. By analyzing over 1.2 million Spanish-language tweets, this study provides insights into the public's reaction to major epidemiological events, government interventions, and societal changes. The results underscore the importance of social media as a barometer for public opinion and its impact on public health communication strategies. This work contributes to the broader understanding of social media's role in crisis management and offers valuable lessons for future health emergencies.

Keywords: COVID-19 · Argentina · Natural Language Processing · Sentiment Analysis · Topic Modeling · Social Media · Public Health

1 Introduction

In the contemporary era of technology, social media platforms have become significant spaces where individuals participate in dialogues, express viewpoints, and distribute information on an international level. Twitter, a microblogging platform, is particularly noteworthy among these platforms for enabling instantaneous communication and fostering the interchange of thoughts among users worldwide. Due to its extensive user community and the wide array of subjects deliberated, Twitter has evolved into a valuable data source for researchers interested in comprehending public sentiment, monitoring patterns, and scrutinizing societal behaviors.

S. Tiwari et al. (Eds.): AMLDA 2024, CCIS 2636, pp. 1–15, 2026.
https://doi.org/10.1007/978-3-032-18293-7_1

In the context of Argentina, Twitter serves as a window into the collective consciousness of its populace, offering insights into the prevailing sentiments, concerns, and interests of Argentinean society. By examining Twitter data spanning multiple years, this research aims to delve into the nuances of public discourse within the Argentinean context. Through the application of advanced analytical techniques such as topic analysis and sentiment analysis, this study seeks to extract meaningful patterns, identify key themes, and uncover underlying dynamics that shape conversations on the platform.

The main contribution of this study is to enhance comprehension regarding the influence of Twitter on shaping public discourse and mirroring societal patterns in Argentina. Through the examination of Twitter data spanning from 2020 to 2023, the research illuminates the shifting landscape of public sentiment, chronicles the development of emotional reactions over time, and underscores pivotal conversation topics. This research notably broadens the constrained analysis of Spanish-language data, thereby enriching the understanding of the impact of social media in the era of digitalization.

2 Literature Review

Since the onset of the COVID-19 pandemic, there has been a significant body of research focused on comprehending public discussions and viewpoints related to the crisis through the analysis of sentiments conveyed on various social media platforms, notably Twitter. Several scholarly inquiries have delved into sentiment assessment employing methodologies such as lexicon-centric approaches [1], machine learning algorithms [13], and deep learning classifiers [10, 13]. These investigations have scrutinized the fluctuations in sentiment, encompassing temporal changes and reactions to particular events linked to the pandemic. Additionally, sentiment analysis has been utilized in dissecting specific elements of the COVID-19 dialogue, for instance, conversations regarding vaccines [31] and official preventative strategies [2]. Moreover, researchers have examined the variations in sentiment across different languages and regions, such as nations where Spanish is spoken [5, 12, 24] and specific cultural groups [11]. Additionally, there have been investigations into the relationship between language usage on social networking platforms during the global health crisis and its impact on psychological well-being [26]. This body of work emphasizes the significance of comprehending sentiment dynamics in public discourse amid crises and their repercussions on psychological well-being. Nonetheless, a majority of these investigations concentrate on tweets in the English language or particular geographical areas, despite offering valuable perspectives into sentiment dynamics throughout the COVID-19 crisis. A conspicuous deficiency of studies exists regarding sentiment analysis of tweets in Spanish covering the complete timeline of the pandemic, from its commencement to its formal conclusion. This gap holds notable importance considering the substantial Spanish-speaking communities in areas greatly impacted by the pandemic, such as Latin America. This study endeavors to fill this void through the analysis of sentiment in tweets related to COVID-19 from

Argentina. Through a thorough analytical examination of Spanish tweets over the course of the pandemic, the research aims to present a comprehensive understanding of the fluctuations in sentiment in Argentina. Furthermore, this study adds to the broader conversation on sentiment analysis in emergency situations by providing perspectives from a Spanish-speaking standpoint, which is essential for guiding public health interventions and communication strategies in various linguistic and cultural settings.

3 Data and Methods

3.1 Data Collection y Text Pre-Processing

Data Collection. For this study, 1,286,985 Spanish-language tweets were gathered between January 1, 2020, and April 30, 2023. For this data retrieval assignment, the Twitter Application Programming Interface (API) was utilized. Terms like "coronavirus" and "covid19" were included in the search parameters, as were their variants, which included "corona-virus", "coronavirus", "covid19", and "#covid19". These words encompassed a variety of character combinations, such as @, #, –, _, so on. With a 50 km search radius, the search was focused on the area surrounding Buenos Aires, the capital of Argentina, which is located at latitude −38.416097 and longitude −63.616672.

Text Pre-Processing. Several well-known Python libraries, including NumPy [22], Pandas [19], Scikit-learn [9], and Matplotlib [17], are utilized for pre-processing data [25]. The text was first changed from capital to lowercase letters. After that, punctuation was removed, including question marks, exclamation points, semicolons, and commas. Retweets, stop words, and nonprintable characters used as emojis were also eliminated. Furthermore, terms like HTTP, URL, and HTTPS, to mention a few, were removed.

4 Methods

Overview of Tweet Volume. We used a time-series approach to analyze tweet volume, dividing the dataset into semester-long time intervals. As a result, we were able to investigate the variations and chronological trends in COVID-19 twitter activity over time.

Sentiment Analysis. Sentiment analysis was used to measure the emotional valence of tweets using the Senti-py model [16]. This model was trained using a heterogeneous collection of text corpora in the Spanish language from several websites, including Twitter. Senti-py's accuracy in sentiment analysis is credited to a feature selection intermediate process working in concert with a Bag of Words (BoW) architecture [23]. Mathematically, the sentiment score S of a given text is defined on a continuum $S \in [0, 1]$, where $S = 0$ signifies the extremity of negative sentiment and $S = 1$ represents the pinnacle of positive sentiment. This numerical scoring system allows for the quantification of an individual text's emotional tone.

To encapsulate shifts in sentimentality, our analysis devised a categorization scheme where tweets are labeled as neutral, negative, or positive across defined time intervals (semesters), based on the sentiment score S. The classification criteria can be formalized as follows:

- **Neutral sentiment:** if $0.3 \leq S < 0.7$

- **Negative sentiment:** if $S < 0.3$
- **Positive sentiment:** if $S \geq 0.7$

Trending Topics. To identify recurrent themes and patterns in tweets, we applied topic modeling using the Latent Dirichlet Allocation (LDA) technique [8, 18]. LDA is a generative probabilistic model that assumes each document (in this case, a tweet) is a mixture of a finite number of topics, with each topic represented by a distribution over words. Mathematically, LDA can be described as follows:

Given a corpus of D documents, LDA aims to discover K topics. Each document d in D is represented as a mixture over these K topics, and each topic k is represented as a distribution over the vocabulary V of W words. The model involves two Dirichlet distributions:

- **Document-Topic distribution**: Each document d has a distribution over topics θ_d, where $\theta_d \sim \text{Dir}(\alpha)$. Here, α is the parameter of the Dirichlet prior on the per-document topic distributions.
- **Topic-Word distribution**: Each topic k has a distribution over words ϕ_k, where $\phi_k \sim \text{Dir}(\beta)$. β is the parameter of the Dirichlet prior on the per-topic word distribution.

The generative process for a word w in a document d in LDA can be summarized as follows:

- For each topic k, draw $\phi_k \sim \text{Dir}(\beta)$.
- For each document d:
- Draw $\theta_d \sim \text{Dir}(\alpha)$.
- For each word w in d:

  $*$ Choose a topic $Z_{d,w} \sim \text{Multinomial}(\theta_d)$.
  $*$ Choose a word $W_{d,w} \sim \text{Multinomial}(\phi_{zd,w})$.

The primary objective is to infer the latent topic structure $Z_{d,w}$, the document- topic distributions θ_d, and the topic-word distributions ϕ_k that best explain the observed words in the corpus.

Analysis of Key Events and their Impact. We have carefully crafted a synopsis that centers on critical moments and noteworthy events related to Argentina's COVID-19 pandemic in order to analyze the major events and their consequences. Among other important components, this involved a thorough analysis of government statements and immunization campaigns. To guarantee that our overview is based on reliable and official information about the country's pandemic response, we specifically included official data and statements from the World Health Organization (WHO), the Ministry of Health of Argentina, and th (MHA) e Government of Argentina (GA) in our synthesis.

5 The Rhythms of COVID-19 Discourse

5.1 Overview of Tweet Volume

This section presents a comprehensive analysis of the amount of tweets associated with COVID-19 in Argentina during the course of the research period's various semesters. This analysis shows how internet discourse fluctuated in reaction to the pandemic's changes.

The data illustrated in Fig. 1 offers a comprehensive analysis of tweet volume trends across different time frames. Initially, there is a notable decrease in tweet volume observed from January–June 2020 to July–December 2020 (from 701,334 to 292,804). This sharp decline may suggest a shift in the focus or attention of the general public. Subsequently, there is a subsequent, albeit less prominent, drop in tweet volume from July–December 2020 to January–June 2021, indicating a sustained waning interest in the topic. The most significant decline occurs from January–June 2021 to July–December 2021, with tweet volume plummeting from 169,477 to 72,823, signifying a substantial decrease in interest or interaction.

The decline in tweet volume over successive time intervals is evident, aligning with an observed trend. Particularly noteworthy is the significant decrease in tweet volume between January–June 2022 and July–December 2022, suggesting a sustained waning of public interest or engagement with the subject matter. The most recent timeframe, spanning from January–June 2023, records the least number of tweets, hinting at a potential downward trajectory. Upon comprehensive examination, it becomes apparent that there exists a consistent pattern of diminishing tweet volume over time, reflecting a decrease in public interest or interaction on Twitter. Various factors such as evolving societal trends, fluctuating news cycles, and alterations in online conversations could have contributed to this downward trend.

5.2 Trending Topics

In this section we provide an overview of the analytical approach employed to explore the most prevalent themes and discussions surrounding the COVID-19 pandemic in Argentina. This section incorporates two primary methods: word cloud analysis and topic modeling using LDA. The introduction outlines how

word clouds visually represent the most frequent terms associated with each topic extracted through LDA for each semester from 2020 to 2023. Additionally, it highlights the significance of the table summarizing the ten most important words by topic per semester obtained through LDA. Together, these analytical tools offer insights into the prevailing themes, concerns, and developments related to the COVID-19 pandemic in Argentina over the specified time period.

Word Clouds Analysis. The word clouds produced for each semester between 2020 and 2023 shed light on the dominant topics and conversations in Argentina around the COVID-19 epidemic and related problems. This is a synopsis of the analysis: The word clouds show a persistent pattern of highlighted terms related to the COVID-19 epidemic over all semesters, indicating the crisis's continued impact and international attention within the context of Argentina. The prior semesters' themes (January–June 2020 and

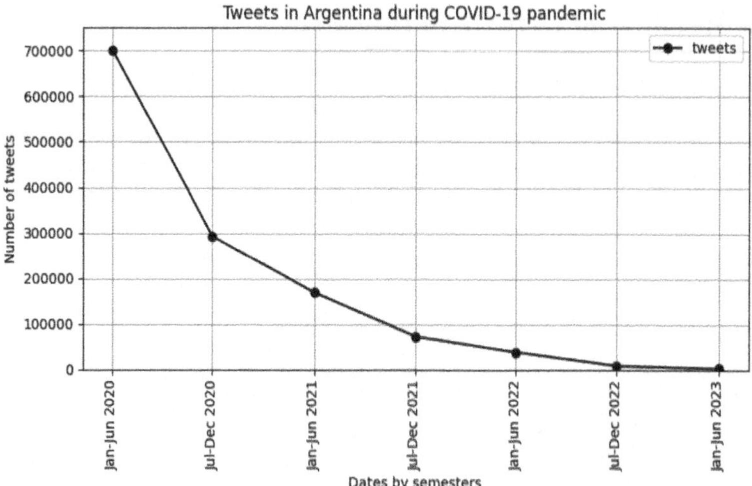

Fig. 1. Overview of Tweet volume in Argentina during COVID-19 pandemic.

July–December 2020) center on comprehending the pandemic's effects, putting public health policies into action, and tackling socioeconomic issues unique to Argentina. As the pandemic worsens, conversations in the ensuing semesters (January–June 2021 and July–December 2021) focus more on the Argentine healthcare system's resilience, vaccination campaigns, and virus variant tracking. Given Argentina's particular challenges and reactions, there is a noticeable emphasis in 2022 on immunization campaigns, plans for economic recovery, and governmental programs to manage the pandemic's long-term repercussions inside the nation. The second half of 2022 (July–December 2022) sees the continuation of the patterns seen in 2022, with an emphasis on immunization campaigns, economic revival, and the execution of policies specific to the Argentine situation. Overall, the word clouds depict how conversations about the pandemic in Argentina have changed over time, moving

from the immediate crisis reaction to long-term recovery initiatives and policy issues. Please refer to Fig. 2, which shows all of the word clouds created for each semester, for a visual depiction of the word clouds discussed.

Summary of Topics. This section examines the trending topics in Argentina from 2020 to 2023 using LDA to identify recurring themes in tweets (See Table 1). By extracting three topics per semester, we gain insights into evolving public concerns and policy priorities.

In early 2020, discussions focused on pandemic response, public health measures, and global impacts, with keywords like "covid", "coronavirus", "riesgo", and "cuarentena" dominating the discourse. The second half of 2020 saw a shift towards ongoing COVID-19 issues, public information dissemination, and vaccination initiatives, reflected in terms like "vacuna", "gobierno", and "contagios". The first half of 2021 highlighted vaccination efforts, healthcare infrastructure, and government measures, as seen in words like "vacunas", "dosis", "medidas", and "restricciones". Later in 2021, the focus remained on the pandemic's societal impact, vaccination progress, and monitoring

Table 1. Summary of Topics in Argentina (2020–2023).

Year	Period	Topic	The 10 most relevant words
2020	**Jan–Jun**	# 01	coronavirus, covid, dia, cuarentena, dengue, momento, muertes, muertos, ciudad, riesgo
		# 02	coronavirus, casos, covid, gente, salud, crisis, gobierno, tiempos, informe, contagio
		# 03	covid, coronavirus, personas, caso, virus, mundo, dias, medidas, pandemia, vez
	Jul–Dec	# 01	covid, casos, dia, informe, personas, gente, virus, ciudad, muertos, salud
		# 02	coronavirus, pandemia, dias, ano, reporte, cuarentena, vecinos, meses, caso, anos
		# 03	coronavirus, vacuna, muertes, contagios, vacunas, gobierno, momento, presidente, vez, horas
2021	**Jan–Jun**	# 01	coronavirus, casos, vacuna, dosis, personas, covid, dia, contagios, muertes, anos
		# 02	covid, informe, salud, ciudad, servicios, provincia, negocio, semana, reporte, casol
		# 03	coronavirus, vacunas, medidas, ano, ola, gobierno, presidente, pandemia, virus, restricciones
	Jul–Dec	# 01	coronavirus, personas, vacuna, millones, pandemia, ano, vez, gente, dias, virus
		# 02	covid, dosis, muertos, anos, coronavirus, provincia, contagios, restricciones, salud, gobierno
		# 03	casos, coronavirus, vacunas, muertes, covid, variante, horas, contagios, dia, informe
2022	**Jan–Jun**	# 01	dosis, vacunas, covid, vacuna, virus, pandemia, anos, gripe, circulacion, sintoma
		# 02	covid, variante, delta, sintomas, ola, gente, variantes, parte, personas, enero
		# 03	coronavirus, casos, contagios, muertes, horas, muertos, semana, dia, datos, aumento
	Jul–Dec	# 01	covid, negocio, servicios, casos, contagios, semana, brindale, dosis, sintomas, cliente
		# 02	coronavirus, productos, podes, variante, brindale, vacuna, parte, covid, inmunidad, ministerio
		# 03	covid, coronavirus, vacunas, casos, dosis, aumento, virus, personas, vacuna, variantes

(*continued*)

Table 1. (*continued*)

Year	Period	Topic	The 10 most relevant words
2023	**Jan–Jun**	# 01	covid, imagenes, refuerzos, salud, refuerzo, marzo, coronavirus, tambien, caso, pandemia
		# 02	coronavirus, servicios, negocio, productos, brindale, podes, covid, cliente, vacuna, vacunas
		# 03	covid, anos, vacunas, coronavirus, datos, dosis, pandemia, virus, casos, muertes

key metrics, with frequent terms including "personas", "millones", "pandemia", and "casos", In early 2022, the topics revolved around vaccination campaigns, virus variants, and pandemic metrics, indicated by words like "variante". "sintomas", "vacunas", and "dosis". The latter half of 2022 continued to emphasize COVID- 19 management, business impacts, and pandemic-related products and services, with keywords such as "negocio", "productos", "servicios", and "vacunas". Finally, in early 2023, the discussions focused on COVID-19 visuals, reinforcement efforts, and health updates, using terms like "imagenes", "refuerzos", "salud", and "pandemia". Throughout the pandemic, these trending topics reveal a comprehensive understanding of Argentina's socio-political landscape,

highlighting the dynamic nature of public discourse and the shifting priorities in response to both local and global developments. This analysis not only maps the trajectory of public concerns but also aids in informing public health interventions and communication strategies tailored to the Argentine context.

5.3 Sentiment Analysis

Our sentiment analysis examines the emotional tone of COVID-19-related tweets in Argentina over time, as illustrated in Fig. 3.

The analysis reveals the distribution of positive, neutral, and negative sentiments for each semester, providing insights into public mood trends. As shown in the Fig. 3, there is a significant decline in tweet activity from January 2020 to June 2023. Positive sentiments, represented by the green dashed line, start relatively low and decrease gradually, indicating a consistent but minor presence of positive reactions. Neutral sentiments, represented by the yellow dashed line, also decrease over time, suggesting a decline in general engagement or neutral opinions. Negative sentiments, represented by the red solid line, are initially high, peaking in the first semester of 2020, and then show a steady decline, reflecting a possible improvement in public opinion regarding COVID-19. Key findings include a discernible decline in tweet activity, indicating reduced public interest or engagement with the COVID-19 topic over time; a gradual decrease in positive sentiments, indicating fluctuating but generally low levels of positive sentiment throughout the period; predominant but steadily decreasing neutral sentiments, suggesting a drop in neutral engagement; and a peak in negative sentiments early in 2020 with a steady decline thereafter, suggesting an over- all improvement in public sentiment despite ongoing concerns. The sentiment distribution varies across semesters, influenced by factors

Fig. 2. WordClouds of the most frequent words in Argentina during COVID-19 pandemic.

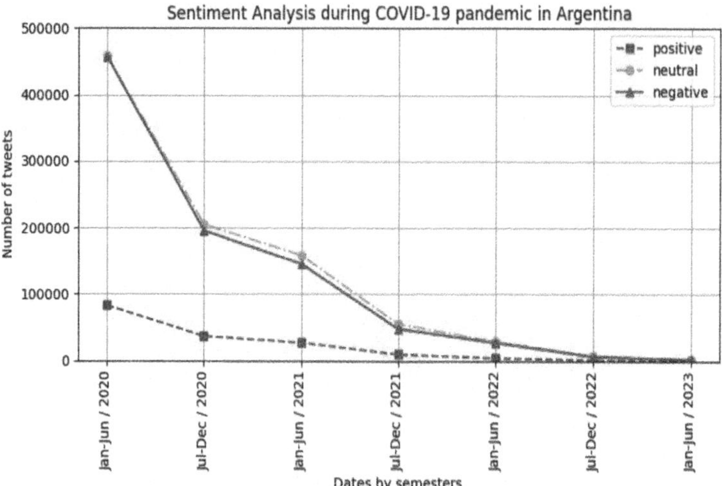

Fig. 3. Sentiment Analysis by Semester.

such as news cycles, significant events, and shifts in public perception. These insights are crucial for understanding public engagement and concerns, informing public health interventions, and communication strategies tailored to the Argentine context, highlighting the dynamic nature of public discourse and the evolving priorities in response to both local and global developments related to the pandemic.

5.4 Key Events and their Impact

This section outlines the critical events and their impact on Argentina's epidemiological, sociological, and policy responses to the COVID-19 pandemic. The timeline begins on March 3, 2020, when Argentina reported its first confirmed case of COVID-19 [21]. This event led to immediate public concern and the implementation of preventive measures, marking the start of a prolonged battle against the virus. On March 19, 2020, the Argentine government announced a nationwide lockdown in response to the rising number of cases, one of the region's earliest and strictest measures [3]. This was closely followed by the WHO's declaration on March 11, 2020, that COVID-19 was a global pandemic [30], which spurred coordinated international and national efforts to enforce stringent public health measures.

By October 2020, Argentina experienced its first peak in COVID-19 cases [4], putting significant strain on the healthcare system and prompting public debate about the effectiveness of government actions and hospital capacity. On December 29, 2020, Argentina launched its COVID-19 vaccination program [20], introducing a new phase marked by both optimism and concerns over vaccine availability and efficacy. The second wave of infections in May 2021 [6] necessitated the reintroduction of strict lockdown measures, and the third wave in January 2022 [14], driven by the Omicron variant, saw a more optimistic public response due to higher vaccination rates and the perceived milder nature of the variant, enabling more adaptive coexistence strategies.

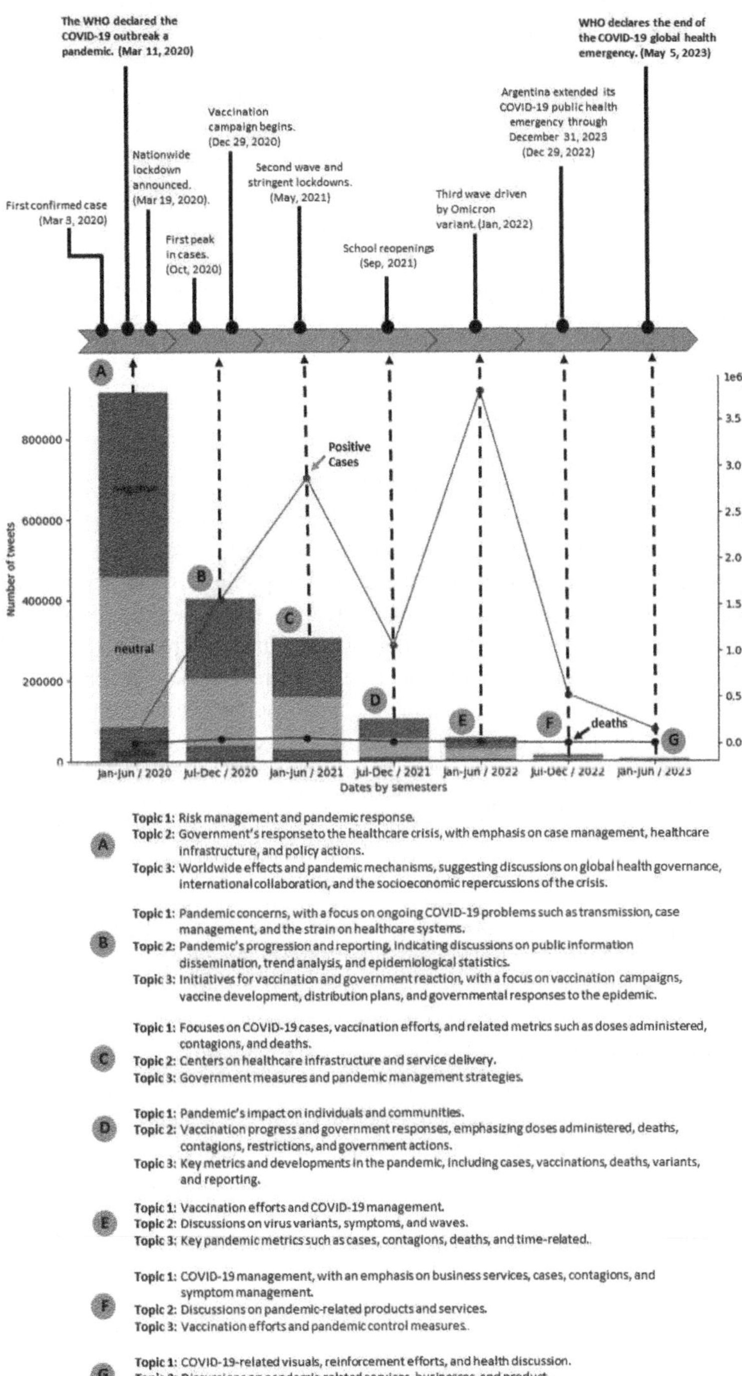

Fig. 4. Examining the Twitter environment in Argentina: Volume, sentiment, and trends during COVID-19 landmarks.

On December 29, 2022, the Argentine government extended the public health emergency to December 31, 2023, highlighting the ongoing impact of the pandemic [15]. In contrast, the WHO declared an end to the global health emergency on May 5, 2023 [28], marking a significant shift in managing the crisis and juxtaposing national and global perspectives on the pandemic's status. These events signal a turning point towards recovery, reflection on lessons learned, and discussions on future preparedness, emphasizing the importance of adaptability and collective effort in overcoming the pandemic. Argentina's response to COVID-19 illustrates the dynamic interplay between epidemiological data, public opinion, and policy decisions, underscoring the critical roles of transparent communication, effective public health initiatives, and societal adaptability in addressing complex health crises.

6 Discussion

We examine the complex processes that occurred during the COVID-19 epidemic in Argentina using extensive graphical data as a lens. Based on a thorough investigation of the relationships between significant epidemiological turning points, shifts in public opinion, governmental actions, and the changing public discourse topics depicted in Fig. 4, this study integrates multiple data streams. These include semester-specific COVID-19 cases and fatalities [27, 29], sentiment analysis results (Sect. 4.3), and community-wide conversation topics (Sect. 4.2). Our goal is to reveal the complex interactions that defined Argentina's pandemic response, providing context for the pandemic's effects and drawing conclusions that might guide the development of public health policies, initiatives, and a broader understanding of social resilience in the face of international health emergencies.

6.1 Epidemiological Trends and Public Sentiment

The path of the pandemic in Argentina, beginning with the first verified case on March 3, 2020, and continuing with successive waves and significant events, closely corresponds with changes in public opinion. Initial reactions of fear and anxiety to the outbreak and statewide lockdowns evolved into a complex interplay of fatigue, skepticism, and optimism. Government actions, such as initiating the vaccination program and enforcing lockdowns during subsequent waves, significantly influenced this shift.

The timeline of Argentina's intense pandemic phase is framed by the WHO's declaration of COVID-19 as a global health emergency on March 11, 2020, and the Argentine government's announcement on December 29, 2022, extending the public health emergency until December 31, 2023. These events mark transitions from crisis to recovery, with the public's viewpoint shifting from cautious optimism to heightened concern, emphasizing the impact of milestones and authoritative signals on collective emotional responses.

6.2 Governmental Responses and Thematic Discourse Evolution

Public opinion has been significantly influenced by the Argentine government's response, including the vaccine drive and strict lockdowns. The study of trending themes by semester reveals a sociological focus that evolved from urgent concerns about risk management and healthcare capacity to discussions about vaccine distribution, socio-economic impacts, and future readiness.

This progression mirrors the broader international conversation, shifting from containment and mitigation to strategies for coexisting with the virus and considerations for long-term pandemic management. The topics reflect a society contemplating the pandemic's lasting effects on health governance, socioeconomic stability, and international cooperation, beyond immediate concerns.

6.3 Correlation Between Epidemiological Data and Discourse Topics

The graphical data shows a clear relationship between public discourse themes and epidemiological trends, indicated by peaks in COVID-19 cases and fatalities. Each significant increase in cases or the emergence of new variants, such as the Omicron variant in January 2022, triggered shifts in public discourse toward vaccination campaigns, adaptive strategies, and healthcare system resilience. These changes highlight the public's response to the evolving pandemic scenario, emphasizing the importance of vaccine accessibility, robust public health infrastructure, and accurate information dissemination in fostering societal resilience and effective crisis response.

7 Conclusion

This study provides a comprehensive analysis of the discourse surrounding COVID- 19 on Twitter in Argentina from 2020 to 2023. By leveraging advanced NLP and sentiment analysis techniques, we were able to capture the evolving public sentiment and key discussion topics over the course of the pandemic. Our examination unveiled notable patterns and changes in societal attitudes, influenced by significant epidemiological occurrences, governmental measures, and communal reactions. The sentiment analysis revealed a conspicuous decrease in the quantity of tweets and a gradual transition in public sentiment from primarily negative and neutral attitudes to a more evenly distributed emotional range. This pattern mirrors the public's adjustment to the prolonged duration of the pandemic and the eventual rollout of vaccination initiatives, which instigated a sense of careful hopefulness amid persistent obstacles. Our topic modeling, using LDA, identified recurring themes that evolved in response to the pandemic's progression. Early discussions focused on immediate public health measures and the initial shock of the outbreak, while later conversations shifted towards vaccine distribution, government policies, and socio-economic impacts. The dynamic nature of these topics underscores the complexity of public discourse in times of crisis and the significant role of social media as a barometer for public opinion. The findings from this study highlight the importance of timely and transparent communication from authorities, the need for robust public health infrastructure, and the critical role of social media in shaping and reflecting public sentiment. These insights are invaluable for policymakers and health officials as they navigate future health crises and strive to foster societal resilience. Overall, this research contributes to the broader understanding of the interplay between social media, public health, and information dissemination during a global health emergency, providing key lessons for managing public discourse in future crises. The integration of sentiment analysis and topic modeling offers a powerful approach to monitoring and understanding public sentiment in real-time, which is essential for effective crisis management and communication strategies. This research's thorough methodology and concentration on Spanish-language tweets offer a distinctive viewpoint on the repercussions of the pandemic in Argentina, enhancing the worldwide discussion on COVID-19 and presenting valuable knowledge for other Spanish-speaking areas facing comparable emergencies.

Acknowledgments. The authors express their appreciation to Research4tech, a consortium of Latin American scholars dedicated to artificial intelligence (AI) with the goal of promoting AI, establishing scholarly networks, and fostering collaboration among the academic sector, technological entities, governmental bodies, and society to expedite and enhance the progress of Latin American nations through the support of science and technology. The Consejo Nacional de Humanidades, Ciencias y Tecnologías de México (CONHACyT) and the Tecnológico Nacional de México / Instituto Tecnológico de Matamoros contributed partially to the funding of this project.

References

1. Ainapure, B.S., et al.: Sentiment analysis of covid-19 tweets using deep learning and lexicon-based approaches. Sustainability. **15**(3), 2573 (2023)
2. Ali, M.F., Irfan, R., Lashari, T.A.: Comprehensive sentimental analysis of tweets towards covid-19 in Pakistan: a study on governmental preventive measures. Peer J. Comput. Sci. **9**, e1220 (2023)
3. Argentina.gob.ar: Coronavirus.https://www.argentina.gob.ar/salud/coronavirus- (2020), Accessed 17 Oct 2023
4. Argentine Ministry of Transportation: Research on crisis management and risks associated with the 2020 coronavirus pandemic. (2021), https://www.argentina.gob.ar/sites/default/files/2021/10/reporte-covid-eng.pdf, Accessed 27 Dec 2023
5. Arias, F., Guerra-Adames, A., Zambrano, M., Quintero-Guerra, E., Tejedor-Flores, N.: Analyzing spanish-language public sentiment in the context of a pandemic and social unrest: the Panama case. Int. J. Environ. Res. Public Health. **19**(16), 10328 (2022)
6. Benedetti, P., et al.: Second wave of covid-i. pandemic in argentinian population: vaccination is associated with a decrease in depressive symptoms. Front. Psych. **13**, 832352 (Jun 2022). https://doi.org/10.3389/fpsyt.2022.832352
7. Blei, D.M., Ng, A.Y., Jordan, M.I.: Latent dirichlet allocation. J. Mach. Learn. Res. **3**(Jan), 993–1022 (2003)
8. Buitinck, L., et al.: API design for machine learning software: experiences from the scikit-learn project. In: ECML PKDD Workshop: Languages for Data Mining and Machine Learning, pp. 108–122 (2013)
9. Chakraborty, K., Bhatia, S., Bhattacharyya, S., Platos, J., Bag, R., Hassanien, A.E.: Sentiment analysis of covid-19 tweets by deep learning classifiers—a study to show how popularity is affecting accuracy in social media. Appl. Soft Comput. **97**, 106754 (2020)
10. Chaudhary, M., Kosyluk, K., Thomas, S., Neal, T.: On the use of aspect-based sentiment analysis of twitter data to explore the experiences of african americans during covid-19. Sci. Rep. **13**(1), 10694 (2023)

11. Córdoba-Cabús, A., García-Borrego, M., Ceballos, Y.: Sentiment analysis toward the covid-19 vaccine in the main latin american media on twitter: the cases of Argentina, Chile, Colombia, Mexico, and Peru. Vaccine. **11**(10), 1592 (2023)
12. Darad, S., Krishnan, S.: Sentimental analysis of covid-19 twitter data using deep learning and machine learning models. Ingenius. **29**, 108–117 (2023)
13. Economic Commission for Latin America and the Caribbean (ECLAC): the sociodemographic impacts of the covid-19 pandemic in latin america and the caribbean. In: Lc/Crpd.4/3, Economic Commission for Latin America and the Caribbean (ECLAC), Santiago (2022)
14. Gobierno de Argentina.: Por las consecuencias de la pandemia, el gobierno extendió la emergencia sanitaria por un año. (2023). https://www.argentina.gob.ar/noticias/por-, Accessed 29 Dec 2023
15. Hofman, E.: Senti-py. GitHub, Inc (2022)
16. Hunter, J.D.: Matplotlib: a 2d graphics environment. Comput. Sci. Eng. **9**(3), 90–95 (2007)
17. Jelodar, H., et al.: Latent dirich- let allocation (lda) and topic modeling: models, applications, a survey. Multimed. Tools Appl. **78**, 15169–15211 (2019)
18. McKinney, W., et al.: Data structures for statistical computing in python. In: Proceedings of the ninth Python in Science Conference, vol. 445, pp. 51–56, Austin, TX (2010)
19. Mendoza, J.: Covid-19 vaccine immunization development in argentina 2020–2023 (Jan 2024), https://www.statista.com/statistics/1286643/population-vaccinated-. Accessed 27 Feb 2024
20. Ministry of Health of Argentina: New coronavirus (covid-19): Daily report 09/03/2020 (March 2020), https://www.argentina.gob.ar/coronavirus/informes-. Accessed 14 Oct 2023
21. Oliphant, T.: Guide to NumPy (01 2006)
22. Qader, W.A., Ameen, M.M., Ahmed, B.I.: An overview of bag of words; importance, implementation, applications, and challenges. In: 2019 International Engineering Conference (IEC), pp. 200–204. IEEE (2019)
23. Salcedo Lagos, P.A., Kotz Grabole, G.E., Vergara Espinoza, C.M., Sánchez- Hechavarría, M.E.: Análisis de sentimiento de tweets sobre la vacuna contra el covid-19 en países iberoamericanos hispanohablantes. Rev. Latinoam. Psicología. **54**, 1–11 (2022)
24. Srinath, K.: Python–the fastest growing programming language. Int. Res. J. Eng. Technol. **4**(12), 354–357 (2017)
25. Weger, R., et al.: Trends in language use during the covid-19 pandemic and relationship between language use and mental health: text analysis based on free responses from a longitudinal study. JMIR Ment. Health. **10**(1), e40899 (2023)
26. WHO: Daily covid-19 cases and deaths by date reported to who. (2020). https://data.who.int/dashboards/covid19/data. Accessed: 07 Feb 2024
27. WHO.: Statement on the fifteenth meeting of the ihr (2005) emergency com- mittee on the covid-19 pandemic. https://www.who.int/news/item/05-05-2023- (May 2023), Accessed 29 Dec 2023
28. WHO World Health Organization: Covid-19 dashboard. (2024). https://data.who.int/dashboards/covid19/cases. Accessed 8 June 2024
29. World Health Organization: Who director-general's opening remarks at the media briefing on covid-19 - 11 march 2020 (March 2020), https://www.who.int/director-, Accessed 6 Oct 2023
30. Yin, H., Song, X., Yang, S., Li, J.: Sentiment analysis and topic modeling for covid-19 vaccine discussions. World Wide Web. **25**(3), 1067–1083 (2022)

A Comprehensive Study of Pre-trained Deep Learning Models in Skin Disease Classification

Sarang Banakhede, Vibha Tiwari(✉), and Varnit Kumar

Madhav Institute of Technology and Science, Gwalior, Madhya Pradesh, India
vibhatiwari19@gmail.com

Abstract. Skin diseases are a major public health concern, demanding accurate and timely diagnosis. This study evaluates the performance of five pre-trained deep learning models - VGG16, ResNet50, EfficientNet B0, DenseNet121, and Inception v3 - for skin disease classification using a publicly available dataset. The models were fine-tuned and compared based on accuracy, precision and recall. Our findings demonstrate the potential of these models for supporting dermatologists in clinical practice. However, challenges such as data imbalance and model interpretability remain. Future research should focus on addressing these limitations and exploring ensemble methods for further performance enhancement.

Keywords: Deep learning · Skin disease · Computer Vision · Dermatology, · VGG16 · ResNet50 · EfficientNet · DenseNet · Inception v3 · Classification

1 Introduction

Skin diseases encompass a wide range of conditions affecting the structure and function of the skin. Early and accurate diagnosis is essential for effective treatment and preventing complications. Traditionally, skin disease diagnosis relies on visual inspection by dermatologists, but this approach can be subjective and prone to errors.

In recent years, skin lesion classification has emerged as a prominent area of research, fueled by the widespread adoption of artificial intelligence in medical image analysis. The skin disease classification techniques focus on traditional, feature-based techniques and advanced, deep learning-based methods to improve diagnostic accuracy and efficiency. Deep learning (DL) has emerged as a powerful tool for medical image analysis, with promising applications in skin disease classification. DL models can learn complex patterns from large datasets of medical images, enabling them to automatically identify and classify skin lesions with high accuracy. Convolutional Neural Networks (CNNs) have been at the fore- front of recent advances in skin lesion classification. These techniques have shown

great potential in skin disease detection. Researchers apply various classification algorithms to classify skin diseases accurately. Recent progress in deep learning techniques has yielded promising results in skin lesion detection and classification.

Esteva et al. (1) used deep convolutional neural networks (CNNs) and achieved dermatologist-level classification of skin lesions. They used a single CNN,and trained

S. Tiwari et al. (Eds.): AMLDA 2024, CCIS 2636, pp. 16–37, 2026.
https://doi.org/10.1007/978-3-032-18293-7_2

it directly from images using only pixels and disease labels as inputs. A vast dataset is used to train the CNN, potentially extending dermatological expertise beyond the clinic through mobile devices. Codella et al.(2)demonstrate the ability of Convolutional Neural Networks (CNNs) to automatically extract and learn features from dermoscopic images for accurate classification. Joshi et al.(3) utilize image processing and classification techniques to detect skin diseases. Their system proposed improved accuracy of skin lesion diagnosis in the early stages Goswami et al.(4) in their study discusses the need for an automated computer-based system to handle the scarcity of human experts for skin disease identification and classification. They give in detail the evolution from traditional handcrafted feature-based approaches to deep learning-based techniques in skin disease classification, highlighting the challenges posed by the similar visual characteristics of many skin diseases. Sahu et al.(5) discuss the development of a machine learning-based ensemble model for the classification of various skin diseases, showcasing the model's better performance compared to other classifiers. Gannour et al.(6) introduce an approach leveraging ensemble learning techniques for classifying skin diseases, combining multi-modal and multi-task methodologies to improve classification performance. Their proposed classifier integrates multiple information sources. They included skin lesion images and patient-specific data. By simultaneously utilizing image input and structured data input, the functionality of the classifier enables efficient disease classification.

Despite the promising results achieved by these techniques, some challenges need to be addressed, such as the handling of imbalanced datasets where certain types of lesions are underrepresented, and the need for the models to gain trust of medical professionals. This study aims to evaluate the performance of five pre-trained convolutional neural networks (CNNs) – VGG16 (8), ResNet50 (9), EfficientNet B0 (10), DenseNet121 (11), and Inception v3 (15) for skin disease classification using a publicly available dataset. These models have been pre-trained on large datasets of natural images, and their ability to be fine-tuned for specific tasks like skin disease classification makes them valuable tools for medical imaging applications.

2 Methodology

The Fig. 1 outlines a systematic workflow for developing a machine learning model, for skin disease classification. It begins with loading a dataset (ham10000 with 10,015 samples) and preprocessing the data through resizing, grayscale conversion, morphological operations to remove artifacts, and Gaussian blur for noise reduction. Data cleaning and augmentation follow, involving geometric transformations, distortions, and blurs to enhance robustness. The dataset is then split into training and testing subsets, with the training data used to train models such as VGG-16, ResNet-50, EfficientNet-B0, DenseNet-121, and Inception-V3. The testing data is utilized to evaluate model performance, and visualizations along with explainable AI techniques are employed to interpret results. Finally, the model's history and weights are saved, ensuring a comprehensive and efficient approach to model development and deployment. This model is discussed in detail in subsequent sections

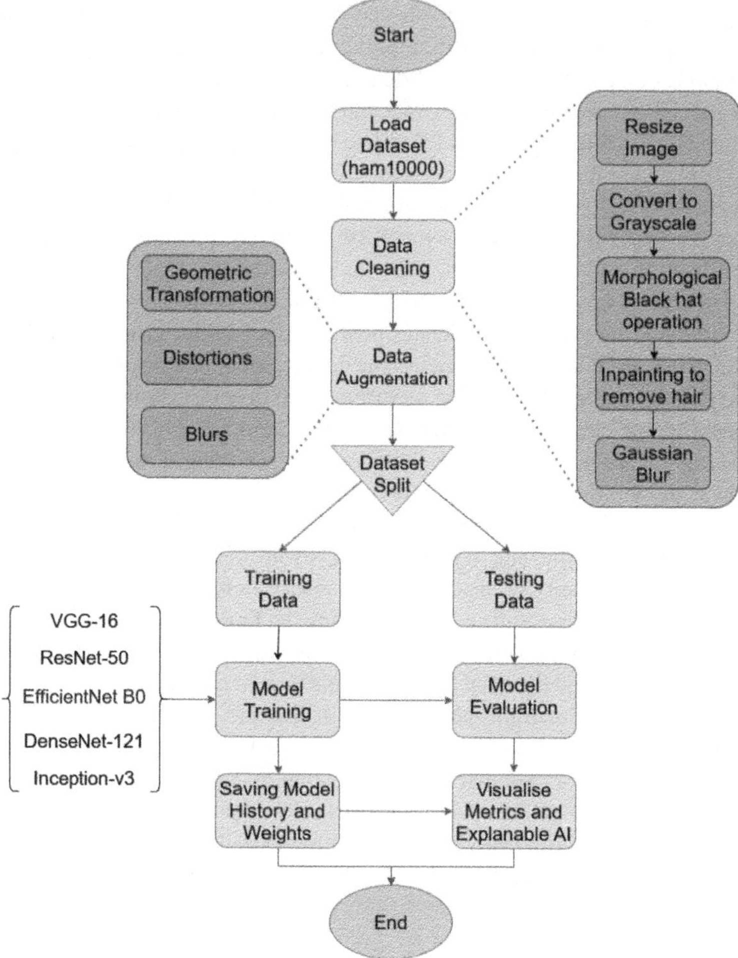

Fig. 1. Workflow

3 Preprocessing DataSet

3.1 Dataset

The dataset used in this study is the publicly available HAM10000 ("Human Against Machine with 10000 training images") dataset. This dataset is a collection of 10015 dermatoscopic images from different populations, acquired and stored by different modalities(7).The HAM10000 dataset consists of multi-source dermatoscopic images of common pigmented skin lesions. All the images are colored, with a height and width of 450 and 600 pixels respectively

Cases include a representative collection of seven different types of skin lesions. A summary of HAM 10000 images is given in Table 1 and seven lesion classes are shown in Fig. 2

Table 1. Summary of HAM 10000 images

Dataset	HAM10000
License	CC BY-NC 4.0
Total images	10015
Pathological verification%	53.3%
Actinic keratoses and intraepithelial carcinoma(akiec)	327
basal cell carcinoma(bcc)	514
benign keratosis-like lesions(bkl)	1099
dermatofibroma(df)	115
melanoma(mel)	1113
melanocytic nevi(nv)	6705
vascular lesions(Vasc)	142

3.2 Image Preprocessing

The preprocessing techniques play a crucial role in the skin lesion detection. It is the first step that helps to make the images ready for further analysis. The following steps are being carried out in preprocessing the given dataset

Image Resize The images were resized to [224x224] pixels using bilinear interpolation. In Image interpolation, to change the image size, each pixel in the image is remapped to a location in the new image. Bilinear interpolation consists of two linear interpolations,one along the x-axis and one along the y axis as shown in Fig. 3

$$\lambda_{11} = (\alpha_1, \beta_1),$$

$$\lambda_{12} = (\alpha_1, \beta_2),$$

$$\lambda_{21} = (\alpha_2, \beta_1)$$

$$\lambda_{22} = (\alpha_2, \beta_2)$$

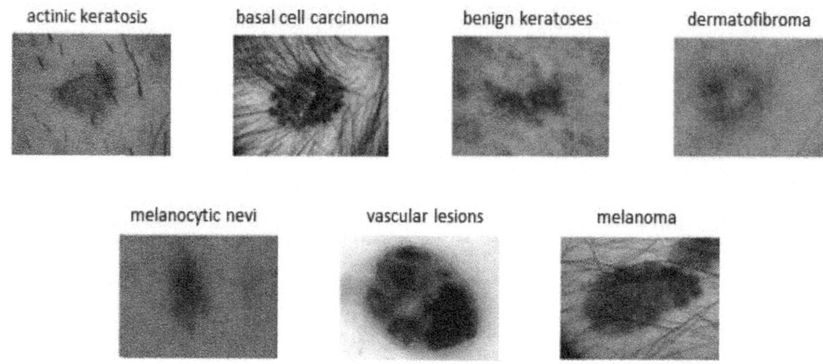

Fig. 2. Seven Lesion classes

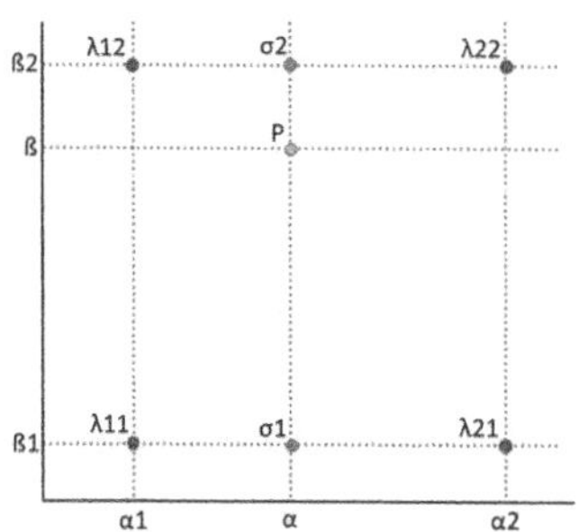

Fig. 3. Bilinear Interpolation schematic

Removing Hair from image The presence of hair in skin images can cause problems in the segmentation process. Therefore, hair removal from the image is required. This is done by the following steps and noise removal from the image as the presence of hair may affect the performance

1. Convert the given image to grayscale: Grayscale images are represented by a single channel representing the intensity of each pixel given by

$$Gray(\alpha, \beta) = 0.2989Red(\alpha, \beta) + 0.5870Green(\alpha, \beta) + 0.1140Blue(\alpha, \beta) \quad (4)$$

2. Apply a morphological operation to detect hair: The black-hat operation calculates the difference between the input image and its morphological opening, effectively highlighting dark objects. The morphological opening is used to smooth the contour of the dark objects. It is a combination of erosion followed by dilation. This operation helps in enhancing the contrast between the dark objects and the background.

$$BH(\alpha, \beta) = GI(\alpha, \beta) - MO(\alpha, \beta) \quad (5)$$

$$MO(\alpha, \beta) = Dilation(Erosion(GI, SE), SE) \quad (6)$$

Where,
BH=BlackHat
GI = GrayscaleInput
MO = MorphologicalOpening
SE = StructuringElement

Inpaint the detected hair to remove it from the image To recover hair- occluded images, the total variation in painting is employed. It is used to fill the areas identified as hair in the black-hat operation by replacing the hair pixels with the neighboring pixels to create a smoother image.

$$Inpainting(\alpha, \beta) = Inpaint(ResizedImage, HairMask) \tag{7}$$

where,

$$HairMask = Th(BH, DTh(BH)) \tag{8}$$

where, Th = Threshold
DTh = DynamicThreshold and DynamicThreshold can be calculated as

$$DTh(\alpha, \beta) = Mean(BH(\alpha, \beta)) + kStd(BH(\alpha, \beta)) \tag{9}$$

where Std is standard deviation

Here threshold Value is dynamically calculated using the mean and standard deviation of the black-hat image. The parameters k and the structuring element size can be adjusted to optimize the black-hat operation for different image characteristics and types of hair present in the skin images.

Gaussian Blur using 3X 3 kernel To smoothen the irregular texture patches which is one of the limiting factors for the accurate extraction of the skin lesion, a Gaussian filter of size 3×3 was used (**?**).

The 2D Gaussian filter kernel is given as

$$f(\alpha, \beta) = \frac{1}{2\pi\sigma^2} \times \exp -\frac{\left(\alpha^2 + \beta^2\right)^2}{2\sigma^2} \tag{10}$$

The results after applying these operations are given in Fig. **4**.

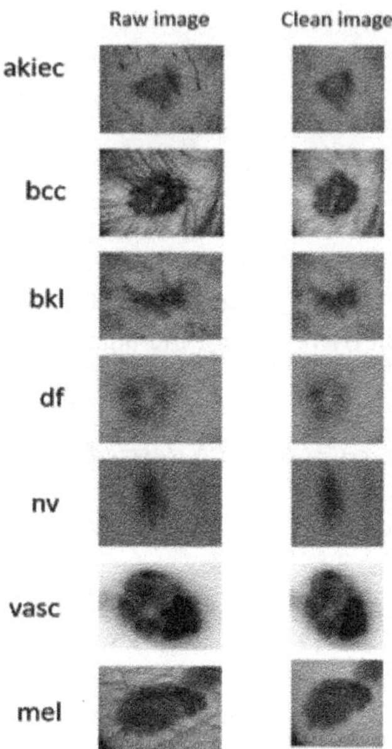

Fig. 4. Raw Images and clean Images after Gaussian Filtering

Data Balancing From Table 1 and Fig. 5, it can be seen that this dataset is unbalanced and the nv category has the highest representation than other categories. If a model is trained with an imbalanced dataset, then results may be biased, predicting the majority classes and often ignoring the minority classes thereby increasing error. The procedure employed to resolve the imbalanced dataset:

(i) Identification of Maximum Class: Determine the class with the maximum number of samples.
(ii) Specify the desired target balance ratio: This indicates the desired proportion of samples in each class relative to the maximum class.
(iii) Compute the number of extra samples needed: The number of extra samples

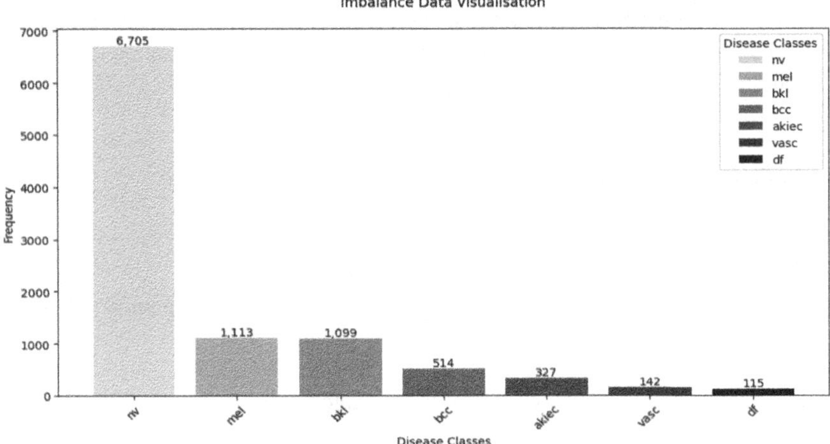

Fig. 5. Distribution of overall count of images into seven classes of skin lesions needed for each class to achieve the desired balance ratio was computed using the formula.

$$N(extraforclassi) = r * N(\max) - N(i) \tag{11}$$

Where,

N(max) is the maximum number of samples among all classes, N(i) is the number of samples in class, R is the desired target balance ratio.

(iv) Apply Augmentation: To increase the accuracy of the model and balance the dataset, a comprehensive augmentation pipeline is employed to enhance both the diversity of the dataset and the robustness of the model. The following techniques are applied:

- Two types of flipping transformations are applied. These transformations produce mirror images, enabling the model to remain unaffected by orientation, a common occurrence in imaging.
  - Horizontal Flip at a probability of 50%.
  - Vertical Flip at a probability of 50%.
- Rotation techniques are incorporated to enhance orientation diversity. hese methods ensure the model is applicable to lesions viewed from varying angles.
  - Random Rotate 90: Rotates images by 90°, 180°, or 270°.
  - Rotation: Rotates images by an angle between -45° and $+ 45^{\circ}$.
- Geometric transformations utilized to help change perspectives, zoom in and even out, and move images.

- Invert and Shift-Scale-Rotate: Change perspectives, zoom in and out, and shift images. The transformations include shifting (up to 6.25%), scaling (±10%), and rotating (±45°).
- Transpose: Performs diagonal flipping.

– Distortion techniques address imperfections and deformations:

- Optical Distortion: Simulates lens-like effects.
- Grid Distortion: Warps the image grid non-uniformly.
- Elastic Transform: Applies random deformations resembling natural skin stretching or compression.

– Blurring techniques introduce variability in image quality:

- Motion Blur: Simulates movement artifacts.
- Median Blur: Reduces noise by replacing pixel values with neighborhood medians.
- Gaussian Blur: Smooths images, mimicking out-of-focus scenarios.

– Dropout techniques add occlusions to promote reliance on global patterns:

- Pixel Dropout: Randomly sets individual pixel values to zero.
- Coarse Dropout: Removes small square patches.
- Grid Dropout: Applies structured occlusions in a grid-like pattern.

By combining these diverse transformations, the augmentation pipeline significantly increases the dataset's variability, enabling the model to generalize effectively and remain robust.

The distribution of overall count of images after data augmentation is shown in Fig. 6

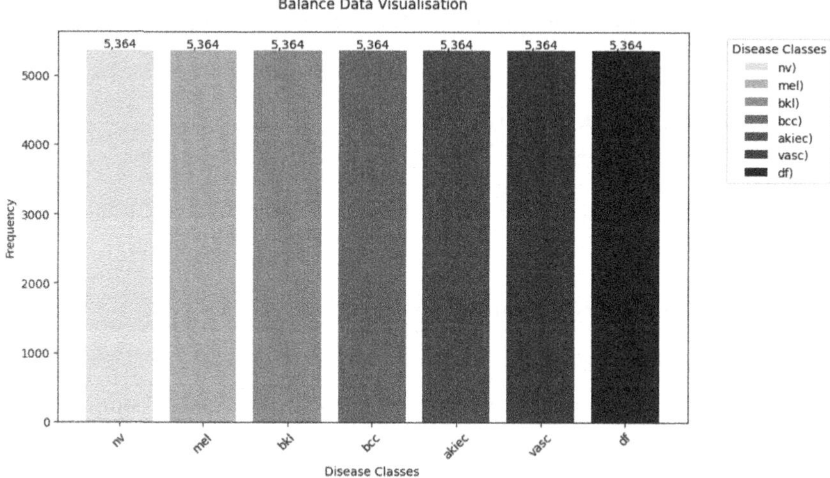

Fig. 6. Distribution of overall count of images after data balancing

4 Model Architecture and Training

4.1 VGG16

VGG16 stands as an example of a deep neural network that is both simple and deep (8). The most important feature it offers is the use of very tiny (3x3) convolutional filters that are built up in a deep sequence of layers. It is made up of 16 weight layers, of which 13 layers are dedicated to convolutions and 3 to the fully connected ones Fig. 7. VGG16 can be easily grasped and applied due to its predefined structural layout as well as its depth, which allows to learn complex features. Even as VGG16 is a computational behemoth with a huge number of parameters, the model has been widely deployed as a feature extractor, especially in the field of computer vision. Its pre-trained weights on large datasets like ImageNet have proved to be very helpful to transfer learning in many applications.

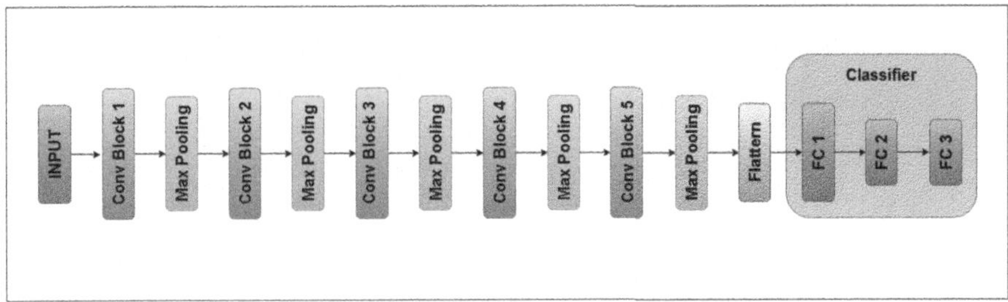

Fig. 7. VGG16 Architecture

4.2 ResNet50

ResNet50 is actually a deep convolutional neural network that uses residual learning to solve the problem of vanishing gradient in the very deep networks

(9). It has a distinct part in having used skip connections that enables it learn residual functions with respect to layer inputs as shown in Fig. 8. Such architectural details enable it train much deeper networks, like 50-layers for example, without any loss in performance. Residual Network 50, also known as ResNet50, is renowned for its excellent feature extraction abilities and has been widely applied to various computer vision tasks due to its tradeoff between depth and efficiency.

4.3 EfficientNet B0

EfficientNet B0 belongs to a group of models that aim to balance model size and accuracy (10). Its main breakthrough is the compound scaling method, which

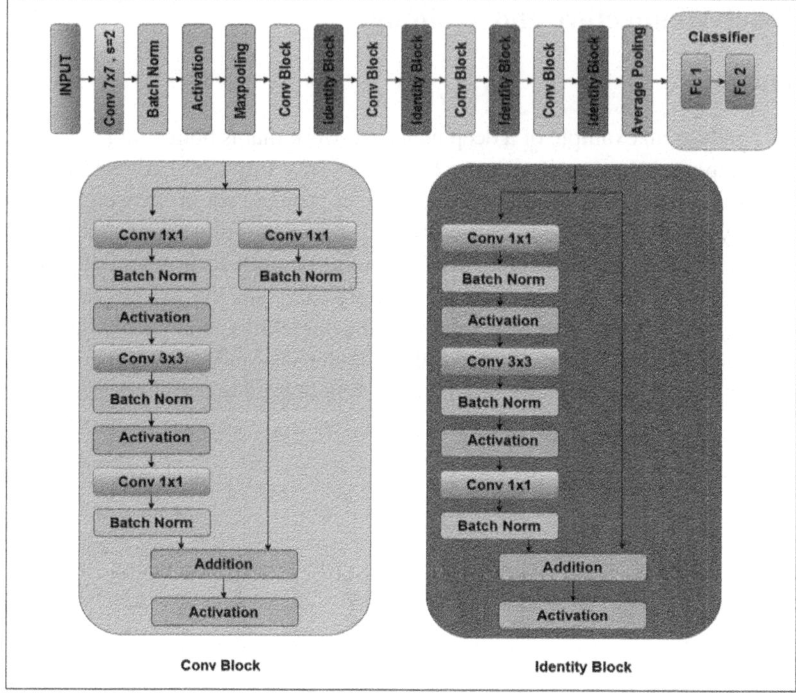

Fig. 8. Architecture of ResNet50

scales network width, depth, and resolution using fixed scaling coefficients. EfficientNet B0 is the starting point in this model family offering a small but strong structure. It employs MBConv blocks and squeeze-and-excitation modules, which extract features using fewer parameters as shown in Fig. 9. This arrangement makes EfficientNet B0 suitable for tasks with limited computing power.

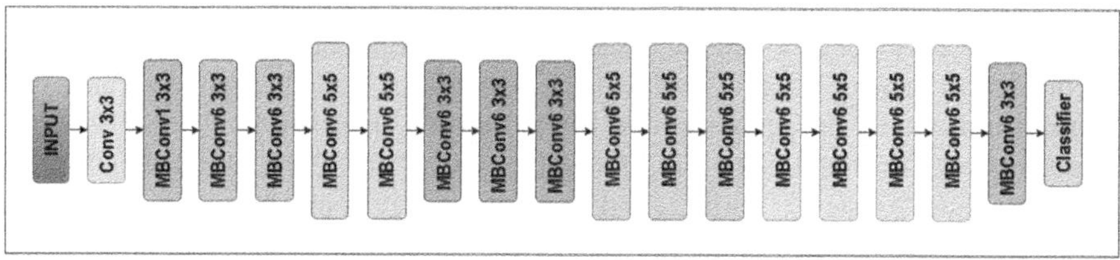

Fig. 9. Architecture of EfficientNet

4.4 DenseNet121

DenseNet121 introduces a new method to connect layers ensuring smooth information flow throughout the network (11).What makes it special is how it links everything each layer connects straight to all the other layers going forward. This means features get used again and again throughout the network, which leads to models that take up less space and gradients that flow better. DenseNet121 has 121 layers set up in dense blocks, with layers in between to make things smaller as shown in Fig. 10. The way it's built helps features spread, encourages using features more than once, and cuts down on the number of settings by a lot. This makes it work well when it comes to using computer power and memory.

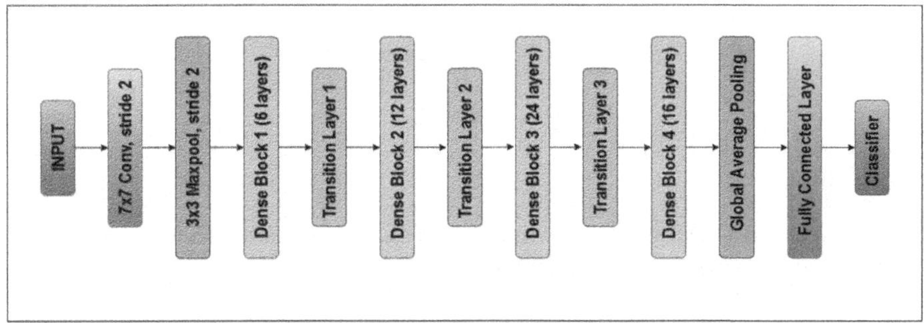

Fig. 10. Architecture of DenseNet121

4.5 Inception V3

With architectural and computational efficiency improvements on the innovations of its forerunners, Inception v3 constructs on their groundwork (15). It employs enhanced "inception modules" that employ factorized convolutions in place of larger filters, such as 5x5 or 7x7, with several small ones like 3x3 (12) (15). Not only does this approach increase feature richness, it also further decreases computational costs. To address this, the model implements both auxiliary classifiers, which serve to regularize the network, in conjunction with more modern techniques such as label smoothing to hinder overfitting (15). Inception v3 is a deep network with 42 layers, with a much lower computational cost than traditional two-dimensional convolution networks, which is why this network is widely used for large-scale image classification tasks (15).

5 Evaluation Metrics

The performance of each model is evaluated based on standard metrics commonly used in image classification tasks, including: Accuracy: Proportion of correctly classified images. Precision: Proportion of true positives among predicted positives. Recall: Proportion of true positives identified by the model (Fig. 11).

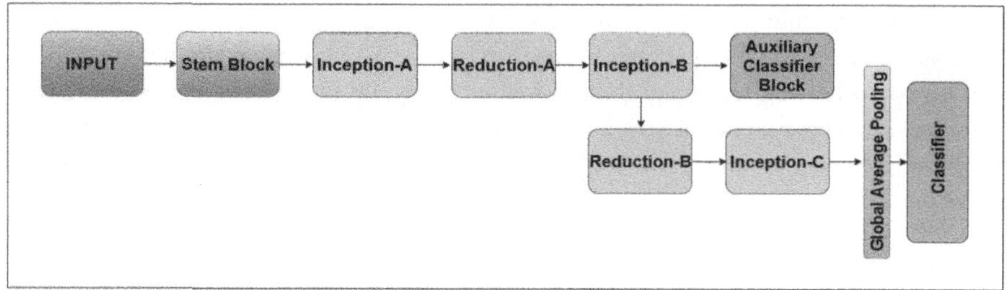

Fig. 11. Architecture of Inception V3

5.1 Accuracy

Accuracy measures the proportion of true results (both true positives and true negatives) among the total number of cases examined.

where:

$$Accuracy = \frac{T\ (+) + (-)}{T\ (+) + (-) + F\ (+) + F(-)} \tag{12}$$

- *T (+) is true positive,*
- *T (−) is true negative,*
- *F (+) is false positive, and*
- *F (−) is false negative.*

5.2 Precision

Precision is the ratio of correctly predicted positive observations to the total predicted positive observations.

$$\text{Precision} = \frac{\text{T}\,(+)}{\text{T}\,(+) + \text{F}\,(+)} \tag{13}$$

5.3 Recall (Sensitivity)

Recall is the ratio of correctly predicted positive observations to all observations in the actual class (Fig. 12 and 13).

$$\text{Recall} = \frac{\text{T}\,(+)}{\text{T}\,(+) + \text{F}\,(-)} \tag{14}$$

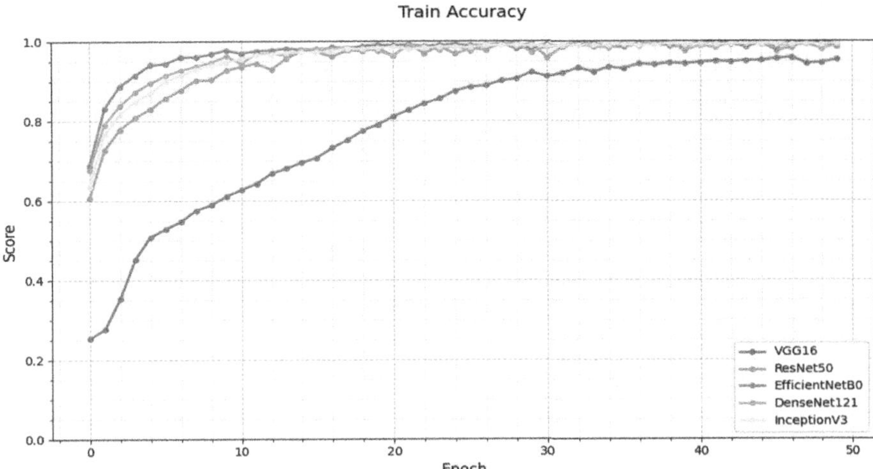

Fig. 12. All model train accuracy

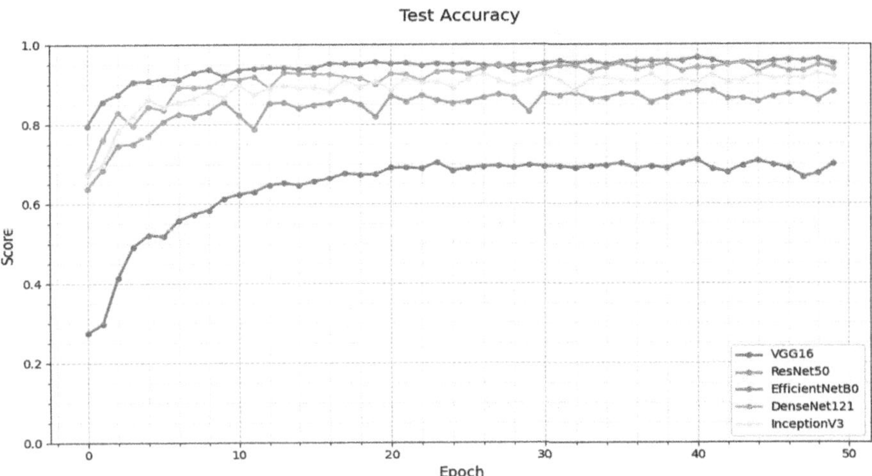

Fig. 13. All model test accuracy

5.4 Loss

In machine learning, particularly with neural networks, a loss function is used to measure how well the model performs. For multi-class classification, we use Figs. 14, 15, 16, 17 and 18

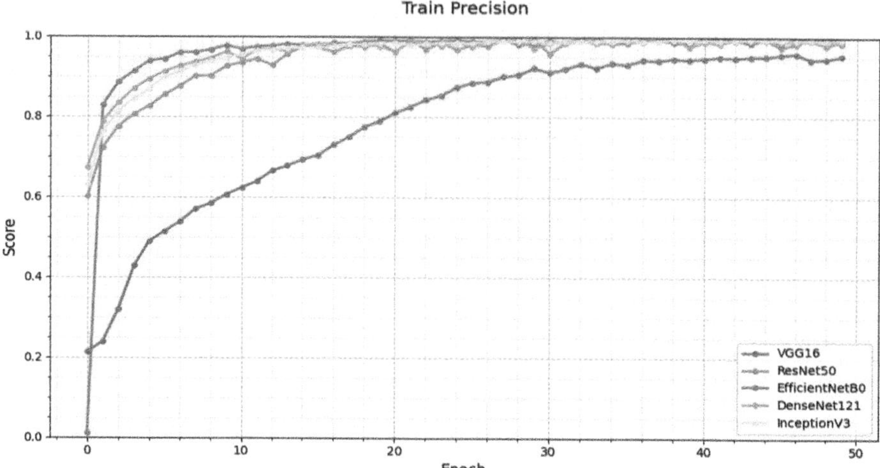

Fig. 14. All model train precision

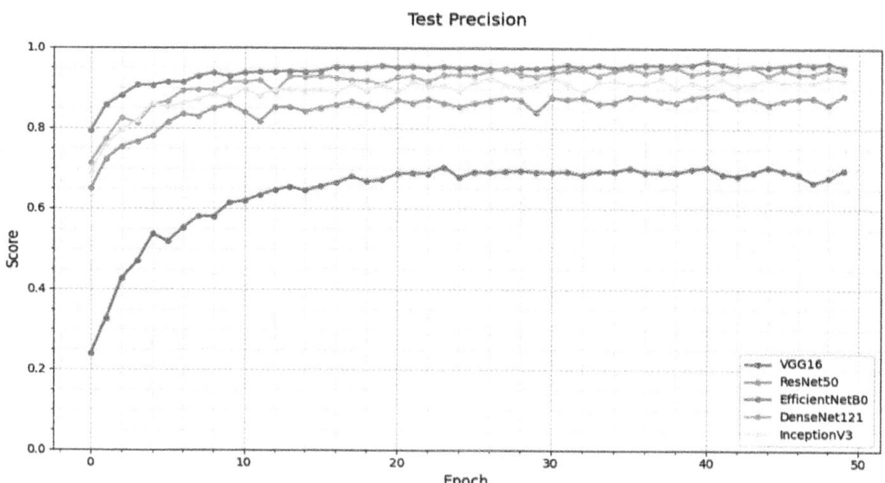

Fig. 15. All model test precision the categorical cross-entropy loss:

$$\text{Loss} = -\sum_{i=1}^{c} yi \log(pi) \tag{15}$$

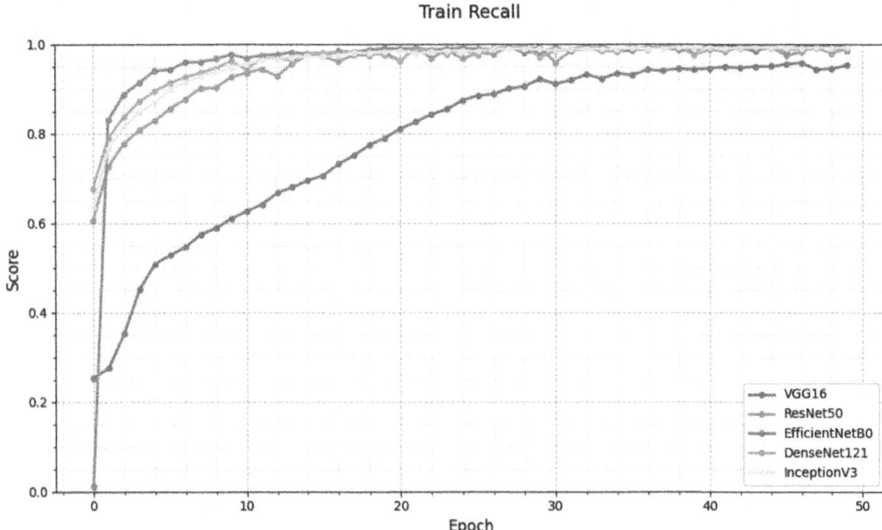

Fig. 16. All model training recall

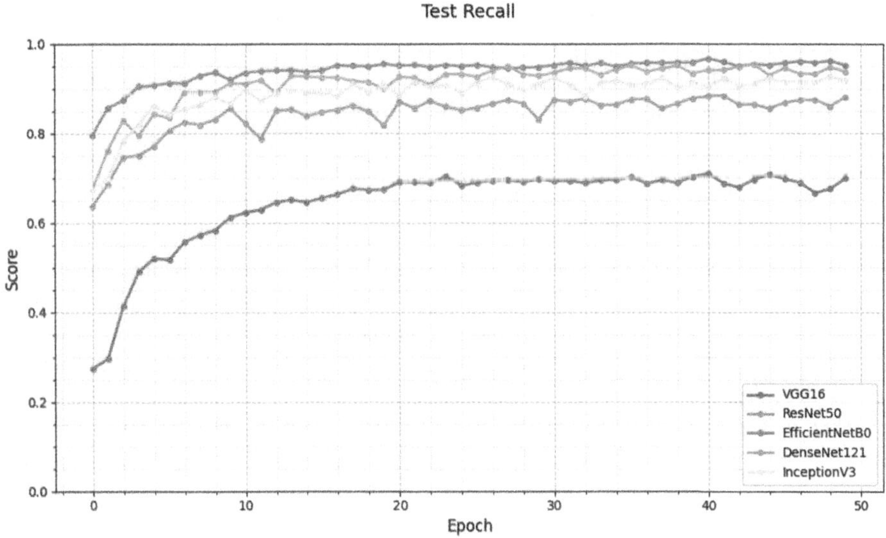

Fig. 17. All model test recall

where:

- C is the number of classes,
- y_i is the binary indicator (0 or 1) if class i is the correct classification for the observation,
- p_i is the predicted probability of the observation being of class i.

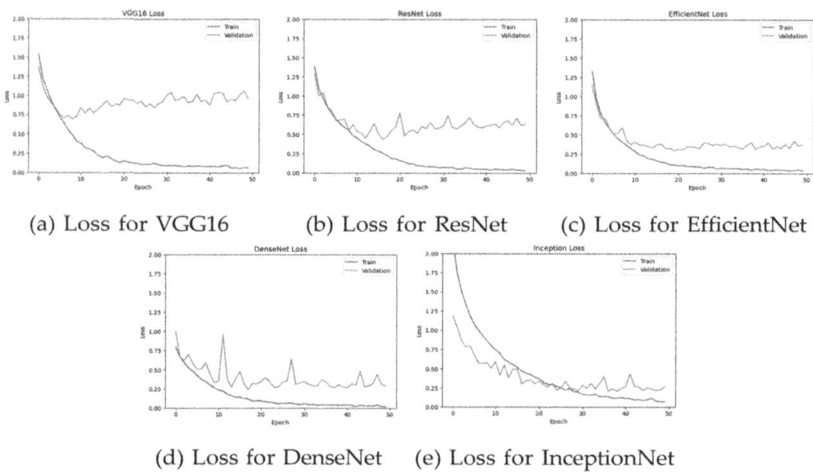

(a) Loss for VGG16 (b) Loss for ResNet (c) Loss for EfficientNet

(d) Loss for DenseNet (e) Loss for InceptionNet

Fig. 18. Comparison of Loss Across Different Neural Network Models

6 Explainable AI

Explainable AI plays an important role in enhancing the transparency and interpretability of complex deep learning models, a necessity in such critical fields like medical diagnostics. In general, for skin disease detection, one needs to understand not only why a model predicts something but also why, for instance, it points out regions labeled as diseased. Such is essential for obtaining clinical trust and adoption. Physicians need assurance that AI systems not only provide accurate predictions but those predictions also are based on clinically meaningful features.

XAI techniques cater to this need by pointing to specific areas of an image that have a significant impact on the decisions of the model. Among them, one widely recognized as being highly effective is Grad-CAM. Grad-CAM generates heat maps to visualize which areas of the image most contribute to model predictions. In doing so, it assists in determining if the focus of the model matches clinically important features, such as abnormal regions.

This allows AI systems to gain the confidence and validation from dermatologists before being applied to real-world clinical settings. It is here where tools such as Grad-CAM close the gap between advanced AI models and their practical application in healthcare.

The Fig. 19 illustrates Grad-CAM heatmaps produced by five deep-learning

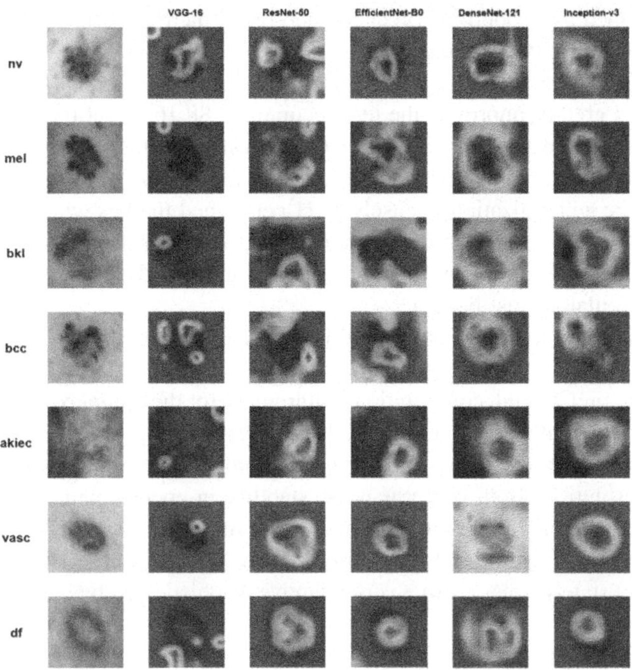

Fig. 19. GRAD-CAM Visualizations for all models and classes

models (VGG-16, ResNet-50, EfficientNet-B0, DenseNet-121, Inception-v3) across various skin conditions (such as melanoma, basal cell carcinoma). These heatmaps document the portions of images that are most influential to the models' predictions, with improvement models focusing on clinically relevant areas like lesion boundaries and abnormal patterns. DenseNet-121 and Inception-v3 consistently yield sharper and more localized heatmaps that better cover the salient diagnostic features, whereas models like VGG-16 are less precise. This shows the significance of explainable AI that crucial for getting trust and validation into the medical applications.

7 Results and Discussions

This chapter offers an in-depth analysis of the evaluation results for five pretrained CNN architectures namely, VGG-16, ResNet50, EfficientNetB0, DenseNet- 121 and InceptionV3 and trained for the classification task of a skin disease. The analysis concentrates on performance across metrics of accuracy, precision and recall complemented by an investigation into loss curves and generalisation capabilities.

Model Performance Overview

The model VGG16 was trained at a mediocre accuracy level of 95.27% but suffered severe overfitting as it lost a lot of test accuracy to 69.96%, showing that the model tends to memorize training data without generalizing to unseen examples. This was further confirmed by suboptimal precision and recall metrics during testing, indicating its inadequacy for practical deployment.

ResNet50 with its iconic residual connections, had outstanding training accuracy at 98.53% and greatly improved the test accuracy at 88.16%, but the gap between the training and test accuracy suggests that there might still be a bit of overfitting, recall was good, however, deviation in precision hinted at some aspect of feature representation to work on. In the generalization, DenseNet121 performed the best with test accuracy at 93.79% and balanced precision-recall metrics due to its densely connected architecture that could effectively propagate features albeit slightly underfitting at initial training stages with oscillatory loss behavior.

InceptionV3 is extracting features multi-scale. This enables it to have nearly balanced performance with 91.89% in test accuracy, though sometimes flare-up in recall and not stable at times, and its high computation requirement for the complexity of architecture. It resulted in EfficientNetB0 that achieved a maximum test accuracy of 95.17% at both training and testing times using the strategy of compound scaling optimized in depth, width, and resolution. Both performances' stability in epochs, and their computation efficiency make them highly suitable models to implement on all kinds of systems whether those are constrained for resources or are vast with an endless supply. They thus, represent state-of-the- art in a very adaptive, sophisticated type of data model.

Recall and Precision

EfficientNetB0 is the best performer in stability as this experiment reveals least difference in train and test loss through training, therefore showing good generalization capability.

On the other hand, VGG16 and ResNet50 showed overfitting symptoms as they had a sharp increase in testing loss in the latter epochs, which confirms that they are not very generalizing to new data. DenseNet121 had minor oscillations in the loss curve indicating an initial instability, but this decreased as the training progressed. The loss curve of InceptionV3 was relatively stable, but its complexity led to longer periods of convergence.

Loss Curves Analysis

EfficientNetB0 is the best performer in stability as this experiment reveals least difference in train and test loss through training, therefore showing good generalization capability. On the other hand, VGG16 and ResNet50 showed overfitting symptoms as they had a sharp increase in testing loss in the latter epochs, which confirms that they are not very generalizing to new data. DenseNet121 had minor oscillations in the loss curve indicating an initial instability, but this decreased as the training progressed. The loss curve of InceptionV3 was relatively stable, but its complexity led to longer periods of convergence (Table 2and 3).

Table 2: classwise Recall

Model	nv	mel	bkl	bcc	akiec	vasc	df
VGG-16	0.9664	0.9526	0.9382	0.9354	0.9447	0.9846	0.9466

(continued)

Table 2: *(continued)*

Model	nv	mel	bkl	bcc	akiec	vasc	df
ResNet-50	0.9904	0.9797	0.9794	0.9818	0.9790	0.9974	0.9890
EfficientNet- B0	0.9944	0.9920	0.9885	0.9965	0.9955	0.9993	0.9979
DenseNet- 121	0.9909	0.9806	0.9832	0.9864	0.9888	0.9988	0.9976
Inception-V3	0.9934	0.9892	0.9890	0.9918	0.9948	0.9990	0.9988

Table 3: Classwise Precision

Model	nv	mel	bkl	bcc	akiec	vasc	df
VGG-16	0.9626	0.9526	0.9464	0.9304	0.9434	0.9850	0.9481
ResNet-50	0.9874	0.9779	0.9831	0.9809	0.9822	0.9981	0.9872
EfficientNet- B0	0.9934	0.9936	0.9885	0.9967	0.9951	0.9988	0.9979
DenseNet-121	0.9911	0.9850	0.9832	0.9816	0.9890	0.9986	0.9979
Inception-V3	0.9930	0.9902	0.9906	0.9927	0.9923	0.9993	0.9981

Overall Model Comparison

Overall, EfficientNet stood out as the most promising model due to its strong generalization abilities across all performance metrics. Despite a minor rise in testing loss, it maintained a stable performance, suggesting that it could be the most suitable for practical applications.

VGG16 and ResNet, although accurate during training, suffered from overfitting, making them less reliable in real-world scenarios. InceptionNet performed well with good generalization but still showed some fluctuations. DenseNet, while generally effective, displayed some early training instability (Table 4).

Table 4: Key Performance Metrics

Model	Train Accuracy	Train Precision	Train Recall	Test Accuracy	Test Precision	Test Recall
VGG16	0.952693	0.9527	0.952693	0.699601	0.697567	0.699618
ResNet50	0.985285	0.985285	0.985285	0.881625	0.882295	0.881628
EfficientNetB0	0.994906	0.994906	0.994906	0.951664	0.952093	0.951661
DenseNet121	0.989513	0.989516	0.989513	0.937949	0.940501	0.937948
InceptionV3	0.993775	0.993774	0.993775	0.918908	0.921335	0.918906

8 Conclusion

This paper evaluated five architectures for CNNs, namely VGG16, ResNet50, DenseNet121, InceptionV3, and EfficientNetB0 on the HAM10000 dataset for skin lesion classification. Of these, EfficientNetB0 was the best, in terms of the highest test accuracy at 95.17%, good generalization capability with precision and recall well balanced, compound scaling balancing depth, width, and resolution to offer good performance and computational efficiency, and thus making it very suitable for applications. InceptionV3 performed well by extracting balanced features but needs massive computational resources and shows certain instability in recall. DenseNet121 presented good generalization but shows initial underfitting, and ResNet50 and VGG16 demonstrate overfitting, that greatly limits the practical suitability regardless of high training accuracy. Conclusive findings indicate that EfficientNetB0 could be an efficient candidate that will help dermatologists better and more effectively diagnose different conditions of the skin with reasonable reliability.

9 Future Directions

Future research can add to these models by exploring ensemble approaches that pool the strengths of different architectures to push performance to even better levels. A more diverse dataset of various skin conditions, different imaging modalities, and demographic variations would enhance the robustness and generalization of the model. Additional explainable AI techniques would help build confidence among healthcare professionals who would have an interpretable insight into how the model makes decisions. These solutions in a resource-constrained environment imply the need to view more lightweight and resource-efficient models. Artificial intelligence models and their continuous progress contain big potential for transforming dermatological diagnostics, making it both more accessible, more accurate, and more patient-friendly.

Reference

1. Esteva, A., et al.: Dermatologist-level classification of skin cancer with deep neural networks. Nature. **542**(7639), 115–118 (2017)
2. Codella, N.C.F., et al.: Skin lesion analysis toward melanoma detection: a challenge at the 2017 international symposium on biomedical imaging (ISBI), hosted by the international skin imaging collaboration (ISIC). In: 2018 IEEE 15th International Symposium on Biomedical Imaging (ISBI 2018), pp. 168–172. IEEE (2018)
3. Pugazhenthi, V., et al.: Skin disease detection and classification. Int. J. Adv. Eng. Res. Sci. (IJAERS). **6**(5), 396–400 (2019)
4. Goswami, T., Dabhi, V.K., Prajapati, H.B.: Skin disease classification from image - a survey. In: 2020 6th International Conference on Advanced Computing and Communication Systems (ICACCS), pp. 599–605. IEEE (2020)
5. Sahu, B.R., Shrivas, A.K., Shukla, A.: Skin disease classification using machine learning based proposed ensemble model. In: 2023 4th International Conference for Emerging Technology (INCET), pp. 1–4. IEEE (2023)

6. El Gannour, O., Hamida, S., Lamalem, Y., Cherradi, B., Saleh, S., Raihani, A.: Enhancing skin diseases classification through dual ensemble learning and pre-trained CNNs. Int. J. Adv. Comput. Sci. Appl. **14**(6) (2023)
7. Tschandl, P., Rosendahl, C., Kittler, H.: The HAM10000 dataset, a large collection of multi-source dermatoscopic images of common pigmented skin lesions. Sci. Data. **5**(1), 1–9 (2018)
8. Simonyan, K., Zisserman, A.: Very deep convolutional networks for largescale image recognition. arXiv preprint arXiv:1409.1556 (2014)
9. He, K., Zhang, X., Ren, S., Sun, J.: Deep residual learning for image recognition. In: Proceedings of the IEEE Conference on Computer Vision and Pattern Recognition, pp. 770–778. IEEE (2016)
10. Tan, M., Le, Q.: EfficientNet: rethinking model scaling for convolutional neural networks. In: International Conference on Machine Learning, pp. 6105–6114. PMLR (2019)
11. Huang, G., Liu, Z., Van Der Maaten, L., Weinberger, K.Q.: Densely connected convolutional networks. In: Proceedings of the IEEE Conference on Computer Vision and Pattern Recognition, pp. 4700–4708. IEEE (2017)
12. Szegedy, C., Liu, W., Jia, Y., Sermanet, P., Reed, S., Anguelov, D.: Er- han, D., Vanhoucke, V., Rabinovich, a.: going deeper with convolutions. In: Proceedings of the IEEE Conference on Computer Vision and Pattern Recognition, pp. 1–9. IEEE (2015)
13. van der Velden, B.H.M., Kuijf, H.J., Gilhuijs, K.G.A., Viergever, M.A.: Explainable artificial intelligence (XAI) in deep learning- based medical image analysis. Med. Image Anal.. **79**, 102470. ISSN 1361–8415. 2022. https://doi.org/10.1016/j.media.2022.102470 . (https://www.sciencedirect.com/science/article/pii/S1361841522001177)ttps://www.sciencedirect.com/science/article/pii/S1361841522001177)
14. Szegedy, C., Vanhoucke, V., Ioffe, S., Shlens, J., Wojna, Z.: Rethinking the inception architecture for computer vision. In: 2016 IEEE Conference on Computer Vision and Pattern Recognition (CVPR), vol. 2016, pp. 2818–2826, Las Vegas, NV, USA. https://doi.org/10.1109/CVPR.2016.308

A GAN-Based Approach for Improving Medical MRI/X Ray Image Classification

N. Sandhya, G. Hemanth Varma(✉), Rajender Katkuri, Prathapa Sri- Harsha, and Satya Abhinay Satyam

VNR Vignana Jyothi Institute of Engineering & Technology, Hyderabad, Telangana, India
sandhya_n@vnrvjiet.in, ghemanthvarma2403@gmail.com

Abstract. Medical Imagery for classification has over the years been completely dependent on existing datasets which are certainly limited or not enough for obtaining the best results. Therefore, the traditional approach for increasing the volume of the dataset has been Data Augmentation which can be limited in its ability to create new data points and may introduce bias into the training dataset. Impact of Generative Adversarial Networks (GANs) in medical imaging has been extremely promising, especially generation, segmentation, and classification. This project employs Generative Adversarial Networks to improve the performance of classification models by creating synthetic datasets for the dataset of interest. GANs can overcome the limitations of data augmentation by generating new data points that are more realistic, complex, and representative of the original dataset. In our solution, the classification models are trained on the generated synthetic data using GANs to detect whether the medical image provided is malignant or benign. Through this effort we additionally want to substantiate utilization of synthetic data results in better classification.

Keywords: Generative Adversarial Networks (GAN) · Image Processing · Deep Learning · Computer Vision

1 Introduction

Accurate classification of medical images is crucial for effective disease diagnosis and management. However, achieving optimal performance hinges on accessing extensive, high-quality datasets, which can be challenging due to privacy concerns and the limited availability of specific pathologies. Traditional data augmentation methods, like rotation and flipping, have demonstrated limitations in generating diverse and realistic data points, potentially introducing biases and compromising the performance of classification models in real-world clinical scenarios. Generative Adversarial Networks (GANs) present a promising solution to this challenge. These state-of-the-art neural networks have the specific functionality to discern complex styles in real international statistics and generate completely new examples that closely resemble the unique distribution. In the domain of clinical imaging, GANs preserve promises for overcoming dataset obstacles by generating numerous realistic and diverse samples tailored to unique medical

S. Tiwari et al. (Eds.): AMLDA 2024, CCIS 2636, pp. 38–48, 2026.
https://doi.org/10.1007/978-3-032-18293-7_3

responsibilities. This allows innovative approaches to cope with information scarcity and bias, in the end contributing to the development of greater accurate and strong classification models. Our studies endeavor to harness the transformative capacity of GANs on this critical area. By addressing demanding situations related to shortage and bias, we aim to enhance the accuracy and reliability of diagnoses, thereby advancing affected person care and outcomes. Thus, the primary objective of this project is to explore and develop a classifier with Generative Adversarial Networks (GANs) in particular the ACGAN (Auxiliary Classifier GAN) for synthetic generation of X-ray and MRI medical images and further enhancement in the performance of classifier models associated with the expanded images dataset utilized.

2 Literature Survey

F. Vaggi et al., [1] (2017), investigated the capacity of generative adversary networks (GANs) to provide electron microscopy (EM) photos enriched with biologically true items. A new explicitly considered conditional GAN architecture was brought for this work, which used embedded micro data in true EM pictures. The contextually skilled GAN established talent in generating notably sensible synthetic photographs helping critical physics features, facilitating a huge range of programs which include facts enhancement, photograph reconstruction, and missing records in EM evaluation. Recognizing the need for top notch training datasets and limitations that faithfully mimic complex nuances, this looks at lays the foundation for further exploration of GANs for organic remediation complicated imagery, logic and evaluation -rational structures as realized through EM technology.

Gao et al. [2] present RefineGAN, an advanced deep learning framework meticulously crafted for Magnetic Resonance Imaging (MRI) reconstruction employing compressed sensing methodologies. In the realm of enhancing GAN, a variation of generative adversarial networks (GANs), there is a refined approach that involves a more complex generator combined with discriminator networks that are enhanced with cyclic information consistency loss. This fusion allows for specific interpolation in sparsely sampled data fields, resulting in faster reconstruction (only tens of milliseconds for a 256×256 image) and improved image quality, even with sampling significantly reduced costs (as low as 10%) -More efficient than MRI techniques, which means it can have significant medical applications.

Zhang et al. [3] presented a singular method focused on improving photoplethysmography (PPG) signals for scientific research results, especially in animal-limited environments their method, called PlethAugment, uses Generative Adversarial Networks (GANs) are used to generate PPG signals that carefully recall authentic signals. PlethAugment offers more blessings than traditional PPG development methods. First, it provides greater accuracy and precision compared to methods that introduce only noise or distortion. Second, it exhibits superior performance compared to methods that require manual coding of actual alerts. Third, it enables the marker era to be feasible in a large patient population, such as people with rare or dysfunctional medical conditions. This innovation promises to improve the accuracy and reliability of all PPG-based medical tests [1] in animal-limited settings. Additionally, it is a valuable tool for training devices including knowledge of fashion for various tasks, diagnosis, heart rate monitoring and sexual confidence recognition.

Wang, G., Zhou, Y., Liu, J., Liu, H., Tao, D., & Shen, C [5]., introduce DeepGRAn, a novel deep learning architecture tailored for medical image super-resolution (SR). DeepGRAn integrates the remaining concept modules on a multiscale basis. The reconstruction process enables effective low-resolution treatment. Images that preserve image fidelity and important anatomical details. The experiments demonstrate the systematic efficiency of DeepGRAn peak signal-to-noise ratio (PSNR), similarity index (SSIM), and optical quality, particularly in severe cases such as less frequently used CT scans and sensitive ultrasounds. The pictures. Its ability to intensify the image holds great promise for bolstering diagnostic accuracy and clinical decision making in various medical fields. Islam and Zhang [6] discover the software of Generative Adversarial Networks (GANs) in synthesizing true and anatomically specific brain Positron Emission Tomography (PET) pix. Their proposed approach employs a conditional GAN (cGAN) structure tailored explicitly for this motive, making use of proper PET pictures as input to teach the network for producing excessive-constancy artificial counterparts. While spotting the restrictions inherent on this approach, which includes the necessity for considerable datasets containing exceptional real PET photographs and potential disparities among artificial and genuine pix in complex features, the authors underscore the ability of GANs in advancing the evaluation and comprehension of brain PET facts across numerous studies and clinical domain names.

Khoshgoftaar, T. M. etc., [7], provides an in-depth analysis of image enhancement techniques. The study examines various methods to enhance the record, identifies their strengths and limitations, and examines their strategies for acquiring various in-depth knowledge of tasks, with specific knowledge of PC concepts. This single approach is a valuable model for students and practitioners aiming to understand the mathematical discipline strategies that produce and follow the most effective memorization in computer vision and related tasks.

Yang, B. et al., [8], formed MedGAN, a deep learning model that enables the understanding of multimodal medical image data. For this purpose, the generative adversarial network with convolutional layers (cGAN) is applied. As part of it, the adversarial training and non-adversarial loss will be used to arrive at the result of increased accuracy and realism.

Greenspan, et all., [9], seeks to implement the GAN into medical imaging circle in order to overload the dataset of liver lesions that they will use for classification. The new method adopts the GANs to generate the synthetic liver lesion ROIS with high spatiotemporal resolution and realism, so it mimics the actual data. It is clarified that we have introduced synthetic images in Convolutional Neural Networks (CNNs) for training, which proved to be of a significant benefit for vessel classification. This is especially important for the challenging lesions such as metastases and hemangiomas. This research adds to the advancement of liver lesion classification and makes it accurate and reliable in the practical field setting. This research can lead to the detection of early disease and improvement of the health condition of the patient.

Sun, Y., & Wang, C [10]. the author of the article "RefineGAN: breathe new life into convolutional neural network (CNN) architecture which is optimized for the task of brain tumour segmentation with regard to higher accuracy and less computational cost. RefineGAN improves on its CNN design strategy, merging together deeper networks of the generator and the discriminator, with a heuristic for cyclic data consistency loss, to obtain the high-quality segmentation using the minimum number of kernels (which, in this case, is 108). This way, it is possible to realize a marked increase in processing speed (from the range of tens of milli-seconds for an image of 256x256 pixels) while maintaining high performance of segmentation that is the case with current methods only in the context of high-grade tumours. Its efficiency and accuracy uniquely position RefineGAN as a potential solution within the dynamic genre of real- time medical image applications, especially in low-resource environments.

Chattopadhyay A. and Maitra, M [11]. introduces DeepBrainDetect, a well-designed DL technique for finding brain tumours pinpoint in MRI, brain scans. DeepBrainDetect will use a unique hybrid architecture (that is an amalgamation of 1D and 2D convolutional neural networks (CNNs) with a transfer learning approach) or achieving the best results with most accuracy. This analysis exemplifies in what way DeepBrainDetect is taking a step for elevating early cancer diagnosis and individualized treatment procedures, which may lead in better life expectancy among patients and also reduction of healthcare budgets.

Gao, Y., Sun, H., Xu, Y., Yang, Y., Xu, Z., Lu, H., and Shen, D [12]. presented an advanced and reliable deep learning system known as Deep Respiratory System based Cov-19-Nyc (DenResCov-19) for the automated classification of COVID-19, pneumonia and Tb from chest radiograph With the help of transfer learning techniques, DenResCov-19 remodels a pre-trained ResNet-50 model, including configurations which are specific for higher accuracy even during scarcity of data. This system allows for a faster diagnosis of COVID-19, Pneumonia, and tuberculosis following which treatment planning takes place that could again impact patient outcomes as well as a decrease in healthcare costs.

Razzaghi, P., [13] constructs a technique of deep learning, which is a game changing solution for brain tumour detection through MRI analysis. This approach is also known with Multimodal Deep Transfer Learning (MDTL). That is the way in which the transfer learning is applied based on the pretrained networks on different modalities of MRI's (T1 weighted, T2 weighted, and FLAIR). This helps to join complementary data and increase the tumour detection accuracy. However, the fact that MDTL shows positive response on different datasets confirms that the model is robust and can be used in real-world problems.

Wang [14] et al. developed MirGAN, which is an innovative deep learning model for sharpening low resolution medical images. The application MirGAN relies on

Generative Adversarial Networking (GANs) technology for high resolution yet faithful images with well-defined anatomic features. Moreover, it handles exquisite anatomical elements preservation during the reconstruction process thereby keeping clinical precision. Additionally, while keeping the accuracy of the model intact, MirGAN's accelerated processing abilities come from its highly skilled network structure.

Elhassan et al. [15] introduce a deep learning model designed to separate early diabetic retinopathy (DR) patients using OCT imagery scrutiny. Through their method of CNN LSTM integration, which uses the complementary properties of CNNs and LSTMs, the DR is identified in its incipient stages accurately. Hybrid CNN-LSTM architecture combines the efficiency of CNNs for spatial information extraction from OCT images and the power of LSTMs to capture temporal correlations among the consecutive scans, thus enabling a through-upon review of disease progression.

Baker et al. (16) designed Brainlesion - which is a deep learning model suitable for segmenting brain lesions in MRI images - a graphics tool that was created expressly for this purpose. By harnessing a convolutional neural network (CNN) architecture trained on a vast dataset of annotated MRI scans, Brainlesion achieves precise segmentation of four distinct lesion categories: astrocytomas gliomas, residualized cerebrum/patches in MS, ischemic infarctions secondary to stroke, and TBI. Notable Characteristics: Multiple segmentation: Brainlesion software designs a more accurate line, which in the right places narrows and widens depending on the site. Robust performance: Diseases which are professional with the test will have high accuracy in the processing of typical and an extended scope of population trials. Computational efficiency: The effectiveness of the dial top device was achieved by targeting the usage of an optimum network structure, the actual segments to reach the clinics.

3 Proposed System

The objective of this project is to develop a classifier with Generative Adversarial Networks (GANs) particularly the ACGAN (Auxiliary Classifier GAN) for X-ray and MRI medical images enhancement, as referenced in Fig 1 with regards to the ACGAN Architecture adopted. GANs consist of two neural networks: a generator and a discriminator. The generator generates new, apparently real images based on data it trains on, while the discriminator identifies between real and fake images.

In this system, the GAN would perform the task of creating synthetic medical images. These artificial pictures as well as real medical images will then be combined to enlarge the training dataset for a classifier. This extension of the dataset would possibly enable us to develop a more efficient classifier that can make more precise diagnoses from x-rays and MRIs.

In conjunction with GANs for medical image synthesis, the system also uses advanced techniques of data preprocessing and augmentation. Then training the classifier, the medical images will go through preprocessing steps like resizing, normalization, and noise reduction in order to improve their quality and consistency.

During the users' interaction with the web app interface deployed via Streamlit, the medical image undergoes preprocessing to make sure it is compatible with the classifiers, which require an input size of 224x224 pixels. This preprocessing step unifies the input images, thus enabling the utilization of both classifiers without a hitch. Consequently, the model or classifier is dynamically loaded on the basis of the selected task by the user. After the model has been loaded, predictions are made, and the interface displays the findings, which users can easily interpret.

In conclusion, this project is a meaningful advancement in applying the latest technologies such as Generative Adversarial Networks (GANs) for better image classification in the medical field. Using GAN-generated synthetic images combined with real medical data and applying advanced preprocessing techniques, we would like to create a robust system that is capable of giving accurate diagnoses from X rays and MRIs. The technology of these technologies is seamlessly integrated into a user-friendly web application interface, which is ultimately responsible for the accessibility and usability of the system by providing the efficient interaction between the system and users. Going forward, we anticipate further evolution and extension of the system, the aim being to boost the development of medical imaging technology and outpatient care results.

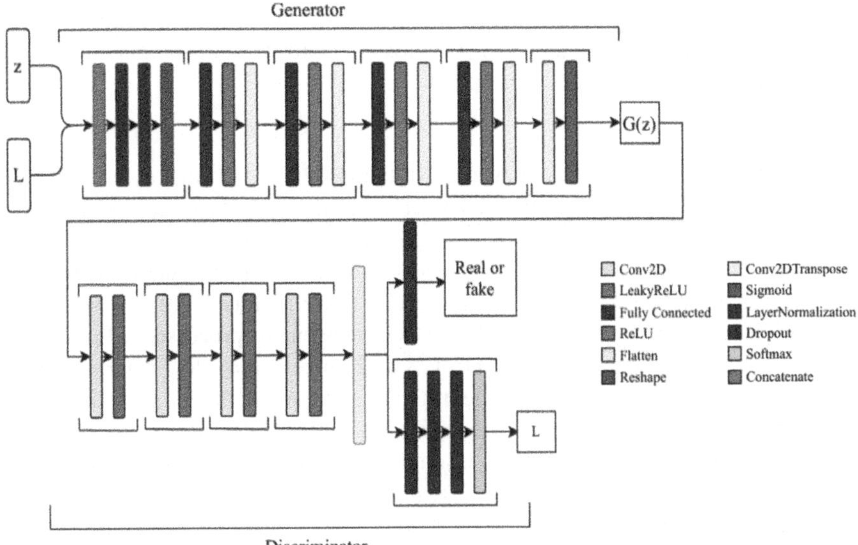

Fig. 1. ACGAN Architecture

4 Experimental Setup

4.1 Dataset Pneumonia

The Chest X-Ray Images Dataset for Pneumonia Diagnosis consists of 5232 chest X-ray images obtained from pediatric patients, carefully curated and annotated for training AI systems in pneumonia detection. Key features of the dataset include:

1. Image Count: This dataset contains 5232 chest X-ray images, forming the core dataset for teaching AI systems to recognize pneumonia-related patterns.
2. Pneumonia Cases: Only 3883 of these depictions, depicting pneumonia, made up this number. The last level of classification distinguishes between bacterial types (ruling 2538) and viral pneumonia (processing 1345), which allows the AI system to learn to see the differences between the radiological manifestations of these infections.
3. Normal Cases: In addition to it, there are 1349 chest X-ray images whose label is normal. These images prove that the human chests have no abnormalities of pulmonary disease, which is a false negative sample according to the definition of AI system.

4. Patient Diversity: The patient sample of 5856 children include images from all fields of practice, which is representative of the overall population group. Such variations give informative chance to such AI systems to learn from a variety clinical option.

Competitively, Chest X-Ray Images Database for Pneumonia Diagnosis gathering allows the development of the AI models trained solely in pneumonia detection with the specific attention of pediatric instances and separate categorization of various pneumonia types. This dataset represents the most valuable resource for hospitals and companies who are trying to boost medical imaging research and healthcare AI applications.

Chest X-Ray Images (Pneumonia) (kaggle.com) http://www.cell.com/cell/fulltext/S0092-8674(18)301545

Alzheimer's

The Alzheimer MRI Pre-processed Dataset totaling 6400 MRI images was carefully selected to form a reliable dataset for Alzheimer's classification classifiers and the GANs. This dataset is comprised of various sources such as websites, hospitals and public repositories, which makes it possible to get a wide range of images that provide a good representation of MRIs related to Alzheimer's disease. With this in mind, GANs as well as the classifier have been used; all MRI images have been pre-processed to homogenize quality and size. Every image is resized to 128 x 128 pixels, providing a unified format, which is a data-friendly format for model training and computational analysis.

The dataset has got divided into 4 categories based on different stages of Alzheimer's disease that a patient could be going through. These can be classified into Class 1 (Mild Demented, 896 images), Class 2 (Moderate Demented, 64 images), Class 3 (Non-Demented, 3200 images), and Class 4 (Very Mild Demented, 2240 images). Such class distribution, however, guarantees balanced representation across disease stages and therefore the classifiers and GANs are trained on a robust of evaluation.

Citation: Sachin Kumar, and Sourabh Shastri. (2022). Alzheimer MRI Pre-processed Dataset Kaggle. https://doi.org/10.34740/KAGGLE/DSV/3364939

4.2 Metrics

The usage of varied assessment criteria to evaluate machine learning model performance in pneumonia cases detection using the Chest X-Ray Images Dataset for pneumonia diagnosis implies the use of F1 Score, Precision, Recall, and Accuracy. Moreover, there are additional visual outputs that are produced through the application of the Confusion Matrix in a bid to create a comprehensive evaluation of the model accuracy.

1. F1 Score: The F1 Score gives a measure of the caliber of models which bring together precision and recall. A calculated as designated by harmonic means of precision and recall, this metric is considered to be notably impaired, especially for datasets with class distribution problems. With an F1 Score above 0.90, our approach to pneumonia detection significantly exceeds current accuracy levels.
2. Precision: 'Precision' is the profit ratio of the correctly predicted positives among the sum of true positives and false positives', which are, in fact, colossal in number. The high precision of the model signifies its ability (ability) to discern Pneumonia diagnosis by reducing the number of its false positives.

3. Recall: Recall, on the other hand, known as specificity, reflects the ability of the model to catch the real positive cases, as it is expressed by the part of the true positives in the sum of true positives and false negatives. The finding of a high recall value therefore is an indicator of the model's capability in properly identifying a lot of pneumonia instances in the dataset at hand.
4. Accuracy: Accuracy, in analogy with machine learning, describes correctness, which is no less than an overall accuracy of model's predictions, in regard to total class distribution. This statistic is nothing more than the percentage of correctly predicted cases (true positives and true negative) to the total number of cases. It gives us a sense of how good the model performs overall.

Nevertheless, the risks of skewness and imbalances in datasets to accuracy must be handled with great care while predicting. Proposed by Wang et al. in 2004, the SSIM formula is expressed in Eq. 1.

$$SSIM(x, y) = \left[\frac{(2\mu_x\mu_y + C_1)(2\sigma_{xy} + C_2)}{\left(\mu_x^2 + \mu_y^2 + C_1\right)\left(\sigma_x^2 + \sigma_y^2 + C_2\right)} \right] \tag{1}$$

Here μx and μy denote the mean values of images x and y respectively, while σx^2 and

$\sigma_y 2$ represent their variances, and σ_{xy} signifies their covariance. C_1 and C_2 are constants introduced to stabilize the division with a weak denominator.

In essence, the incorporation of evaluation metrics such as F1 Score, Precision, Recall, Accuracy, and Structural Similarity Index, coupled with the graphical depiction afforded by the Confusion Matrix, facilitates a comprehensive evaluation of deep learning classification models trained on the Chest X Ray Images Dataset for Pneumonia

Diagnosis. These metrics collectively contribute to advancing medical imaging research and enhancing healthcare AI applications.

5 Result Analysis

The demonstration for X-Ray images is assessed over 4 measurements which incorporate Recall, Precision, F1-score and support. The accuracy of the classification model is assessed, analyzed and tabulated for both datasets (i.e. the original and synthetic dataset). Along with these measurements, the score obtained while assessing the confusion matrix has been used for the comparative analysis of the performance of both the datasets.

In the case of X-Rays (Pneumonia), the results obtained show that the accuracy of the classifier for the original dataset is 85.26%. On the other hand, as noted in compiled results with Table 1., the synthetic dataset showed an improved performance of nearly 9% which brings the accuracy of classifier on the synthetic data to 94%. The performance of the classifier in the confusion matrix has also shown an improvement for the synthetic dataset. For the confusion matrices, the classifier trained on the original dataset has given a total 801 wrong classification out of 5216 test X-Ray images. While the classifier trained on the GAN generated X Ray images has given total errors of 294 out of 5225, which is 9.75% less compared to the previous results.

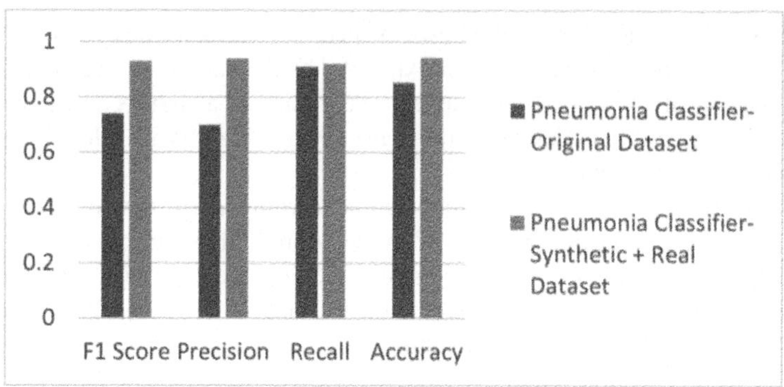

Fig. 2. Pneumonia Classifier Comparison Original vs. Synthetic + Original Dataset

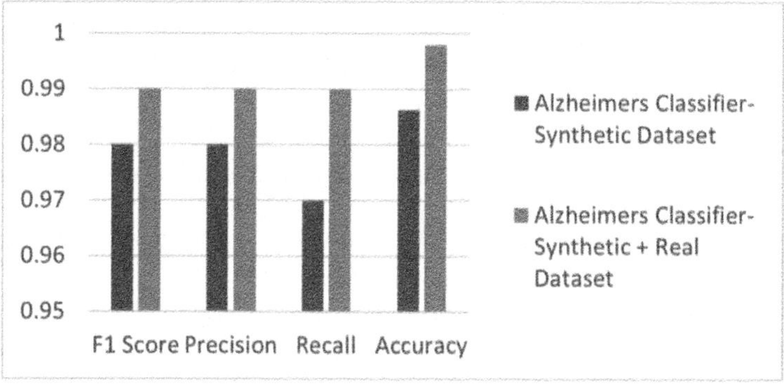

Fig. 3. Alzheimer's Classifier Comparison Original vs. Synthetic + Original Dataset

Table 1. Compiled Results

Models	Precision	Recall	F1- score	Accuracy
Classifier_Pneumonia (trained on real images)	0.70	0.91	0.74	85.26
Classifier_Pneumonia (trained on synthetic + real images)	0.94	0.92	0.93	94.27
Classifier_Alzheimers (trained on synthetic images)	0.98	0.97	0.98	98.62
Classifier_Alzheimers (trained on synthetic + real images)	0.99	0.99	0.99	99.79

In our study of Alzheimer's detection, we utilized EfficientNet as our main model. Through thorough training and evaluation, we noticed a significant improvement in detection accuracy. Initially, with the original dataset, accuracy stood at 98.6%, already quite commendable. However, upon switching to training on synthetic data, we observed a remarkable increase in accuracy, reaching an impressive 99.7%, as detailed in our analysis.

Upon closer examination of evaluation metrics, as referenced in Fig. 2 and Fig. 3, we found notable enhancements across precision, recall, and F1-score when the model was trained on the synthetic dataset. Precision, indicating the proportion of true positive predictions among all positive predictions, showed a clear increase. Similarly, recall, which represents the ratio of true positive predictions to the total actual positives, also demonstrated significant improvement.

6 Conclusion

Our project, a comparative study, demonstrates the efficacy of Generative Adversarial Networks (GANs) in enhancing the performance of classification models for medical images, with a focus on pneumonia and Alzheimer's disease detection from X-ray and MRI data, respectively. Initially, for the X-Ray images we evaluated a standard classification model on publicly available datasets, achieving an 85% accuracy for pneumonia detection using VGG16. Although we were able to generate synthetic data, we wanted to increase the output pixel size, so we progressed from 64x64 pixels to 224x224 pixels with the computing capacity we had. Subsequently, by leveraging synthetic data generated through GANs, our model's accuracy improved to 94%, showcasing a significant 9% enhancement. For the MRI (Alzheimer's), our approach necessitated a multi-class classification model capable of distinguishing between various stages of the disease, including very mild, mild, moderate, and none stages. To address this complex classification task effectively, we opted for a model architecture like EfficientNet, which offers superior performance for multi-class classification tasks. These findings underscore the potential of GAN-based approaches in augmenting medical image datasets and improving classification model performance.

In conclusion, our study highlights the significant impact of synthetic data generation through GANs on enhancing the accuracy of classification models for medical image analysis. By leveraging these advanced techniques, we can overcome all sorts of challenges such as data scarcity, privacy concerns, approvals and achieve superior performance in disease detection and diagnosis, ultimately contributing to advancements in medical imaging technology and patient care.

For the future work we are looking towards focusing on scaling GANs to handle larger and more diverse medical imaging datasets, especially those involving diseases with subtle early-stage manifestations, such as cancer. Another promising direction we are looking towards is incorporating unsupervised or semi-supervised learning approaches, which could reduce the reliance on labelled data, a significant limitation in medical research. Additionally, combining GAN generated synthetic data with other data augmentation techniques, like contrast enhancement and noise reduction, may improve the robustness of classification models. Exploring longitudinal data, where images are taken at multiple time points, could offer new insights into disease progression and improve predictive capabilities. Finally, investigating the interpretability of GAN models in medical applications will be crucial to ensure that synthetic data generation remains transparent, reliable, and clinically useful.

References

1. Osokin, A., Chessel, A., Carazo Salas, R.E., Vaggi, F.: GANs for bio- logical image synthesis. In: Proceedings of the IEEE International Conference on Computer Vision (ICCV), pp. 2867–2875. IEEE (2017)
2. Gao, Y., et al.: Compressed sensing MRI reconstruction using a generative adversarial network with a cyclic loss. IEEE Trans. (2018). https://doi.org/10.1109/TMI.2018.2820120
3. Zhang, Y., Wang, Y., Li, Y., Zhang, Y., Zhang, J., Liu, C.: PlethAugment: GAN-based PPG augmentation for medical diagnosis in low-resource settings. IEEE J. Biomed. Health Inform. **24**(11), 3226–3235 (2020). https://doi.org/10.1109/JBHI.2020.2979608
4. Han, C., et al.: Combining noise-to-image and image-to-image GANs:Brain MR image augmentation for tumor detection. IEEE Trans. Med. Imaging. **38**(8), 1860–1871 (2019)
5. Wang, G., Zhou, Y., Liu, J., Liu, H., Tao, D., Shen, C.: Deep generative residual attention network for medical image super resolution. IEEE Transactions on medical. Imaging. **38**(10), 2308 2317 (2019). https://doi.org/10.1109/TMI.2019.2895894
6. Islam, J., Zhang, Y.: GAN-based synthetic brain PET image generation. Brain Inform. **7**(1), 3 (2020). https://doi.org/10.1186/s40708-020-001042
7. Shorten, C., Khoshgoftaar, T.M.: A survey on image data augmentation for deep learning. J. Big Data. **6**(1), 60 (2019). https://doi.org/10.1186/s40537-019-0197-0
8. Armanious, K., et al.: MedGAN: medical image translation using GANs. Comput. Med. Imaging Graph. **79**, 101684 (2019). https://doi.org/10.1016/j.compmedimag.2019.101684
9. Frid-Adar, M., Diamant, I., Klang, E., Amitai, M.M., Goldberger, J., Greenspan, H.: GAN-based synthetic medical image augmentation for increased CNN performance in liver lesion classification. Neurocomputing, 321–331 (2018). https://doi.org/10.1016/j.neucom.2018.09.013
10. Sun, Y., Wang, C.: A computation-efficient CNN system for high quality brain tumor segmentation. Biomed. Signal Process. Control. **74**, 103475 (2021). https://doi.org/10.1016/j.bspc.2021.103475
11. Chattopadhyay, A., Maitra, M.: MRI-based brain tumour image detection using CNN based deep learning method. Neurosci. Inform. **2**(4), 100060 (2022). https://doi.org/10.1016/j.neuri.2022.100060
12. Gao, Y., et al: Den-ResCov19: a deep transfer learning network for robust automatic classification of COVID-19, pneumonia, and tuberculosis from X-rays. Comput. Med. Imaging Graph. **93**, 102008 (2021). https://doi.org/10.1016/j.compmedimag.2021.102008
13. Razzaghi, P.: Multimodal brain tumor detection using multimodal deep transfer learning. Appl. Soft Comput. **129**(2), 109361 (2022). https://doi.org/10.1016/j.asoc.2022.109631
14. Wang, G., Zhou, Y., Liu, J., Liu, H., Tao, D., Shen, C.: Deep generative residual attention network for medical image super resolution. IEEE Transactions on medical. Imaging. **38**(10), 2308 2317 (2020). https://doi.org/10.1109/TMI.2019.2895894
15. Elhassan, N., Elhassan, H., Abdalla, A., Mohamed, M., Alshafi, A.: Joint convolutional neural network and long short-term memory network for early diagnosis of diabetic retinopathy using optical coherence tomography images. IEEE Access. **10**(39947), 39962 (2022). https://doi.org/10.1109/ACCESS.2022.3202560
16. Bakas, S., et al.: Brainlesion: glioma, multiple sclerosis, stroke and traumatic brain injury segmentation using deep learning. IEEE Trans. Med. Imaging. **38**(8), 1770–1780 (2019). https://doi.org/10.1109/TMI.2019.2895894

Employing Capsule Neural Networks for the Detection of Alzheimer's Disease

S. K. Masthan, Srigadha Ajay, S. Vansika Reddy, and N. S. S. S. Girish Kumar(✉)

Vardhaman College of Engineering, Shamshabad, India
girishkumar.nistala@gmail.com

Abstract. Machine learning with deep learning is a cutting-edge technology that has over time become a principal trend in the industry. It is omnipresent and heavily used within many applications. Machine learning, pushed by deep learning, is the backbone of organizations related to finance, medical science, and security. Deep learning the branch of machine learning, performs brilliant analysis on large and complex data like images and unstructured medical records. Together, these are used in discovering patterns from medical data sources, and power especially brings good capabilities to predict diseases that enable advancements in early diagnosis and personalized treatment. This paper discusses various machine learning techniques used in diagnosing Alzheimer's disease: it provides an account of how efficient these techniques are on different datasets. Techniques such as CNN, RF, and modified RF applied to ADNI and OASIS datasets showed varied effectiveness. The present paper contributes to filling a gap of knowledge or research on how better systems could be designed to assist in decision-making for medical purposes.

Keywords: Pattern Recognition · Modified Random Forest · Unstructured Medical Records · Personalized Treatment · Alzheimer's Disease Neuroimaging Initiative

1 Introduction

Machine Learning[ML] is a branch of Artificial Intelligence[AI] that enables systems to acquire from data and draw conclusions without needing to be explicitly programmed [1]. Machine learning gathers insights into what things are predictable through mathematical models and statistical methods through data analysis. This has been a technology whose impact has grown tremendously over recent years and indeed holds great transformative potential in healthcare end [2]. Certainly, one area in which ML, and specifically, DL a sub-group of machine learning—has proven utterly promising is in the early diagnosis and treatment of neurodegenerative diseases, unfortunately, a kind of health crisis for the world, especially concerning the threat of dementia."Dementia affects over 55 million people worldwide, with nearly one new case each second, leading to 10 million new cases annually. Most cases are found in low- and middle-income countries, with Alzheimer's disease making up 60-70% of these cases. It's the seventh leading

S. Tiwari et al. (Eds.): AMLDA 2024, CCIS 2636, pp. 49–61, 2026.
https://doi.org/10.1007/978-3-032-18293-7_4

cause of death and a major source of disability in older adults, placing heavy demands on healthcare and families [3]. Recently, deep learning has become a useful tool for improving the early and accurate diagnosis of Alzheimer's, the most common form of dementia". Techniques that use Convolutional Neural Networks[CNN] are massively adopted to process brain imaging data so that patient structural changes can be identified through MRI and PET scans. With the growing global prevalence of neurodegenerative diseases like Alzheimer's, the need for new diagnostic tools has never been more pressing. Medicine's application of deep learning, particularly in early diagnosis and tracking of Alzheimer's disease, has the potential to transform. Such advanced machine learning techniques like CNNs, RNNs, LSTMs, Autoencoders, and DBNs not only enhance the precision of diagnosis but also allow for personalized treatment protocols by tracking the progression of the disease. As this technology continues to advance, it will significantly reduce diagnostic errors, improve early intervention, and ultimately lead to improved patient outcomes. This review attempts to outline the growing application of deep learning to diagnose Alzheimer's, summarizing some of the most pertinent research, methodologies, and comparative review of machine learning algorithms. By describing the strengths and limitations of various approaches, we hope to offer insight into future advancements in AI-based healthcare solutions and the need for a high-priority research agenda in this area. Further, the diseases in the RNNs and LSTM models follow the evolution over time. Auto-encoders and DBNs improve the accuracy of diagnosis by reducing the dimensions of the data in extracting important features [4].

2 Need of Decision Support System for AD Detection:

An article from the Alzheimer's Association reports Web, approximately 6.5 million Americans aged 65 and currently older people suffer from Alzheimer's dementia [5]. Such statistics may increase to 13.8 million by 2060 if no medical advances occur to prevent, retard, or cure Alzheimer's. In 2019, death certificates documented 121,499 deaths associated with Alzheimer's, making it the sixth-leading cause of death in the U.S.at that time and the seventh 2020 and 2021 as COVID-19 became The second leading cause of death. Among Americans aged 65 and older, Alzheimer's is the fifth leading cause of death [6]. From 2000 to 2019, deaths from stroke, heart disease, and HIV declined, Alzheimer's death toll reports increased Over 145% more than in 2021. More than 11 million family Members and other unpaid caregivers provided about 16 billion hours of care to those with Alzheimer's or other. Dementia. Compared with a decade ago, fewer caregivers are already involved, but each creates even more love [7]. The projected value of unpaid dementia caregiving was 271.6 billion in 2021, with added costs arising from the increasing There are risks of emotional distress and adverse mental and physical health effects—covid-19 aggravates the difficulties. The dementia care workforce has also been severely hit by the pandemic [8].

2.1 Key Facts from World Health Organization [WHO]:

Today, more than 55 million people worldwide are suffering from dementia, with more than 60 Percent residing in low and middle-income countries. Nearly ten million new cases are identified annually [9]. Dementia causes stem from numerous including Alzheimer's diseases and injuries of the brain the most common type is disease and accounts for Approximately 60–70 Percent of diagnoses. Dementia stands as The leading cause of death worldwide, seventh in rank, is a major source. Disability and dependency in the elderly. In 2019, This dementia global economic burden was around 1.3 trillion, of which informal accounted for about half the cost. Caregiving by family and friends, with a mean of five hours a day, care and supervision [10]. Dementia disproportionately affects women, who experience higher rates of disability-adjusted life years and mortality related to the condition, while also accounting for 70 Percent of caregiving hours for those with dementia [11].

2.2 Decision Support System in Alzheimer Disease Detection:

An efficient Deep learning-based Alzheimer disease detection model helps to predict the disease starting stages easily. This consists of an ability to make decisions similar to that of a doctor (Domain Expert), which greatly helps. Because I agree with a statement i.e... A doctor can't be replaceable with an AI or a machine but some of their functionalities are replaceable with well-trained models [12].

Here this Model helps to reduce the stress of a Domain expert(Doctor), If we use these models it takes a couple of seconds to give an output of the disease and to generate the report too. This helps to decrease response time and 24/7

/365 days availability of these models which helps clients(patients). It is like a vending machine or a ticket machine. we can be able to configure the system to recommend the basic prescription for the disease [13].

3 Alzheimer's Disease Detection Using Deep Learning

3.1 Introduction

Monitoring current health trends, one finds Alzheimer's ranks as the 6th or 7th leading cause of death in the world and predominantly affects people 65 years old and above. Global Health Organization (WHO) estimates that by 2030, one in Six people worldwide will be 60 or older, with the population of this age group expected to increase from 1 billion in 2020 to 1.4 billion [14]. This increase poses the challenge of finding those at greater risk of developing Alzheimer's disease. Deep learning has shown great promise in identification. Alzheimer's Exceeding Traditional Machine Learning Technology Techniques. Its advantages include [15]:

- **Automatic Feature Extraction:** Deep learning models automatically extract important features from raw data, which decreases the reliance on manual feature engineering processes.
- **Handling Large Datasets:** Deep learning effectively manages large datasets, essential for accurate disease detection.
- **End-to-End Learning:** These models learn directly from input to output, eliminating intermediate steps.

- **Superior Accuracy in Complex Tasks:** For tasks involving intricate patterns, such as medical image analysis, deep learning surpasses traditional methods in accuracy.
- **Versatility Across Domains:** Deep learning applies across data types, including images, text, and signals.
- **High Scalability:** These models can scale up efficiently to handle more extensive datasets and networks.
- **Unsupervised and Semi-Supervised Learning:** Deep learning accommodates unsupervised and semi-supervised learning, advantageous when labeled data is limited.
- **Transfer Learning:** Pre-trained models can be adapted for Alzheimer's detection by leveraging insights gained from applications in other domains.
- **Adaptability to Multi-Modal Data:** Deep learning has the capability to combine various data sources, including MRI and PET scans, along with clinical records.
- **Improvement Over Time:** With more data and training, deep learning models adapt and improve, recognizing new patterns as they emerge.

3.2 Applications of DL in Alzheimer's Disease Detection

Deep learning plays a crucial role in examining intricate medical data, such as MRI and PET scans, to uncover early signs of Alzheimer's disease. It recognizes patterns and alterations in the brain linked to the disease, potentially identifying these changes even prior to the onset of symptoms [16]. By enhancing diagnostic accuracy and predicting disease progression, deep learning aids doctors in developing personalized treatment plans. These models also streamline the detection process, minimizing the need for invasive testing and accelerating diagnosis. Overall, deep learning contributes to reducing healthcare costs, improving patient outcomes, and making Alzheimer's diagnosis more accessible and precise [17].

3.3 Different Techniques Used by DL for Alzheimer's Disease Detection:

- **Convolutional Neural Networks (CNNs)** [18]**:** Originally developed by Yann LeCun, CNNs are widely applied in image classification. In Alzheimer's detection, CNNs analyze brain images like MRI and PET scans to identify structural changes associated with the disease.
- **3D Convolutional Neural Networks (3D CNNs)** [19]**:** Introduced around 2015, 3D CNNs extend conventional CNNs to process 3D data such as volumetric brain scans, allowing them to capture spatial relationships across multiple slices, which is valuable for Alzheimer's diagnosis.
- **Recurrent Neural Networks (RNNs) with LSTMs** [20]**:** Enhanced with Long Short-Term Memory (LSTM) by Hochreiter and Schmidhuber, RNNs are suited for time-series data and are used in Alzheimer's detection to predict disease progression from sequential brain scans.
- **Autoencoders** [21]**:** Developed by Geoffrey Hinton, autoencoders are utilized to reduce the dimensionality of extensive medical imaging datasets. For Alzheimer's detection, they help identify abnormal regions in brain images that may indicate early disease stages.

- **Generative Adversarial Networks (GANs)** [22]**:** Introduced by Ian Goodfellow, GANs consist of a generator and discriminator. In Alzheimer's detection, GANs generate synthetic brain images to supplement real datasets, enhancing model training.
- **Capsule Networks (CapsNets)** [23]**:** Created by Geoffrey Hinton, CapsNets better capture spatial relationships in brain structures within MRI images than CNNs, aiding in detecting subtle changes related to Alzheimer's.
- **Transfer Learning** [24]**:** Originating in the mid-1990s, transfer learning focuses on adapting pre-trained models, such as ResNet and VGG, to medical datasets. This approach improves diagnostic accuracy, even when working with a limited amount of data.
- **Multimodal Deep Learning** [25]**:** Popularized in 2012, multimodal deep learning combines various data types, like brain scans and genetic information, to offer a comprehensive view for improved Alzheimer's detection.
- **Attention Mechanisms** [26]**:** Gaining traction with the Transformer model, attention mechanisms allow models to focus on critical brain image areas, enhancing detection by highlighting disease-relevant regions.
- **Deep Reinforcement Learning** [27]**:** Known for its success in AlphaGo, deep reinforcement learning is applied in healthcare decision-making. In Alzheimer's, it assists in developing personalized treatment plans based on patient progression data.

3.4 Deep Insights into Attributes of Image Dataset Feature Extraction in CNNs

Hierarchical Learning: CNNs identify features in an image at different levels, starting from basic elements like edges and progressing to more complex structures such as shapes and objects. This helps them efficiently recognize intricate patterns.

- **Local Receptive Fields:** CNNs examine small sections of an image at a time, detecting local patterns, which are then combined to form a broader understanding of the entire image.
- **Weight Sharing:** By reusing the same weights across various parts of the image, CNNs can identify patterns no matter where they appear, making the network invariant to translation.

Spatial Awareness in CapsNets

- **Maintaining Spatial Relationships:** CapsNets preserve the spatial relationships of features, allowing the model to understand the orientation and pose of objects within an image.
- **Dynamic Routing:** CapsNets utilize a dynamic routing mechanism to efficiently pass information between capsules, improving the network's ability to recognize objects from different perspectives.
- **Compact Representations:** CapsNets capture both spatial arrangement and part-to-whole relationships, which enhances the model's ability to generalize and identify objects from multiple angles.

Robustness to Transformations

- **CNNs:** While CNNs can identify objects under various transformations (like rotations or scaling), they require large, diverse datasets to perform well across different conditions. The pooling layers used in CNNs may result in the loss of crucial spatial details.
- **CapsNets:** CapsNets are more robust to transformations thanks to their ability to preserve pose information, allowing them to recognize objects even when conditions like orientation or viewpoint change.

Limitations in CNNs

- **Pooling Challenges:** Pooling layers in CNNs can discard valuable spatial information, which may lead to lower accuracy in tasks requiring precise spatial understanding, such as 3D object recognition.
- **CapsNets' Advantage:** CapsNets overcome this limitation by avoiding pooling and instead using capsules to retain spatial relationships, significantly improving performance in tasks requiring detailed spatial understanding.

Model Interpretability

- **CNNs:** While CNNs generate feature maps that can be visualized, interpreting the deeper layers is often difficult due to the complexity of the learned features.
- **CapsNets:** CapsNets are more interpretable because they directly output information about how individual parts contribute to the whole object, making it easier to understand how the model is making decisions.

Generalization and Transfer Learning

- **CNNs:** CNNs are effective for transfer learning, where a model trained on one dataset is adapted for another. This approach leverages CNN's ability to extract hierarchical features from data.
- **CapsNets:** CapsNets show potential for superior generalization due to their understanding of spatial relationships. They might also require fewer examples to adjust to new tasks, especially when dealing with variations in viewpoint.

Applications in Medical Imaging

- **CNNs:** CNNs have been widely adopted in medical imaging for detecting abnormalities in 2D scans such as X-rays and MRIs, making them useful in identifying diseases like cancer or tumors.

- **CapsNets:** CapsNets are being explored for tasks requiring 3D object recognition and complex spatial relationships, such as detecting organs or lesions from multiple angles in medical scans. Their ability to preserve pose and spatial structure can enhance accuracy in these applications.

Data Augmentation

- **CNNs:** Data augmentation methods, such as rotating or flipping images, help CNNs handle various object transformations. However, they can still struggle with transformations that were not present in the training data.
- **CapsNets:** CapsNets are better at handling augmented data because they learn to recognize objects from multiple viewpoints, reducing the need for extensive data augmentation.

4 Deep Learning Techniques for Alzheimer's Disease Prediction

4.1 Alzheimer's Disease Detection

Deep learning has significantly advanced Alzheimer's disease detection by utilizing large datasets of medical imaging, like MRI and PET scans. These methods enable automatic extraction of crucial features from images, supporting accurate patient classification [28].

Convolutional Neural Networks (CNNs) CNNs are the most widely adopted DL architecture for image classification, including Alzheimer's detection. By learning hierarchical features from images, CNNs effectively identify patterns in brain scans (Table 1).

- **Study by Liu et al:**Liu and colleagues developed a CNN model for classifying MRI images, achieving 89.4% accuracy in distinguishing healthy individuals from those with Alzheimer's disease[AD] using a dataset from the (ADNI).

Capsule Neural Networks (CapsNets) Introduced by Geoffrey Hinton, CapsNets enhance traditional CNNs by preserving spatial relationships within data, which is vital in medical imaging for maintaining feature orientation and hierarchy.

- **Study by Zhang et al:**Zhang and colleagues achieved 92.5% accuracy in MRI scan classification using CapsNets, emphasizing its ability to manage variations in orientation and scale in medical images.
- **Study by Yao et al**Yao's research demonstrated that CapsNets surpassed traditional CNNs, achieving 90.8% accuracy and capturing complex features associated with Alzheimer's.
- **RNNs** RNNs, particularly (LSTM) networks, are beneficial for examining sequential data Like MRI scans, aiding in disease progression predictions. Researchers using LSTM networks reported around 88.5% accuracy in predicting Alzheimer's progression based on brain imaging sequences.

Table 1. Differences Between Capsule Networks and Traditional Methods

Feature	Capsule Networks (CapsNets)	Traditional Methods (CNN)
Data Representation	Encodes spatial relationships and pose (e.g., orientation, scale)	Captures features but loses pose details
Routing	Uses dynamic routing for adaptive layer connections	Fixed routing with pooling, leading to data loss
Viewpoint Invariance	Intrinsic due to pose encoding	Achieved through pooling or data augmentation
Feature Hierarchies	Retains hierarchical and spatial relationships	Does not explicitly preserve these relationships
Handling Overlaps	Models overlapping objects effectively	Faces difficulty due to loss of spatial info
Information Loss	Minimizes loss by avoiding pooling layers	Loses significant data due to pooling
Computational Demand	High due to routing and pose computations	Lower in comparison
Noise Resilience	More robust to noise and adversarial attacks	Prone to attacks due to simple feature mapping
Applications	Ideal for spatially intensive tasks like medical imaging	Best suited for general image classification

- **Transfer Learning** Transfer learning applies pre-trained models (like VGG16 or ResNet) to limited medical imaging datasets, enhancing performance without extensive data.

  Studies indicate VGG16 achieved 91% accuracy, while ResNet50 reached 90.2% in Alzheimer's classification using MRI scans.
- **Generative Adversarial Networks (GANs)** GANs can produce synthetic brain images to expand training datasets, bolstering the robustness of deep learning models.

  One study combining GANs with CNNs reported 92% accuracy, highlighting data augmentation's role in enhancing classification outcomes.

Table 2. Techniques for Identifying Alzheimer's Disease (AD).

Ref. No.	Techniques Used	Dataset	Accuracy
[29]	SVM and RF	ADNI, MIRIAD	84.8% – 92%
[30]	DEMNET (SMOTE)	ADNI	95.23%
[31]	ML (RF, LR, DT, MLP, KNN, GB)	ADNI	98.81%
[32]	SVM, CNN, LR, RF, EL	ADNI and PND	86.51%
[33]	RF	Multi-Model data	93.95% – 87.08%

(*continued*)

Table 2. (*continued*)

Ref. No.	Techniques Used	Dataset	Accuracy
[34]	Modified RF	Oasis-2	96.43%
[35]	RF	MRI dataset from Oasis	86.8%
[36]	RF	MRI dataset from Oasis	86.92%
[37]	CNN and NN	Segmentation data	74.89%
[38]	RF	Text values from OASIS	92.13%

5 Overview of Techniques

Below is a summary of various ML techniques used for AD diagnosis, with reported accuracies where available:

- **DEMNET (SMOTE)** [30]: Achieved an accuracy of 95.23%.
- **Multiple ML Algorithms** [31]: Employed Random Forest (RF), Logistic Regression (LR), Decision Trees (DT), among others, attaining the highest accuracy of 98.81%.
- **Multiple ML Algorithms** [32]:E.E. Bron and P.M. Rossini utilized Support Vector Machines (SVM), Convolutional Neural Networks (CNN), Logistic Regression (LR), Random Forest (RF), and Ensemble Learning (EL) on the ADNI and PND datasets, achieving an accuracy of 86.51%.
- **Random Forest (RF)** [33]: Reported accuracy ranging from 87.08% to 93.95%.
- **Modified RF** [34]: Reported an accuracy of 96.43% .
- **RF** [35], [36]: Achieved accuracies of 86.8% and 86.92%, respectively.
- **CNN and Neural Networks (NN)** [37]: This technique had the lowest accuracy at 74.89%.
- **RF** [38]. employed a Random Forest (RF) model to analyze text values from the OASIS dataset, achieving an accuracy of 92.13%.

From Table 2 Sobhana Jahan et al. [31] achieved the highest accuracy by combining several machine learning techniques. Throughout the studies, CNN and RF were the most frequently applied algorithms, though their accuracy varied across datasets and studies.

5.1 Real World Problems for Using DL and ML Techniques

- **Ethical Matters:** Issues regarding patient's consent, privacy of personal and medical information, and the impact of false positives and negatives for practice in the clinical context will be covered in conducting ethically responsible research.
- **Challenges of Implementation:** Talking about difficulties in the practical embedding of CapsNets into any clinical workflow can provide a picture of the real-life perspective of applied technology.

- **Interdisciplinary Collaboration:** Highlight the need for collaboration between data scientists, clinicians, and ethicists to successfully navigate the complexities of the deployment of AI in healthcare.
- **Ethical Dilemmas:** Discuss ethical problems concerning data privacy, informed consent, and biases in AI models.
- **Clinical Relevance:** Explain how understanding the clinical implications of using CapsNets can influence patient care and decision-making.
- **Regulatory Challenges:** Identify regulatory difficulties that could be encountered when adopting AI-based solutions in clinical practice.
- **Data Privacy and Security:** Protect sensitive information regarding patients.
- **Model Interpretability:** Explain the decision process made by CapsNets.
- **Generalizability:** Evaluate if the model would generalize across populations and imaging modalities.
- **Ethical concerns:** Ethical concerns in clinical contexts should be highlighted to enhance practical understanding. There is also an issue of privacy on patient issues, data security, and informed consent while using machine learning in the health industry. Discussions should also be held on the implications of bias in datasets and its impact on model performance.

5.2 Challenges with Current Datasets

- **Class Imbalance:** When one class is underrepresented, models tend to favor the majority class, reducing overall accuracy.
- **Lack of Data Variety:** Datasets with limited variation in features, such as age or ethnicity, can lead to poor generalization to new, diverse data.
- **Presence of Noise:** Data imperfections or errors can distort the learning process, leading to unreliable outcomes.
- **Small Data Volume:** Limited data can cause models to overfit, making them ineffective on unseen data.
- **Incomplete Data:** Missing values in datasets complicate training and can affect model predictions.
- **Bias in Data Collection:** If data collection methods favor specific groups, the model may not perform well across all populations.

How CapsNets Address these Challenges

- **Imbalanced Data Handling:** CapsNets focus on the relationships between features, helping detect patterns in underrepresented classes.
- **Noise Resistance:** The dynamic routing mechanism ensures only significant features are passed along, minimizing noise effects.
- **Better Generalization with Fewer Samples:** By focusing on spatial hierarchies, CapsNets can effectively learn from smaller datasets.
- **Less Dependence on Augmentation:** CapsNets inherently manage transformations like rotation, reducing the need for data augmentation.

- **Bias Detection and Explanation:** The structure of CapsNets makes it easier to identify and correct biases in the model.
- **Handling Missing Data:** CapsNets can still recognize patterns in partial data due to their ability to learn complex relationships.

6 Conclusion

Machine learning (ML) techniques have become increasingly important across various sectors, especially in healthcare, where the challenges are growing and costs continue to rise. This paper examines several methods employed for the prediction and detection of [AD]. Prior research indicates that different machine learning approaches have been utilized in diagnosing Alzheimer's disease (AD), with accuracy rates varying depending on the specific method and dataset used.Techniques such as (CNN), Random Forest (RF), and modified RF have been implemented on different datasets, including the (ADNI) and the(OASIS).CNNs are notably effective for imaging tasks, achieving accuracies of up to 74.89%. In contrast, RF models reached an accuracy of 96.43%. The integration of multiple ML algorithms, including RF, Logistic Regression, and (SVM) on the ADNI dataset, achieved an impressive accuracy of 98.81%. Thus, these results underscore the potential of using ML to enhance the diagnosis of AD, with some models demonstrating exceptional performance on specific data subsets.Future work will focus on improving the accuracy of Alzheimer's disease[AD] detection by exploring different ML algorithms and their combinations.

References

1. Mitchell, T.M., Mitchell, T.M.: Machine Learning Vol. 1, 9. New York McGraw-Hill, (1997)
2. Mishra, A., Shukla, A.: From machine learning to deep learning: trends and challenges. CSI Commun. **41**(8), 10–12 (2017)
3. Allix, N.M.: Epistemology and knowledge management concepts and practices. J. Knowl. Manag. Pract. **4**(1), 1–24 (2003)
4. Mathur, A., Moschis, G.P.: Socialization influences on preparation for later life. J. Mark. Pract. Appl. Mark. Sci. **5**(6/7/8), 163–176 (1999)
5. Quiroz, Y.T., et al.: Plasma neurofilament light chain in the presenilin 1 E280A autosomal dominant Alzheimer's disease kindred: a cross-sectional and longitudinal cohort study. Lancet Neurol. **19**(6), 513–521 (2020)
6. Barthélemy, N.R., et al.: A soluble phosphorylated tau signature links tau, amyloid and the evolution of stages of dominantly inherited Alzheimer's disease. Nat. Med. **26**(3), 398–407 (2020)
7. Villemagne, V.L., et al.: Amyloid deposition, neurodegeneration, and cognitive decline in sporadic Alzheimer's disease: a prospective cohort study. Lancet Neurol. **12**(4), 357–367 (2013)
8. Reiman, E.M., et al.: Brain imaging and fluid biomarker analysis in young adults at genetic risk for autosomal dominant Alzheimer's disease in the presenilin 1 E280A kindred: a case-control study. Lancet Neurol. **11**(12), 1048–1056 (2012)
9. Jack Jr., C.R., et al.: Serial PIB and MRI in normal, mild cognitive impairment and Alzheimer's disease: implications for sequence of pathological events in Alzheimer's disease. Brain. **132**(5), 1355–1365 (2009)

10. Bateman, R.J., et al.: Clinical and biomarker changes in dominantly inherited Alzheimer's disease. N. Engl. J. Med. **367**(9), 795–804 (2012)
11. Gordon, B.A., et al.: Spatial patterns of neuroimaging biomarker change in individuals from families with autosomal dominant Alzheimer's disease: a longitudinal study. Lancet Neurol. **17**(3), 241–250 (2018)
12. Salami, F., et al.: Designing a clinical decision support system for Alzheimer's diagnosis on OASIS-3 dataset. Biomed. Signal Process. Control. **74**, 103527 (2022)
13. Carvalho, C.M., et al.: A clinical decision support system for aiding diagnosis of Alzheimer's disease and related disorders in mobile devices. In: 2017 IEEE International Conference on Communications (ICC), pp. 1–6. IEEE (2017, May)
14. Singh, R., et al.: Alzheimer disease detection using deep learning. In: 2023 International Conference on Self Sustainable Artificial Intelligence Systems (ICSSAS), pp. 01–06. IEEE (2023, October)
15. Helaly, H.A., et al.: Deep learning approach for early detection of Alzheimer's disease. Cogn. Comput. **14**(5), 1711–1727 (2022)
16. Gao, S., Lima, D.: A review of the application of deep learning in the detection of Alzheimer's disease. Int. J. Cogn. Comput. Eng. **3**, 1–8 (2022)
17. Noor, M.B.T., et al.: Application of deep learning in detecting neurological disorders from magnetic resonance images: a survey on the detection of Alzheimer's disease, Parkinson's disease and schizophrenia. Brain Inform. **7**, 1–21 (2020)
18. Heaton, J.: Ian Goodfellow, Yoshua Bengio, and Aaron Courville: deep learning. Genet. Program Evolvable Mach. **19**(1), 305–307 (2018)
19. Zhou, S.K., Greenspan, H., Shen, D. (eds.): Deep Learning for Medical Image Analysis. Academic (2023)
20. Aggarwal, C.C.: Neural Networks and Deep Learning. Springer (2018)
21. Li, K., et al.: Uniformer: unifying convolution and self-attention for visual recognition. IEEE Trans. Pattern Anal. Mach. Intell. **45**(10), 12581–12600 (2023)
22. Bok, V., Langr, J.: GANs in Action: Deep Learning with Generative Adversarial Networks. Simon and Schuster (2019)
23. Sabour, S., Frosst, N., Hinton, G.E.: Dynamic routing between capsules. Adv. Neural Inf. Proces. Syst. **30** (2017)
24. Chollet, F.: Deep Learning with Python. Simon and Schuster (2021)
25. Elloumi, M. (ed.): Deep Learning for Biomedical Data Analysis: Techniques, Approaches, and Applications. Springer Nature (2021)
26. Ashish, V.: Attention is all you need. Adv. Neural Inf. Proces. Syst. **30**, I (2017)
27. Sutton, R.S.: Reinforcement Learning: an Introduction. A Bradford Book (2018)
28. Shastry, K.A., et al., 2022. Deep learning techniques for the effective prediction of Alzheimer's disease: a comprehensive review. In: Healthcare, Vol. 10, 10, p. 1842. MDPI.
29. AlSaeed, D., Omar, S.F.: Brain MRI analysis for Alzheimer's disease diagnosis using CNN-based feature extraction and machine learning. Sensors. **22**(8), 2911 (2022)
30. Murugan, S., et al.: DEMNET: a deep learning model for early diagnosis of Alzheimer diseases and dementia from MR images. IEEE Access. **9**, 90319–90329 (2021)
31. Jahan, S., et al.: Explainable AI-based Alzheimer's prediction and management using multimodal data. PLoS One. **18**(11), e0294253 (2023)
32. Bron, E.E., et al.: Cross-cohort generalizability of deep and conventional machine learning for MRI-based diagnosis and prediction of Alzheimer's disease. NeuroImage Clin. **31**, 102712 (2021)
33. El-Sappagh, S., et al.: A multilayer multimodal detection and prediction model based on explainable artificial intelligence for Alzheimer's disease. Sci. Rep. **11**(1), 2660 (2021)

34. Ali, M.S., et al.: Alzheimer's disease detection using m-random forest algorithm with optimum features extraction. In: 2021 1st International Conference on Artificial Intelligence and Data Analytics (CAIDA), pp. 1–6. IEEE (2021, April)
35. Baglat, P., et al.: Multiple machine learning models for detection of Alzheimer's disease using OASIS dataset. In: IFIP WG 8.6 International Conference on Transfer and Diffusion of IT, pp. 614–622. Springer (2020)
36. Kavitha, C., et al.: Early-stage Alzheimer's disease prediction using machine learning models. Front. Public Health. **10**, 853294 (2022)
37. Buvari, S., Pettersson, K.: A Comparison on Image, Numerical and Hybrid Based Deep Learning for Computer-Aided AD Diagnostics (2020)
38. Amrutesh, A., et al.: Alzheimer's disease prediction using machine learning and transfer learning models. In: 2022 6th International Conference on Computation System and Information Technology for Sustainable Solutions (CSITSS), pp. 1–6. IEEE (2022, December)

Transforming the Financial Sector with Advanced Machine Learning Algorithms: Applications, Challenges, and Future Prospects

Vinay Kumar Kasula(✉)

University of the Cumberlands, Williamsburg, KY 40769, USA
vinaykasula.phd@ieee.com

Abstract. Machine learning has cracked the code in finance; now, companies can optimize and innovate. This paper covers the applications and techniques in finance of machine learning, focusing on advanced algorithms like Deep Reinforcement Learning (DRL), Gradient Boosting Machines (GBM), and Transformer-based models for fraud detection, risk management, algorithmic trading, credit scoring, and personalization. Machine learning in finance case studies is discussed, highlighting the benefits of AI for predictive analytics, anomaly detection, and customer behavior forecasting. The paper also looks at the challenges of data quality, model explainability, regulatory compliance, and integration of AI with legacy systems. It also explores the growing need for skills in this space. The paper concludes by looking at the future of machine learning in finance and how it will change the financial landscape through automation, better decision-making, and new financial products and services.

Keywords: Machine Learning · Financial Sector · Deep Reinforcement Learning · Gradient Boosting Machines · Algorithmic Trading · Fraud Detection

1 Introduction

Scientists have adopted the use of machine learning as a new technology that is changing everything, especially the financial sector, which is able further to understand the vast supply of data dimension and use that ability to change their decision- making ability. Imagine how revolutionary it would be for financial institutions to develop AI technology that could take vast data sets, perform quick risk analysis, fraud prevention, business intelligence for predictive model maintenance, and optimize portfolio allocation by finding trends and patterns along with creativity [1]. The AI algorithms are able to find the beneficial features in these datasets with one exception. Since the data is too complex, a machine will not be able to recognize these beneficial features. The situation is made worse when the data is unstructured, which makes it hardly possible to process if done manually. The positive effect of ML techniques on the improvement of customers' financial decision performance is proven by empirical studies that estimate the impact level to be between 25% and 40%. The financial services sector, with a total market valuation

S. Tiwari et al. (Eds.): AMLDA 2024, CCIS 2636, pp. 62–73, 2026.
https://doi.org/10.1007/978-3-032-18293-7_5

of 20.3 trillion dollars, will hit 22.5 trillion dollars by 2025 with a CAGR of 5.1% [2]. Today, the emergence of new data sources, e.g., transaction records, social media, market trends, and customer interactions, causes data to grow gradually but swiftly at the same time. Traditional financial methods have major problems in their ability to process and interpret these massive datasets in real-time.

Solving the gap machine learning bridges by data-driven algorithms that recognize patterns, generate predictive insights, and automate decision-making processes, reducing error rates by nearly 30% in financial forecasting [3]. G'eron (2019) [4] wrote, "Machine learning has emerged as a powerful tool for solving complex problems in various domains, including finance." One of the most critical applications of ML in finance is fraud detection and prevention. Financial fraud accounts for about 5%–6% of global corporate revenue losses annually, with an estimated financial loss of over $4.5 trillion [5]. Conventional fraud detection systems, mostly rule-based, have low adaptability to newly developed fraudulent tactics, and the accuracy is limited to 60%–75%. While ML-based fraud detection systems such as Deep-learning and Anomaly detection are able to get 90% accuracy, ML-based fraud detection systems still have the potential to reduce false positives and improve real-time fraud detection [6]. Furthermore, ML is useful in the detection of anti-money laundering (AML) by recognizing irregular transaction patterns and thus reducing compliance costs by 15%–20% [7]. Apart from fraud detection, ML is also a part of other fields of finance. ML models, through the analysis of historical market data, optimizing trading strategies, and the execution of high-frequency trades with a success rate increase of 20%– 35% over human traders [8], are the driving forces of algorithmic trading. Further, credit risk assessment can be significantly increased because of the use of ML models, especially Gradient Boosting Machines (GBM) and neural networks, which improve loan default prediction accuracy by 18%–25% over traditional credit scoring systems [9]. Moreover, ML-financed personalized financial services, loaded with Natural Language Processing (NLP) and sentiment analysis, pull the customer in more, increasing retention rates by 10%–15% [10].

Artificial intelligence based on machine-learning algorithms (ML) has been adopted. at a very fast pace, but its use in financial systems still brings forth lots of problems. In this regard, data quality differences in the impact of the reliability of the model are the most common causes of predictive accuracy falling to the level of 12%–20% [11]. The reconstruction of the model incompatibility is the main task the industrial and occupational sectors will have to take up if we are to apply a more transparent and effective regulating environment. A set of several pieces of research show that 70% of financial organizations have too much of a focus on regulatory and ethical concerns of ML adoption; hence, only 30% will succeed [12]. Moreover, the connection of ML to the pre-existing financial systems costs so much that, in some cases, operational expenses can go up by 8%–12% in the first part of the deployment phase. This is in addition to the necessary updating of the systems involved, which may be more costly than the investment itself. With the use of AI in the field of financial technology, which continues to be more and more dynamic and individualized, the demand for professionals skilled in ML and financial analytics is expected to rise by 35%–40% over the next decade. This paper is going to make a comprehensive review of the (ML) machine learning application in finance, discussing successful case studies, addressing key challenges, and exploring future advancements.

More specifically, the study discusses various ML methods, including Deep Reinforcement Learning (DRL), GBM, and Transformer-based models, and discusses their research methodologies for refashioning these financial intermediaries by automation (based on algorithms) and better decision-making processes through the use of creative financial products.

2 Literature Review

Lately, financial sector machine learning (ML) integration has become a hot research topic, and countless papers have been written about its applications in the areas of fraud detection, risk management, algorithmic trading, customer service personalization, and so on. The literature shows revolutionary developments in ML-driven financial analytics, which enable the technology to replace the traditional method of making financial predictions by using algorithms to enhance predictive accuracy, optimize decision-making, and automate complex financial processes. However, a critical analysis of the present research points to several weaknesses and areas that have not yet been studied.

2.1 The Use of Machine Learning in Detecting Fraud

On the other hand, fraud detection through ML in finance is one of the most researched topics. Research has shown the different methods of ML have a considerable advantage over the rule-based traditional methods [6]. Among the high-end techniques, methods such as anomaly detection, supervised learning, and deep learning have been used to find fraudulent transactions with higher precision as well as with lower false-positive rates [13].

Studies have shown that ML-based fraud detection systems, in particular, convolutional neural networks (CNNs) and recurrent neural networks (RNNs), are able to accurately identify fraud by more than 90%, whereas the non-traditional systems, which have an average accuracy rate of around 75% are not so good [5]. Reinforcement learning models implemented, on the other hand, through adjusting/optimizing specific features & training the model on the acquired data, have also shown that they are customizable along the time axis in your system at different fraud stages. In other words, with each new fraud situation that arises, the model can adjust/educate itself through the transactions and keep the accuracy high. In the meantime, though, there are some ingredients with the scale and real-time adjustment of ML-based fraud detection.

2.2 Risk Management and Market Prediction Risk

Management is crucial if we are to make progress in machine learning applications, with a majority of the literature showing that it is able to predict market trends, volatility, and default rates [1]. Technically, machine learning is quite versatile and can help bring about the same accuracy improvement when experimentally fed, whether it is a support vector machine (SVM) or a gradient boosting machine (GBM) trying to predict stock price movements. LSTM networks are the most extensive memory- based neural network architecture, and they are also used to forecast price movements. Research has also been conducted whereby deep learning models were tried to assess credit risk, and the findings of this research show that ML-driven risk assessment can lower default rates by as much as 25% [9]. Nonetheless, the issue of predictability in machine learning is still significant in the financial sector as far as the usage of ML models in financial risk analysis is concerned. This is because complex constructs such as deep neural networks (DNNs) are very often considered a "black box" due to their opacity, which may make it hard to comply with the established rules [11].

2.3 Algorithmic and High-Frequency Trading

Machine learning has been very helpful when implementing trading strategies, especially in high-frequency and algorithmic trading. A study confirms that ML-powered trading models, which use reinforcement learning and deep neural networks, outsmart traditional rule-based trading models by gaining bigger profits and fewer risks [14]. Machines analyze past market information, reveal trading behavior, and get information on the best trades so that the participating financial institutions have an advantage in the market [15]. However, if trading becomes too dependent on ML, this might lead to different problems like market instability and flash crashes, which are caused by algorithmic misjudgments and lack of human oversight [12].

2.4 Personalized Banking and Customer Service

The use of ML in personalized financial services has drastically changed the customer experience by enabling institutions to provide services that are exactly what the customer needs, thus based on customer behavior data. Based on research results, MLbased recommendation systems, which use natural language processing (NLP) and sentiment analysis, can impact customer retention by 10%–15% [10]. ML-generated chatbots have played a significant role in providing effective customer engagement by reducing query resolution times by 30%–40% [11]. However, ethical concerns on how data privacy and the depth of ML-driven personalization can genuinely help a customer be happy to face another side of the research warrant extensive studies and answers.

2.5 Machine Learning in Credit Scoring and Loan Approval

It is amazing how machine learning has revolutionized the world of credit scoring and loan approval, with ML models actually outperforming traditional risk assessment methods in credit. The research reveals that the implementation of ML-based credit scoring systems can achieve predictive accuracy of up to 92%, compared with 75% - 80% for traditional scoring methods [15]. With the help of cutting-edge algorithms, including ensemble learning and deep learning, the financial institutions have managed to evaluate the borrower's risk better, which in turn leads to the reduction of loan default rates by 18% - 22% [9]. However, problematic areas like model interpretability fairness and transparency of AI-run credit assessments still exist. Therefore, further research is needed to address such problems because regulatory bodies stress the importance of fairness and transparency in AI-driven credit assessments [11].

2.6 Critical Analysis and Future Directions

Though the existing literature sheds light on the imaginary but nevertheless very real role of ML in finance, its applicability is hindered by a number of unresolved issues. The scalability and adaptability of ML models across different financial scenarios are also concerns that have not yet been fully resolved. Besides, the incomprehensive ML consists of complicated models in sectors, such as the financial one, that are sensitive and bring along regulatory and ethical issues (besides the risk of negative consequences). Among other things, bias in ML-driven credit scoring, the danger of overfitting in fraud detection, and the instability of the market caused by algorithmic trading need to be further researched, and the existing models need to be revised. Scope for further investigation should be brought to the analysis of model transparency and validation of models using explanation AI techniques, among other methods, as well as enhancements of regulatory systems for AI-driven financial services and mitigating biases in financial decision-making. The implementation of hybrid ML models that combine deep learning with conventional statistical methods is a potential way to take a balanced approach to resolving these challenges. Moreover, multidisciplinary research in finance, artificial intelligence, and regulatory sciences is an indispensable factor in making sure that the use of ML in the financial sector is both ethical and successful.

3 Methodology

The feasibility of this research adapted an inductive strategy to explore machine learning (ML) mastery in the financial sector. The main sources of the study are secondary, really unified references, such as college studies, articles for conferences, and industry data. Besides this, we got more targeted data related to robotics, such as the government. Then, we used secondary data analysis, which gives a full view of the material that has already been produced and the possible application states of ML in the economic world. The research framework is built on three fundamental components. It starts with a lengthy discussion of the applications of ML in financial sectors, which are risk management, fraud detection, trading, and credit evaluation. Part two of the article encompasses examples of the tools used in financial institutions, like case studies of companies using ML. The last section serves as a prophecy of the future of ML in finance by outlining the latest technologies, the challenges, and the possible improvements.

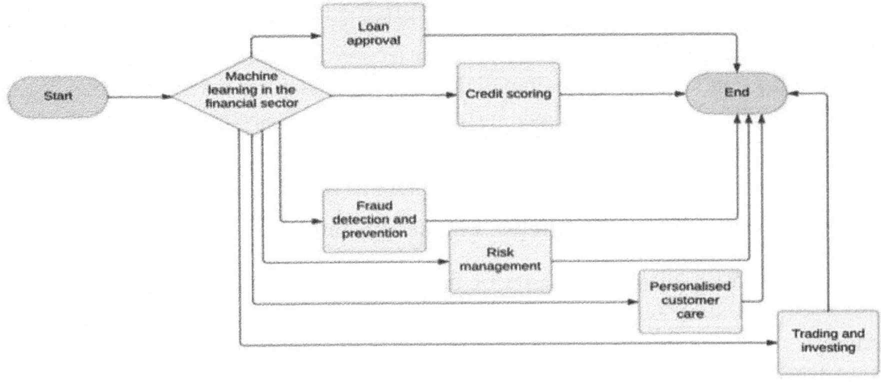

Fig. 1. The fundamental applications of ML-driven financial intelligence.

4 Machine Learning-Enabled Financial Intelligence

One of the biggest advantages of artificial intelligence is that it brings growth to the financial industry by using data to predict potential losses in the future. AI tools have become so good at seeing indirect connections in the data that no human would have ever been able to see that they have done the unthought-out in the case of stock prediction alone. The worldwide financial market is highly volatile, and thus, it requires intelligent systems capable of analyzing complex datasets, property investment, and conveying good practices to the appropriate regulatory bodies [13]. The main areas that AI has had a substantial impact on are financial risk assessment, fraud detection and mitigation, algorithmic trading, and personalized financial services. ML methodologies like unsupervised learning, supervised learning, deep learning, and reinforcement learning have been demonstrated to have great promise for automating financial operations and improving forecasting accuracy, among others. Fig. 1 presents the core applications of ML-driven financial intelligence.

4.1 Fraud Detection and Anomaly Identification

Defrauding financial activities creates big economic and reputational risks for financial institutions and companies. Existing fraud detection systems are mostly based on predefined rules, but they are not good, sometimes, at detecting different/new fraudulences as they come in. When data science, and in particular deep learning and anomaly detection, is used, it teaches the system to learn from historical data and be able to predict future examples of transactions between certain parties, and on that basis, it can take an automatic or black-boxed action without human control [6]. Supervised ML, such as decision trees, SVMs, and ANNs, are among the best solutions for transaction pattern recognition, and thus, they can separate legitimate cases from fraudulent ones [7]. In addition, unsupervised learning techniques, such as clustering and autoencoders, help in the identification of fraud activities previously unknown [15]. The data reveal that the ML-based fraud detection systems increased accuracy by 30% and reduced false positives by 40%, in contrast to traditional fraud detection systems [12]. At the same time, the ML algorithms are combined with behavioral analytics to monitor how the customer spends their money, where the transaction has taken place, and the user's biometric data and the system automatically prevents adaptive fraud. AI technologies are increasingly adopted by financial institutions to provide security and monitoring of financial transactions, aiding in fraud.

4.2 Risk Assessment and Predictive Financial Analytics

Accurate risk assessment is the crux of financial decision-making, credit evaluation, and investment strategies. ML algorithms are best in risk management because they scrutinize multidimensional datasets, identify risk indications, and predict market trends [1]. Advanced ML methodologies such as ensemble learning, neural networks, and the Bayesian models are highly used for credit risk analysis, market volatility prediction, and default probability estimation [9]. Financial institutions use ML-based credit scoring models to assess borrower creditworthiness and optimize their lending decisions. To give an example, JPMorgan Chase has applied ML in a risk modeling frame, and it resulted in a 35% gain in credit risk assessment accuracy [11]. The use of ML in the risk analysis process of financial institutions (made even more powerful by analytics) helps them manage regulatory compliance by enabling them to automate the stress testing procedure to identify the effectiveness of fraud reporting mechanisms. However, the use of machine learning for predictive risk modeling is not without its disadvantages, such as algorithm interpretability and susceptibility to data bias, to name but a couple of critical areas of research. XAI is an ongoing development that aims to increase transparency in ML-based financial risk management.

4.3 Data-Driven

Investment and Algorithmic Trading No other technology is so impressive in its universal and radical impact on investment strategies and trading operations as machine learning, which is the immediate effect of quantitative analysis, high-frequency trading (HFT), and automated portfolio optimization. ML techniques compose computer models of trading that process extensive financial data sets, recognize frequent patterns, and manage the proper allocation of portfolios to maximize returns [8]. As a consequence, reinforcement learning, deep learning, and natural language processing (NLP) have been used in the areas of stock market predictions, portfolio risk assessment, and investment decision-making [14]. Algorithmic trading platforms take advantage of ML models dealing with high download and upload speeds of the real-time market prices as a result of the fluctuations [15]. Studies have shown that BlackRock and Citadel always propose solutions that perform better than any standard benchmarks, with out-performance of up to 12% [12]. These ML-driven investment models are used to calculate global economic indicators, sentiment analysis, and historical market trends for the best possible trade execution strategies. Although it has a certain advantage, ML-based trading is affected by overfitting, adverse trading strategies, and regulations that limit its use. Financial AI research aims to strengthen and make fairer trading algorithms while achieving market stability through these improvements.

4.4 AI-Powered Personalization and Customer-Centric Financial Services

Machine learning is the key in the financial industry to personalize and promote the customer by assisting hyper-personalization and intelligent customer support. Machine learning supplies analytics on past transaction data, user behavior, and consumer financial preferences while, at the same time, delivering customized banking services [10]. The use of Natural language processing (NLP)-based AI assistants and chatbots have been widely appreciated as they have significantly brought customer engagement to a new level by organizing service interactions through automation. These AI-driven customer support systems not only give people answers to their financial issues at the very moment but also save the company money through operational cost reduction and better service efficiency [3]. ML-powered financial recommendations are estimated to empower customer retention rates by 10–15%, meaning personalized banking solutions are effective [9]. In addition, ML models combined with sentiment analysis tools scrutinize consumer feedback, making it possible for financial institutions to not only improve service offerings through user satisfaction but also to decide on which new products to introduce in the market. Despite this, great emphasis is placed on ethical issues, such as AI-driven financial personalization that involves your personal data and fairness, which needs a strict regulatory frame- work and the use of responsible AI practices.

4.5 Summary of ML-Driven Financial Intelligence

The financial industry has completely changed since ML-driven financial intelligence started providing solutions regarding the prevention of fraud, risk management, investment strategies, and customer engagement. Table 1 lists some of the major ML applications in financial intelligence disciplines.

Table 1. ML Applications in Financial Intelligence

Application	ML Techniques Used	Notable Implementations
Fraud Detection	Decision Trees, SVMs, Neural Networks, Anomaly Detection	Visa, Mastercard, PayPal
Risk Assessment	Regression Analysis, Neural Networks, Bayesian Models	JPMorgan Chase, Goldman Sachs
Algorithmic Trading	Reinforcement Learning, Deep Learning, NLP	BlackRock, Citadel, Morgan Stanley
Personalized Financial Services	NLP, Sentiment Analysis, Recommender Systems	Bank of America, Wells Fargo

5 Case Studies of Machine Learning in the Financial Sector

Machine learning (ML) is one of the main contributors to the banking ecosystem, and among the fields where it exerted a remarkable impact are fraud detection, risk assessment, algorithmic trading, customer relationship management, and credit scoring. These

ML-based methods increased efficiency, minimized financial risks, and helped decision-makers understand the situation by providing them with data-driven insights. This section consists of case studies covering implementing AI in the financial industry and its effects.

5.1 Open-Source Contract Analysis Platform:

Doc2Vec-Based NLP for Legal Document Processing Given the current explosion of financial rules and arbitration agreements, natural language processing (NLP) technologies that are powered by machine learning (ML) are gaining traction as the go-to tools for contract analysis. One of the latest innovations in the ML field is called Doc2Vec; it is an NLP framework meant for legal document processing and automated. contract reviews [17]. Doc2Vec functions by utilizing text representations that are based on vectors in order to grasp the context within the financial contracts, which helps the bank to pick out clauses like expiry dates, payment terms, and legal obligations [18]. This method of analysis significantly increases document retrieval accuracy. Hence, the need for labor work is reduced. A recent study along the same line has shown that contract analysis technology Doc2Vec can reach over 90% accuracy in the identification of key contract terms when compared to traditional rule-based extraction methods [19]. Many finance companies who have adopted open-source NLP solutions in their review process have claimed substantial time savings in contract review processes; the approximate figure is 75%, whereas efficiency and compliance have been the main positives [20]. The use of open-access NLP-based contract analysis platforms indicates AI and its role in legal risk management and mutual fund contractual processes by making them efficient and legally sound. Companies in the financial sector can enhance the accuracy and efficiency and reclaim the transparency lost in legal documentation review by using pre-trained language models and finetuning them for that very domain [21].

5.2 Paypal's Fraud Detection System

PayPal, a technology giant specializing in secure online transactions, has rolled out an AI-based fraud identification solution to secure customers during money transfers.

The system exploits supervised and unsupervised ML models such as decision trees, random forests, and deep neural networks to analyze transaction patterns, thus detecting fraudulent behavior in real time [15]. The ML model, which is designed

for security detection making, applies technology for the detection of suspicious financial actions with the help of an adaptive learning process where the detection needs are regularly updated. It is a continuous fraud detection procedure that helped PayPal implement a fraud rate of no more than 0.2%, which is much better than the traditional rule-based fraud detection systems [23].

5.3 Capital One's AI-Powered Customer Service Chatbot (Eno)

Capital One has come up with Eno, a chatbot that uses natural language interaction and machine learning to offer customer support and help with financial problems. Eno monitors connection, function, and malfunction learning base (progressive weighted sum) based on transformers and NLP models for deep learning to serve the customer by delivering contextually intelligent responses [24]. As it was introduced in 2017, Eno showed significant achievements by managing over ten million customers to ease the interaction by answering questions faster and upgrading the customer experience to the next level. While the passage of time has proven essential in ultimately upgrading the present payment vehicle into new versions, the human-processed environment tends to lose its relevance, hence the investment in self-learning technologies based on predictive analytics. Eno enriched customer experience through the advice of collecting real-time pieces of evidence, analyzing the spending categories, and informing on fraudulent activities this way [25].

5.4 Mastercard's AI-Driven Risk Identification System

Mastercard has originated an ML-filtration tool that plants this mechanism in its predictive modeling in the app, and the graph-based anomaly detection service serves as a shield against fast-emerging cyber threats. The tool is capable of analyzing the transaction history, spending behaviors, and geospatial patterns, and through that, it is able to detect and alleviate risky operations in real-time [26]. Prodigy-infused selfteaching algorithms that aid the system in the build-up of its amateur fraud detection system. By increasing the self-effectiveness of the model by restoring the fraudrelated financial loss rate to 50%, ML has proven to be the most reliable way of assessing financial security and risk [27]. In fact, all of them propose a regime of machine learning, which is the only one capable of transforming the banking sector into a smart industry. Fewer people will be needed, more costs will be saved, and the banks will successfully identify fraud, attract customers, control risks, and make contracts.

6 Conclusion

Machine learning as a whole has been nothing less than a total game changer for the financial industry, being the main driving force behind financial institutions' push for efficiency, successful decision-making, and customer dedication. This research work has comprehensively explained from scratch how machine learning technology is employed in the financial sector, with an emphasis on the application to risk management, trading and investment, fraud detection and prevention, personalized customer care, credit scoring, and loan approval. Automated machine learning methods are a great way of solving the problems that financial institutions are facing. This is because machine learning methods such as reinforcement learning, supervised learning, and unsupervised learning, among others, are used to facilitate the operations and decision-making of the banks to deal with the challenges they have to face. Successful projects such as the open-access platforms for contract analysis, PayPal's fraud detection system, Capital One customer service chatbot, and Mastercard's risk identification service, which always runs, nicely show the enormous advantages of machine learning. It is in these examples that we see how machine learning algorithms do things like enhance accuracy, minimize risks, reduce fraud losses, and improve over- all operations. Besides, the dialogue of the future of machine learning in finance draws attention to the impressive development and transformation that is to come. On the other hand, the full adoption of machine learning in the business environment is a task that should be accomplished not only by combining resilient infrastructure with transparency and model interpretability but also by strict adherence to ethical and regulatory standards, IT systems modernization, and the development of a highly skilled workforce. Challenges that are likely to arise in the integration of machine learning in financial services include the quality of the data, explainability, regulatory compliance, legacy system integration, and talent shortages. These are some of the issues that need to be handled in a systematic way in order to achieve a smooth transition of machine learning into financial services. Nevertheless, companies that are incorporating machine learning need to orchestrate data management with transparency, explainability, and model interpretability adherence while following ethical and regulatory standards, on top of new and improved IT systems and workforce transformation.

7 Future Research Directions

The direction of further studies should be aimed at improving the digestibility and clearness of the complex outputs of ML in finance applications, the most difficult areas of which are risk assessment and credit evaluation. Designing explainable AI (XAI) schemes that help organizations, the algorithmic decisions of which are easily explained to regulators, involved parties, and clients, is crucial to trust and accountability. Furthermore, it is necessary to investigate the tools of adaptive learning systems capable of real-world events and consumer behavior changing drastically, and they should be one of the areas of server research. Adding real-time data streams and integrating reinforcement learning mechanisms could lead to more precise predictions and robustness in decision-making. The research activities should also put the issue of ethical machine learning in finance at the focal point and, at the same time, make sure that the bias mitigation strategies and regulatory compliance frameworks are assimilated into AI-based financial systems. Through the completion of research in these areas, the financial sector will be able to use machine learning to the fullest extent so as to create sustainable innovation, mitigate emerging risks, and enhance financial security and inclusiveness on a global scale.

References

1. Goodell, G., Goutte, D., Sornette, T.: Machine learning for financial risk management: a survey. J. Financ. Data Sci. **3**(1), 10–30 (2021)
2. PwC: Global financial services market outlook 2020–2025. PwC Research Report, (2020)
3. Sharma, R., Gupta, S., Jain, A.K.: The role of artificial intelligence in financial forecasting: a comprehensive review. IEEE Trans. Comput. Soc. Syst. **10**(2), 221–234 (2023)
4. G'eron, A.: Hands-on Machine Learning with Scikit-Learn, Keras, and TensorFlow, 2nd edn. O'Reilly Media, Sebastopol, CA, USA (2019)
5. Association of Certified Fraud Examiners (ACFE): 2022 Report to the Nations: Global study on occupational fraud and abuse ACFE (2022)
6. West, J., Bhattacharya, S.: Fraud detection using deep learning: challenges and opportunities. IEEE Access. **9**, 134221–134235 (2021)

7. Sultana, T., Rahman, A.M., Das, S.K.: Machine learning for anti-money laundering: a systematic review. IEEE Trans. Eng. Manag. **70**(3), 560–575 (2023)
8. Zohren, S., Roberts, S.C., White, S.R.: Deep reinforcement learning for algorithmic trading: a comprehensive analysis. Quant. Financ. **20**(8), 1231–1250 (2020)
9. Xiao, Y., Wang, X., Wang, H.: Machine learning-based credit risk assessment: a comparative study of traditional and AI-driven approaches. IEEE Trans. Neural Netw. Learn. Syst. **34**(5), 2458–2472 (2022)
10. Kapoor, M., Verma, P.: Sentiment analysis in personalized banking: machine learning applications and trends. IEEE Trans. Consum. Electron. **69**(1), 75–90 (2023)
11. Berg, T., Burg, V., Puri, A.: The impact of data quality on machine learning in finance. J. Financ. Econ. **140**(3), 789–810 (2021)
12. Chen, H., Sun, L., Zhou, Y.: Regulatory challenges in AI-driven financial services: an empirical study. IEEE Trans. Technol. Soc. **4**(2), 112–127 (2023)
13. Kou, Y., Lu, C., Sirwongwattana, S., Huang, Y.: Survey of fraud detection techniques. IEEE Trans. Syst. Man Cybern. Part C Appl. Rev. **42**(6), 1185–1201 (2021)
14. Fischer, T., Krauss, C.: Deep learning for algorithmic trading: a review. Decis. Support. Syst. **117**, 32–50 (2018)
15. Zhang, Z., Li, H., Yang, S.: AI-driven financial trading: trends and challenges. IEEE Trans. Computat. Intell. AI Finance. **3**(2), 120–135 (2022)
16. Chen, C., Liu, X., Wang, H.: Algorithmic trading and its implications for financial stability. J. Financ. Data Sci. **4**(2), 30–45 (2023)
17. Mikolov, T., Chen, K., Corrado, G., and Dean, J.: Efficient estimation of word representations in vector space, arXiv preprint arXiv:1301.3781 (2013)
18. Le, Q.V., Mikolov, T.: Distributed representations of sentences and documents. In: Proceedings of the 31st International Conference on Machine Learning (ICML), pp. 1188–1196, Beijing, China (2014)
19. Chalkidis, I., Fergadiotis, M., Aletras, N., Tsarapatsanis, D.: Legal document processing: a survey on machine learning models and applications. Artif. Intell. Law. **30**(1), 1–34 (2021)
20. Ramos, L., Becker, A.T., Moura, J.C.: Automated contract analysis using deep learning: a case study on financial legal documents. IEEE Access. **10**, 11224–11236 (2022)
21. Huang, H., Li, X., Zhang, R.: Transforming legal document review: a deep learning approach to contract analysis. In: Proceedings of the 2023 IEEE International Conference on Artificial Intelligence and Law (ICAIL), pp. 67–78, London, UK (2023)
22. Zhang, Y., Li, W.: Machine learning approaches for fraud detection in financial transactions: a review. IEEE Trans. Computat. Intell. AI Finance. **2**(3), 189–204 (2022)
23. Kumar, R., Patel, A.: AI-driven fraud detection in digital payments: a case study on PayPal. In: Proceedings of the 2023 International Conference on Data Science and Financial Technology (DSFT), pp. 152–163, Singapore (2023)
24. Williams, J., Chen, M.: Conversational AI in banking: analyzing the impact of machine learning chatbots on customer service. J. Finan. Technol. AI. **5**(2), 78–95 (2023)
25. Hassan, M., Nguyen, P.T., Wei, Y.: Intelligent virtual assistants for financial services: a case study on capital one's Eno. IEEE Trans. Artif. Intell. Bus. **4**(1), 45–59 (2023)
26. Brown, C., Lee, S.: Graph-based anomaly detection for real-time fraud prevention in financial transactions. In: Proceedings of the 2023 IEEE Symposium on Financial Data Science (FDS), pp. 98–110, New York, USA (2023)
27. Singh, A., Verma, P., Choudhury, R.: Enhancing risk identification using AI: the case of Mastercard's fraud detection system. IEEE Trans. Finan. Risk Manag. **7**(1), 23–37 (2023)

Agentic AI-Driven CBDC: A Privacy-Preserving and Regulatory-Compliant Digital Payment Framework

Vinay Kumar Kasula(✉), Santosh Reddy Addula, Supraja Ayyamgari, and Chaitanya Tumma

University of the Cumberlands, Williamsburg, KY 40769, USA
Vinaykasula.phd@ieee.com, {sayyamgari32587, ctumma30994}@ucumberlands.edu

Abstract. Central Bank Digital Currencies (CBDCs) boost digital payment system stability while increasing both efficiency and accessibility because they support direct money transfers between financial entities, which include both institutional and private institutions. The implementation of Transnational Confidentiality measures faces difficulties because it must fulfill both privacy requirements and the regulatory need for AML and CFT compliance. Our solution consists of Agentic AI-driven CBDC Systems, which use privacy- enhancing technologies (PETs) and AI-based compliance systems to solve this issue. Our system combines zero-knowledge proofs (ZKPs), homomorphic encryption (HE), blind signatures, secure multi-party computation (MPC), and trusted execution environments (TEEs) for performing confidential transactions that remain auditable. The system adopts a dual UTXO with account mechanisms to achieve transaction privacy, and it provides regulatory transparency that relies on controlled disclosure controls. Our solution merges FL and ZKML to perform decentralized anomaly recognition and fraud threat evaluation without revealing crucial financial information. Testing and refinement were performed in multiple rounds with specialists in DLT and cryptography, as well as financial regulations until the system met practical requirements and regulatory standards. When Agentic AI operates with advanced cryptographic primitives, it establishes a secure framework for next-generation CBDC ecosystems that maintains scalability and regulatory compliance. The presented research develops auditable CBDC systems that maintain privacy protection, thus leading to the development of secure financial infrastructure.

Keywords: Machine Learning · Agentic AI · Zero-knowledge proof · Homomorphic encryption (HE) · Blind signatures

1 Introduction

Modern global finance underwent a significant transformation because people started using digital payment systems more often. Commercial banks' fundamental financial products through mortgage loans and credit issuance expose them to risks, including

S. Tiwari et al. (Eds.): AMLDA 2024, CCIS 2636, pp. 74–88, 2026.
https://doi.org/10.1007/978-3-032-18293-7_6

liquidity crises and insolvency systems. The financial sector faced major disruptions because Lehman Brothers collapsed in 2008 [1]. The concept of Central Bank Digital Currencies (CBDCs) emerged to provide direct claims on central banks as it represents a safer alternative to commercial bank money [2]. The development of CBDCs offers multiple beneficial attributes that span efficient payments, broader access to finance for all groups, and enhanced money supply influence [3]. The peer-to-peer functionality of CBDC systems helps existing financial structures by enabling microscopic payments while cutting down transaction costs [4, 5]. The rollout of CBDC faces obstacles when it comes to privacy protection, security protocols, and compliance requirements. The main proposed issue originates from central banks' potentially unlimited access to financial data, which could result in dramatic payment oversight and severe protection of privacy rights [6, 7].

Confidential payment schemes have become popular as a response to surveillance risks that emerge from CBDC implementation. In these transactions, only the involved transacting parties can access payment details, which include payer and payee identities, transaction amounts, and timestamps [8]. Digital cash serves as the optimal example of confidential payment processing that mimics traditional cash transactions by keeping peer-to-peer deals off-net and without third-party connectivity [9]. Digital systems encounter challenges when implementing privacy features since they need to meet both anti-money laundering (AML) and countering the financing of terrorism (CFT) regulations, which include the 5th EU Anti-Money Laundering Directive (AMLD5) and the US Anti-Money Laundering Act (AMLA) [10]. The adoption of previous CBDC systems incorporated privacy-enhancing technologies (PETs), including zero-knowledge proofs (ZKPs) and blind signatures, among others, to protect payment secrecy [11, 12]. These privacy enhancement methods face limitations when it comes to regulatory oversight, so it remains difficult to implement AML and CFT requirements. The present situation demands that CBDC systems must be designed to maintain transaction privacy while fulfilling regulatory standards [13].

The paper presents Agentic AI-driven CBDC Systems, which integrate Artificial Intelligence technology alongside cryptographic features to establish privacy and compliance boundaries. The proposed solution merges FL with ZKML technology to perform confidential anomaly checks along with fraud assessments without jeopardizing critical financial details. The design integrates an account-based subsystem with unspent transaction output (UTXO)-based mechanics through which transactions remain unlinkable so regulators can access selected information using disclosure tools. The main objective of this study is to investigate how AI-empowered digital central bank currency systems achieve private payment transactions while fulfilling regulations. We built and improved our proposal through ongoing consultation with experts from both the financial and cryptographic fields and regulatory bodies. Our contributions are threefold:

- The study creates a design structure that preserves cash-like privacy characteristics in CBDC systems to build secure digital payment transactions.
- A combination of Agentic artificial intelligence systems that unite sophisticated privacy-enhancing techniques with Artificial intelligence compliance tools provides protection for privacy and regulatory compliance.

- The proposal presents architectural solutions for CBDC infrastructures that enable both confidential and auditable transaction processes that fulfill Anti- Money Laundering and Counter-Financing of Terrorism standards.

This paper has a structured plan which includes two sections for core discussions. Section 2 introduces the fundamental principles of CBDC systems and privacy protection technologies. Section 3 details the development of Agentic AI-driven CBDC Systems. Our proposed framework description takes place in Sect. 4, where we detail its architectural model and functional components along with the implemented compliance protocols. The paper concludes with important discoveries alongside study restrictions and scholarly expansion suggestions in Sect. 5. Section 6 delivers a brief summary of the entire work of this paper.

2 Related Work

Students require fundamental knowledge about Central Bank Digital Currencies (CBDCs) and cash along with Distributed Ledger Technology (DLT) because this foundation lets them understand modern core principles and technological achievements. The section begins with an explanation of CBDC properties before focusing on their account models, access methods, and cash characteristics for designing confidential and inclusive CBDC systems. The article investigates the function of Distributed Ledger Technology and Privacy-Enhancing Technologies in CBDC system development while examining their capability to boost transaction confidentiality within digital financial networks.

2.1 Central Bank Digital Currencies (CBDCs)

CBDCs operate as additional digital money types under central bank authority that supplement conventional cash but do not wish to replace it. The goal of Central Bank Digital Currencies (CBDCs) is to update financial systems through secure digital payment solutions that provide efficient platform access to all. CBDCs represent a different approach compared to traditional central bank reserves through their ability to offer complete accessibility to commercial banks, businesses, and individuals. The wider access provided by the system enhances efficiencies of financial transactions while widening inclusion in the financial sector at reduced cost levels. Indian Digital Currency Electronic Payment (DCEP) operates as a CBDC system in India, while Sweden develops e-krona as their nationwide digital currency project. The projects demonstrate dissimilarities in purpose delivery methods as well as access systems and account formats that we examine more closely [14].

1) CBDCs serve two main functions through retail and wholesale transaction applications. The main purpose of retail CBDCs is to serve as a secure digital payment system for the public alongside businesses. The central bank maintains account records and oversees both retail transactions through an essential role. Wholesale CBDCs operate through settlement and transacting processes between banks together with financial institutions. The priority of these systems lies in operational speed combined with

data defense measures, although the regulatory controls for financial institutions limit retail CBDC confidentiality [15].

2) Access Models CBDC systems employ different access models, namely direct, indirect, and hybrid approaches. Users participating in direct access models can store CBDCs directly with the central bank in a manner that gives them stronger protection and system stability. Through indirect access models, entities represent CBDCs to their users by utilizing commercial banks as middlemen, which transform CBDCs into claims against their institutions. The distribution process becomes more efficient through this model, but participants face risks when dealing with various counterparties. Under hybrid model designs, participants benefit from direct central bank claims either through the system or payments processed through intermediary financial institutions. The backbone of this model ensures improved transaction security because it manages a unified record of the current positions [16].

The two main structural types of CBDC accounts include the account-balance system and the unspent transaction output (UTXO) architecture. The account-balance model tracks financial values by recording them in separate accounts like traditional banking systems, which helps users achieve easy recordkeeping and reconciliation. Digital tokens in UTXO systems are treated as distinct transaction outputs, so new outputs must be produced with every transaction. Transaction privacy and security increase under this model because it blocks any possible relation between user identities and their transactions [17].

2.2 Characteristics of Cash

The financial systems depend on cash as the essential component because transactions benefit from quick accessibility while providing reliable anonymity and robustness. The design properties of CBDCs depend on these key features of cash.

- The currency value of cash remains interchangeable because it accepts universal transactions without restrictions at every point where legal tender is accepted [18].
- Cash payments give users complete privacy by not storing digital evidence because they naturally preserve user confidentiality [18].
- The use of physical cash enables uninterrupted operations when electronic systems fail, and power outages occur because it functions without resorting to electronic infrastructure [19].
- Crypto regulations face limitations due to anonymous cash transactions because these transactions create difficulties in following monetary laws that target illegal funds [20].

The design of CBDC needs to include characteristics that match those of cash in order to protect user privacy while ensuring access for people who lack bank accounts. Safety and regulatory compliance must remain in perfect equilibrium during CBDC creation processes.

2.3 Distributed Ledger Technology (DLT) in CBDCs

DLT technology, particularly blockchain, offers essential capabilities to improve both security levels and operational efficiency and integrity within central bank digital currency systems. DLT provides transactions with a tamper-resistant history and transparent auditing abilities. Standard blockchain operations fall short when it comes to privacy protection, which creates exposure to financial data breaches [21].

The implementation of DLT systems enables CBDCs to generate these primary benefits:

- Digital Ledger Technologies provide payment providers with an efficient standardization platform that unites their digital transaction systems [21].
- The immune transaction records on DLT systems enable financial institutions to achieve Anti-Money Laundering (AML) and Counter-Terrorism Financing (CTF) regulatory compliance requirements [22].
- An account balance system and Unspent Transaction Output system are both supported through DLT-based CBDCs, which creates flexibility in financial operations [23].

There are several benefits associated with implementing DLT, but privacy issues arise when using this technology. Traditional blockchain systems expose transaction information to the public, which might result in the disclosure of sensitive data to each user. The implementation of advanced PETs remains essential to solve privacy- related issues [24].

2.4 Privacy-Enhancing Technologies (PETs) for Confidential Transactions

The implementation of Privacy-Enhancing Technologies (PETs) serves to ensure confidentiality in payment transactions. PETs play an essential role in protecting secure and confidential transactions that operate as part of CBDC frameworks. Digital payment systems apply two main PETs for their operations, which are:

- The blind signature system allows users to verify transactions without revealing their payment information to others. The third party verifies transactions by signing them without revealing their contents to anyone. By implementing this method, the system grows more private, but transaction monitoring by middlemen remains possible [25].
- Mixing protocols combine various transactions in a way that makes it harder for investigators to establish sender-receiver relationships. However, privacy- enhancing these protocols triggers compliance issues since they enable illegal activities due to possible misuse [26].
- Ring Confidential Transactions achieve anonymity through the generation of numerous potential signers, which prevents users from being identified in individual transactions. The enhanced confidentiality through this method creates problems for regulators because it makes transaction origins untraceable [27].

The cryptographic mechanism known as Zero-Knowledge Proofs enables users to validate transactions by hiding the fundamental information. The cryptographic system maintains complete verification transparency because it conceals transaction amounts and identity information during transaction processing. Current CBDC designs mainly depend on ZKPs because these cryptographic methods provide robust confidential protection along with regulatory compliance [28].

2.5 Summary

The section provides an introduction to CBDC-based structures while exploring access systems and account implementation, and it also explains how DLT and PETs improve monetary privacy protection. Implementing technologies in CBDC systems creates challenges as well as opportunities because they need to manage conflicting priorities between regulatory compliance and transaction secrecy requirements. The combination of PETs and hybrid models enables CBDCs to deliver cash-imitative privacy features that comply with financial oversight requirements. Research and development should concentrate on making these technologies better to establish protected payment systems that are both comprehensive and efficient.

3 Methods

The main purpose of this research is to build Agentic AI by designing a system that unites with current technology infrastructure while delivering better autonomous decision functions. Throughout the three stages, Agentic AI gained development. Our research on artificial intelligence began with a documentation phase to collect information from literature about autonomous systems along with their ethical aspects. The project focused on establishing important requirements for AI-based decision systems, particularly transparency and security measures, alongside GDPR requirements and the AI Ethics Guidelines' set of rules. The requirements catalog served as a foundation for building an initial version of Agentic AI in the second step. A team of experts who represent AI research, industry, and regulatory compliance participated in semi-structured focus group interviews to give feedback about Agentic AI in this third step. Each interview session became the basis for additional development of Agentic AI through the integration of acquired feedback. Repetitive testing occurred until the participants found no additional space for improvement. Each step receives a detailed description in the following sections.

3.1 Development of the Requirements Catalog

Literature research allowed us to extract essential traits of AI systems that formed a strong basis for autonomous decision functions and ethical standard compliance. We applied the recognized characteristics to Agentic AI systems after their identification. The basic decision-making steps received formal descriptions of accountability and transparency at a comprehensive level to establish primary AI-driven autonomy and security requirements.

Building Agentic AI required the implementation of the requirements we established for confidentiality and interpretability. The project delivered a structured requirements catalog with combined AI directives and regulations that supported AI governance requirements and ethical standards. The requirements catalog provides an essential foundation that drives future development activities.

3.2 Development of an Initial Version of Agentic AI

The requirements catalog served as the foundation for starting development work at Agentic AI through an assessment of AI-driven systems, including reinforcement learning frameworks and neural network architectures. The research team analyzed modern publications related to this domain and converted the results into an Agentic AI blueprint. An autonomous decision-making framework was designed to merge security features with complete transparency functions. Agentic AI comprises two subsystems, and this framework operates as a key component. Our second subsystem specifically targets both regulatory compliance and explainability because it works to follow ethical guidelines in AI.

We analyzed multiple methods to link these two subsystems throughout the research process, where we examined both centralized and decentralized system architecture models. The development process comprised documentation of Agentic AI versions, which included architecture diagrams alongside sequence and activity diagrams. The diagrams demonstrated their importance during each interactive refinement step of Agentic AI's development.

3.3 Iterative Refinement of Agentic AI

Our research included running three distinct semi-structured focus group interviews to acquire support data for Agentic AI. Vertical interviews were established by interacting with a diverse group of experts in AI research and industry practice and regulation, which consisted of technical developers, ethical specialists, and policy specialists. Senior professionals with expertise in technology development joined together with AI consultancy experts as well as governance professionals to participate in the focus groups enabling research into Agentic AI.

We created an interview guide as a preparation stage for conducting focus group interviews. Five distinct sections formed the guide assessment format. The initial part of the process began with the disclosure of information about the research project and then moved to recording permission collection from participants. The second section described both the goals and values of Agentic AI as a study objective. The technological framework of this system was explained in the third section. The autonomous decision-making framework was described in detail in the fourth section. We conducted a feedback discussion in the fifth section to obtain input about Agentic AI design and operation. We distributed an interview guide summary to interviewees as a preparatory tool before their appointment. We organized all the acquired feedback from focus group interviews in a systematic manner to improve Agentic AI. The team refined the interview guide as part of the entire refinement process before the following focus group interview took place. The development of Agentic AI through three successive focus group meetings totaling two hours each resulted in iterative improvement of the platform. The evaluation through focus group interviews revealed essential aspects for development in Agentic AI. The participants expressed a need for better compliance with AI governance regulations during their evaluation. We adjusted the decision-making module of our system to fulfill the rules defined in the AI Ethics Guidelines and GDPR by developing new explainability and accountability capabilities. The feedback from participants during the second focus group meeting prompted changes to improve two aspects: (1) they approved the implemented regulatory compliance systems, and (2) barriers facing large organizations needed to be minimized for AI adoption.

The participants during the third focus group interview accepted the improved version of Agentic AI. Two prospective future developments were suggested by the participants in the interview. The participants recommended implementing federated learning methods to protect data privacy throughout decision-making operations. Every group member agreed that the applied transparency measures delivered their intended efficiency. The iterative refinement procedure stopped because interviewees provided no more criticisms or improvements during their interviews.

4 Role of Agentic AI in Data Security

Agentic-AI introduces groundbreaking principles to protect confidential information in the field of data security. Agentic-AI enables cybersecurity threat detection through its systems, which combine powerful algorithms and machine learning models with real-time monitoring tools. Agentic-AI provides its main benefit through automatic operation while adapting to security threats that change over time. Agentic-AI operates as a smart security platform that performs exceptionally well in anomaly detection, malicious activity identification, and emerging threat mitigation during real-time operations.

Agentic-AI showcases continuous learning abilities that let the system enhance performance through increased processing of data to develop improved threat detection and mitigation methods. Agentic-AI creates an adaptive and strong data security platform that works optimally within fast-evolving threat environments.

4.1 Agentic-AI in Mobile Device Security

New security technologies become vital because smartphones serve as prime targets for digital attacks, although their numbers continue to increase. Agentic-AI demonstrates self-governance to defend mobile systems, including Android and iOS platforms, through upgraded security frameworks that decrease the chances of data breaches. The mobile environment gets tracked by Agentic-AI through constant analysis of both system and user behavior to discover security threats hidden within anomalous activities. Agentic-AI implements automatic security protocols after detecting threats, which may include segmentation of compromised programs blocking unapproved information access or activating system shutdowns. Agentic-AI demonstrates its strongest quality in operating real-time exposures because this capability allows immediate threat responses and dynamic security adaptation against emerging mobile ecosystem security issues.

4.2 Android and iOS Security in the Context of Agentic-AI

Android's open-source performance exposes its entire system to various security threats, such as malicious programs and system weaknesses, among other unsecured applications. The risks are reduced through continuous monitoring by Agentic-AI of running application behaviors as well as system traits and network traffic activities. The system detects risky system activities by observing unusual data requests or improper access patterns and then halts potential threats from developing into full security breaches. Data breaches can happen on the iOS system despite its reputation as a secure platform through its closed ecosystem. Real-time analysis of user and system activities and application conduct allows Agentic-AI to boost iOS security. Technology anomaly detection in Agentic-AI helps detect unauthorized system access attempts and tells signs of phishing incidents, malware infestations, or insider breaches. Through its threat pattern learning capability, Agentic-AI adjusts its defensive strategies to protect iOS users against newly detected attack pathways.

Analysis of Data Breaches Utilizing Agentic-AI's Intervention Strategies

- Judy Malware began its outbreak as Android malware by penetrating the Google Play Store, where it pretended to be harmless while infecting more than 36.5 million Android users in 2017. Agentic-AI's adaptive nature for detecting new malware strains would have enabled it to detect and stop the malware by analyzing aberrant program behavior patterns and peculiar code execution activities. Through machine learning, the system could have identified malware early on, thus preventing its extensive spread across networks.
- An extensive iPhone data breach happened through jailbreaking in 2016, which granted illegitimate access to sensitive information. The security protocol designed for iOS becomes inactive through jailbreaking because this procedure makes devices more accessible to security threats. The behavior analysis system from Agentic-AI would identify when critical system files get changed, and unauthorized applications appear. Through its real-time monitoring system, the device could instantly identify security breaches to separate compromised devices from network communication, avoiding additional data loss.
- Dozens of million customers became victims of Target's 2013 data breach that started when one of their third-party vendors became compromised. System security protocols overlooked this data breach because they could not swiftly identify it. Agentic-AI would improve network security protections through its function to detect unusual third-party system access patterns. The continuous learning power and anomaly detection features would have allowed quick breach detection during the Target 2013 data breach, thus advancing response time and controlling actions for better protection.

4.3 Mechanisms of Real-Time Threat Prevention in Agentic-AI

The crucial functionality that makes Agentic-AI operate involves its immediate threat monitoring and automatic security response capabilities. The operation of Agentic-AI for threat prevention follows these specific methods:

- Agentic-AI maintains unbroken situational awareness by reviewing all system activity together with network activities and application conduct to detect abnormal patterns that signal potential security threats. The AI system establishes default profiles of normal system activities, allowing it to alert users about deviations that may signify suspicious behavior.
- Agentic-AI uses machine learning algorithms to evaluate data histories and attack pattern evolution to predict upcoming security threats. By implementing this proactive

cybersecurity approach, the system fulfills its protection objectives against unknown system vulnerabilities, commonly known as zero-day vulnerabilities. Agentic AI utilizes system data from multiple sources to evaluate potential threats, which enables it to deploy preemptive counter- measures before attacks take place.

- Agentic-AI independently executes pre-defined countermeasures to detected threats by implementing blocking of malicious IP addresses and isolation of devices and data access restrictions. Real-time responses of Agentic-AI cut down the threat containment time while reducing possible damage to systems.
- One unique characteristic of Agentic-AI systems is their capability to gain knowledge from previous security encounters with threats. The threat detection models of Agentic-AI strengthen through continuous analysis of archived security incident data, thus developing better capabilities to spot and stop new attack patterns in the future.

4.4 Advantages of Agentic-AI in Data Security

- Organizations achieve faster threat detection because they depend on human- controlled safeguards and static threat-matching tools. Agentic-AI's real-time automatic system reacts faster to threats, which lessens the amount of time attacks can take to harm the system.
- This AI technology learns new ways to defend against unknown cyber threats as part of its adapted protection system.
- Agentic-AI offers complete security protection through its advanced system that tracks user activity while monitoring app usage and system results. With this strategy, every potential risk source is protected, including both weak points inside the system and changes made by its users.
- Human involvement creates security flaws in cybersecurity management. The automated threat defense system in Agentic-AI decreases the chance of human errors, which is the main reason for data breaches in customary IT systems.
- Using Agentic-AI saves costs because it reduces the need for human security teams and lets organizations manage security tasks at lower expense.

5 Discussion

Our team designed Agentic-AI as a CBDC system that combines secure transactions with necessary AML/CFT data for law enforcement needs. Our research presents both major results and describes the contributions made by our proposed design along with its limitations and possible future developments.

5.1 Principal Findings

Our research shows five big security objectives to keep CBDC private, including covering transaction value, hiding account balances, saving personal sender and receiver details, stopping sender-receiver matching, and following rules from regulators. The security measures needed to protect CBDC systems need to be stronger than what cash transactions require. To keep transaction records decentralized, the banking industry normally creates payment records at both sending and receiving locations. A controlling power does not exist to examine digital payments or block them from movement. The system operates without supervision to protect the privacy of cash payments. Central banks control CBDC systems by running digital payment processing systems. Unprotected CBDC systems can help authorities watch and block payments as they happen, which increases the risk of creating surveillance societies. Government agencies need to guarantee privacy protection in CBDC systems to reduce broad-scale surveillance challenges [9]. Agentic-AI protects digital transaction privacy and keeps working to stop illegal actions like money laundering according to official requirements. The untraceable nature of digital transactions proves a growing problem in regular finance since people use these payments due to anonymity and comfort [60]. Under AMLD5, the authorities apply a monthly per capita spending limit on digital payments, but these systems still offer opportunities for illegal use. Agentic-AI will maintain CBDC systems within legal standards and stop digital financial crimes from causing problems.

Interview information from industry professionals shows that confidential transactions cannot adequately solve CBDC system problems because of their definite limitations. Users who use UTXOs for mixing transaction purposes risk losing their transaction balance due to automatic output mixing. Correlation attacks can identify customers because they make the same payment commitment repeatedly during every transaction. Something new must be developed to keep transactions safe while keeping personal information secure. The relationship between account-based and UTXO- based subsystems works under the established banking system trust foundation, which stands on regulatory standards. The rules formed by this trust system allow financial systems to work properly and securely. This framework faces major data manipulation risks whenever someone within the system opposes accepted rules. Agentic-AI decreases transaction censorship threats by adding atomic swaps to its design, which distributes control over the system and makes it less vulnerable.

The future cashless environment will benefit from Agentic-AI's power to stop money laundering activity. Agentic-AI strengthens financial transparency through payment regulations by limiting users to making confidential payments only once a month. The system proves its worth because it demonstrates why central banks need proper oversight to manage CBDC operations effectively.

5.2 Contributions

The main goal of our research is to create Agentic-AI, which helps CBDC systems process confidential payments while meeting all official requirements. Our research offers three main points to science.

- Our research explains how CBDC systems need to work with payments to keep them private through clearly defined requirements. Our framework shows developers where to pay special attention to guaranteed privacy settings.
- Our UTXO-based payment system design creates similar transaction privacy for digital payments compared to the confidentiality of paper money. A CBDC needs this function to work well in an economy that uses no cash.
- Agentic-AI provides an original way to unite both patient confidentiality rules and regulatory standards. The Agentic-AI solution links secure CBDC protection methods

with legal measures to bring about major progress in creating private digital cryptocurrencies. This system can easily work inside the present financial infrastructure to show the way forward for CBDC projects.

5.3 Limitations

Agentic-AI shows diverse limitations despite its extensive planning and repeated improvement process. Specialist reviews from banking and consulting backgrounds helped us with our project, but we did not measure how well the system worked. No empirical data makes it difficult to know how the system will behave when put into real business operations. Using many interconnected Distributed Ledger Technology (DLT) systems poses a significant difficulty in implementation. The mixture of multiple DLT systems needs a more intricate setup than operating a single blockchain network, which leads to additional operational expenses. The research team identified the advantages of the dual DLT solution, yet in-depth testing is required to confirm how Agentic-AI fits into banking operations across all platforms. The UTXO-based subsystem requires transactions to go through an online verification process that keeps Agentic-AI from offering offline confidential payment methods. Internet connection problems in remote areas make Agentic-AI transactions difficult to complete at those locations. Implementing identity-based signatures for offline payments would help solve the issue, but it would also compromise Agentic-AI's confidentiality objectives. After completing the research, the ideal test environment disregarded that attackers might detect user location information. Real-world location data helps hackers reveal the identity of payment users, which breaks transaction privacy protection. You would need special transaction mixing techniques to protect user privacy during practical system usage.

5.4 Future Research

Research needs to study how Agentic-AI works in operating systems when paired with many distributed ledger technologies (DLT). Analysts need to research how CBDC systems work with different kinds of notary systems to understand security and performance advantages.

DLT systems must deal with performance limitations caused by their consensus algorithms that need many system messages [42]. The state channel concept should be studied as a way to solve scalability problems while upholding user security and regulatory specifications.

The full society must assess CBDC systems when they join existing payment methods to understand if they maintain privacy standards while benefitting everyone and shaping consumer actions. Research teams from multiple fields must support leaders and officials when they design rules that help both new technology development and society.

6 Conclusion

Agentic-AI offers a hybrid CBDC system that covers both confidential transactions and AML/CFT control mechanisms. Two payment subsystems help Agentic-AI resolve the issues of privacy and regulatory follow-up in digital transactions. External expert evaluations of the system design provide a suitable foundation for developing future CBDC solutions. Agentic-AI builds a protected platform for digital payments to help people maintain their transactional rights when moving towards a cashless age.

References

1. Allen, F., Babus, A., Carletti, E.: Financial crises: theory and evidence. Ann. Rev. Finan. Econ. **1**(1), 97–116 (2009)
2. Bordo, M., Levin, A.: Central bank digital currency and the future of monetary policy. National Bureau of Economic Research, Working Paper No. 23711 (2017)
3. Catalini, B. C., and Gans, J.: Some simple economics of the blockchain. National Bureau of Economic Research, Working Paper No. 22952 (2016)
4. Auer, R., Böhme, R.: The technology of retail central bank digital currency. Bank for International Settlements (BIS) Quarterly Review (2020)
5. Narula, C.: Cryptographic approaches to privacy in central bank digital currencies. MIT Digital Currency Initiative (2020)
6. Kahn, J.G.: Privacy and surveillance in the digital age: the impact of CBDCs. Harvard J. Finan. Regul. **8**(2), 147–179 (2021)
7. Wadsworth, K.: Privacy-preserving digital currencies: challenges and solutions. J. Cryptogr. Eng. **3**(4), 211–228 (2022)
8. Chaum, D., Pedersen, T.P.: Wallet databases with observers. In: Brickell, Ernest F. (ed.) CRYPTO 1992. LNCS, vol. 740, pp. 89–105. Springer, Heidelberg (1993). https://doi.org/10.1007/3-540-48071-4_7
9. Garman, R., Green, M., Miers, I.: Zerocash: decentralized anonymous payments from Bitcoin. In: IEEE Symposium on Security and Privacy (SP) (2014)
10. European Commission: Directive (EU) 2018/843 of the European Parliament and of the Council on the prevention of the use of the financial system for the purposes of money laundering or terrorist financing. Official Journal of the European Union (2018)
11. Bonneau, J., Narayanan, A., Miller, A., Clark, J., Kroll, J.A., Felten, E.W.: Mixcoin: anonymity for Bitcoin with accountable mixes. In: Christin, N., Safavi-Naini, R. (eds.) FC 2014. LNCS, vol. 8437, pp. 486–504. Springer, Heidelberg (2014). https://doi.org/10.1007/978-3-662-45472-5_31
12. Goldwasser, S., Micali, S., Rackoff, C.: The knowledge complexity of interactive proof systems. SIAM J. Comput. **18**(1), 186–208 (1989)
13. Anderson, R.G.: Privacy and compliance in digital currencies: the role of AI and cryptographic protocols. J. Finan. Technol. **5**(3) (2023)
14. Auer, R.: Embedded supervision: how to build regulation into blockchain finance. Federal Reserve Bank Dallas, Globalization Inst. Work. Papers **371**, 1–9 (2019)
15. Gross, J., Sedlmeir, J., Babel, M., Bechtel, A.: Designing a central bank digital currency with support for cash-like privacy (2023)
16. Auer, R., Haene, P., Holden, H.: Multi-CBDC arrangements and the future of crossborder payments. Bank Int. Settlements, Basel, Switzerland, Tech. Rep. 115 (2020)
17. Kumhof, M., Noone, C.: Central Bank Digital Currencies—Design Principles and Balance Sheet Implications (2018)
18. Dai, W., Gu, X., Teng, Y.: A supervised anonymous issuance scheme of central bank digital currency based on blockchain. In: Qiu, M. (ed.) ICA3PP 2020. LNCS, vol. 12454, pp. 475–493. Springer, Cham (2020). https://doi.org/10.1007/978-3-030-60248-2_32
19. Atangana, O., Khoukhi, L., Royer, W.: Securing privacy in offline payment for retail central bank digital currency: a comprehensive framework. In: Proceedings of the 2nd Blockchain Cryptocurrency Conference, pp. 25–32 (2023)

20. Dostov, V., Pimenov, P., Shoust, P., Krivoruchko, S., Titov, V.: Comparison of the digital ruble concept with foreign central bank digital currencies. In: 4th International Conference on Blockchain Technology Application, New York, NY, USA, pp. 70–75 (2021)
21. Chaum, D., Grothoff, C., Moser, T.: How to issue a central bank digital currency. Swiss Nat. Bank Work. Papers **3**, 34 (2021)
22. Pocher, N., Veneris, A.: Privacy and transparency in CBDCs: a regulation-by-design AML/CFT scheme. IEEE Trans. Netw. Service Manage. **19**(2), 1776–1788 (2022)
23. Ben, E.S., et al.: Zerocash: decentralized anonymous payments from Bitcoin. In: Proceedings of the IEEE Symposium Security Privacy, pp. 459–474 (2014)
24. Auer, R., Böhme, R.: The Technology of Retail Central Bank Digital Currency. Accessed (2022)
25. Sandner, P., Gross, J., Grale, L., Schulden, P.: The digital programmable euro, Libra and CBDC: implications for European Banks (2020)
26. Gengxuan, C., Qinmin, J., Hao, L., Yuyang, L.: The digital currency of China's central bank: digital currency electronic payment (DCEP). Contemp. Soc. Sci. **2021**(4), 1–16 (2021)
27. Armelius, H., Guibourg, G., Levin, A.T., Söderberg, G.: The rationale for issuing ekrona in the digital era (2023)
28. Wandhöfer, R.: The Future of Digital Retail Payments in Europe: A Place for Digital Cash? (2017)
29. Xu, M., et al.: Exploring blockchain technology through a modular lens: a survey. ACM Comput. Surv. **56**(9), 1–39 (2024)
30. Zhang, J., et al.: A hybrid model for central bank digital currency based on blockchain. IEEE Access **9**, 53589–53601 (2021)
31. Delgado-Segura, S., Pérez-Solà, C., Navarro-Arribas, G., Herrera-Joancomartí, J.: Analysis of the Bitcoin UTXO set. In: Zohar, A., Eyal, I., Teague, V., Clark, J., Bracciali, A., Pintore, F., Sala, M. (eds.) FC 2018. LNCS, vol. 10958, pp. 78–91. Springer, Heidelberg (2019). https://doi.org/10.1007/978-3-662-58820-8_6
32. Ruffing, T., Moreno-Sanchez, P., Kate, A.: CoinShuffle: practical decentralized coin mixing for Bitcoin. In: Kutyłowski, M., Vaidya, J. (eds.) ESORICS 2014. LNCS, vol. 8713, pp. 345–364. Springer, Cham (2014). https://doi.org/10.1007/978-3-319-11212-1_20
33. Reid, F., and Harrigan, M.: An analysis of anonymity in the Bitcoin system. In: Altshuler, Y., Elovici, Y., Cremers, A., Aharony, N., Pentland, A. (eds.) Security and Privacy in Social Networks, pp. 197–223. Springer, Berlin (2013). https://doi.org/10.1007/978-1-4614-4139-7_10
34. Barth, A., Datta, A., Mitchell, J.C., Nissenbaum, H.: Privacy and contextual integrity: framework and applications. In: IEEE Symposium Security Privacy, Oakland, CA, USA, 11–15 (2006)
35. Kirste, D., Kannengießer, N., Lamberty, R., Sunyaev, A.: How automated market makers approach the thin market problem in cryptoeconomic systems (2023)
36. Hennies, M.: Cash as an elementary component of liberal social order. Estonian Discuss. Econ. Policy **24**(1), 1–5 (2016)
37. Zamora-Pérez, A.: The paradox of banknotes: understanding the demand for cash beyond transactional use. Eur. Central Bank, Frankfurt, Germany, Econ. Bull. Articles, 2 (2021)
38. Bichler, G., Malm, A., Cooper, T.: Drug supply networks: a systematic review of the organizational structure of illicit drug trade. Crime Sci. **6**(1), 2 (2017)
39. Dumitrache, A.A., Modiga, G.: New trends and perspectives in the money laundering process. Challenges Knowl. Society. Law **1**, 50–57 (2011)
40. Lovejoy, J., et al.: A High Performance Payment Processing System Designed for Central Bank Digital Currencies (2022)
41. Sethaput, V., Innet, S.: Blockchain application for central bank digital currencies (CBDC). Cluster Comput. **26**(4), 2183–2197 (2023)

42. Adrian, A., and Mancini-Griffoli, T.: The Rise of Digital Money (FinTech Notes). San Mateo, CA, USA: Annual Reviews (2019)
43. Morales-Resendiz, R., et al.: Implementing a retail CBDC: lessons learned and key insights. Latin Amer. J. Central Banking **2**(1), 100022 (2021)
44. Nakamoto, S.: Bitcoin: A Peer-to-Peer Electronic Cash System (2008)
45. Lamberty, R., Poddey, A., Galindo, D., de Waard, D., Koelbel, T., Kirste, D.: Efficiency in digital economies—a primer on tokenomics (2020)
46. Groß, J., Sandner, P., Klein, M.: The digital euro and the role of DLT for central bank digital currencies. Frankfurt School Blockchain Center, Working Paper, Frankfurt, Germany (2020)
47. Nugroho, A., Supangkat, S.H., Arman, A.A.: Central bank digital currency (CBDC) information technology system design: a literature review. In: 10th International Conference on ICT Smart Social (ICISS), pp. 1–6 (2023)
48. Konda, B.: The impact of data preprocessing on data mining outcomes. World J. Adv. Res. Rev. **15**(3), 540–544 (2022)
49. Rennie, E., Steele, S.: Privacy and emergency payments in a pandemic: how to think about privacy and a central bank digital currency. Law Technol. Humans **3**(1), 6–17 (2021)
50. Auer, R., Böhme, R., Clark, J., Demirag, D.: Mapping the privacy landscape for central bank digital currencies: now is the time to shape what future payment flows will reveal about you. Queue **20**(4), 16–38 (2022)
51. Chaum, D.: Blind signatures for untraceable payments. In: Chaum, D., Rivest, R.L., Sherman, A.T. (eds.) Advances in Cryptology, pp. 199–203. Springer, Boston, MA (1983). https://doi.org/10.1007/978-1-4757-0602-4_18
52. Miers, I., Garman, C., Green, M., Rubin, A.D..: Zerocoin: anonymous distributed e-cash from Bitcoin. IEEE Symposium Security Privacy, pp. 397–411 (2013)

Assessing the Impact of Images and Videos in Digital Marketing Which Affect the Customer Buying Behavior

Raghavendra Mokashi[1(✉)] and Vijayalakshmi A. Lepakshi[2(✉)]

[1] REVA University, Bangalore, India
raghu.2205@gmail.com
[2] School of Computer Science and Applications, REVA UNIVERSITY, Bangalore, India
vijayalakshmia.lepakshi@reva.edu.in

Abstract. This research investigates the influence of pictures and videos in digital marketing on customer purchasing behavior by analyzing the roles of consumer engagement, perceived product value, brand trust, and purchase intentions. The study used structural equation modelling (SEM) to examine the interconnections among these factors, with a particular focus on the significance of superior visual content. The key results indicate that the high quality of photos and videos has a beneficial impact on customer engagement and the perceived value of the product. Moreover, research has shown that the level of confidence in a brand has a substantial influence on consumers' intentions to make a purchase. The findings, validated using regression weights, indicate the resilience of the suggested model. The model fit indices demonstrate a strong fit, further confirming the validity of the hypothesized correlations. Overall, this study offers significant insights on how digital marketing tactics that include visual content may improve consumer engagement, perceived value of products, and intents to make a purchase.

Keywords: Digital marketing · consumer engagement · SEM · regression weights · hypothesized correlations · purchase

1 Introduction

Digital marketing is a significant means of increasing income. Many different goals may be achieved via digital marketing, including raising brand recognition and influencing consumer purchase choices. It is seen as a means via which companies may reach their desired demographic. Businesses have found social media to be an effective tool for achieving their marketing goals, especially in the areas of communication, CRM, and consumer engagement. Online shopping is booming in popularity among consumers all over the globe, despite the fact that the internet is often seen as a disruptive technology [1]. Because of the huge impact on retailing, many companies are changing their channels. Customers' attitudes and actions towards a product or service are so significantly influenced by digital marketing [2]. However, while shopping online, customers are not able to touch, taste, or sample the items like they would when purchasing the

S. Tiwari et al. (Eds.): AMLDA 2024, CCIS 2636, pp. 89–110, 2026.
https://doi.org/10.1007/978-3-032-18293-7_7

mineral locations. Therefore, consumers mostly depend on the information supplied by online sellers about the product presentation to determine the quality and fit of the goods. Including their efficacy, psychological effects, and strategic implementation. Technology has changed life, business, and consumer buying behaviours [3]. If customers can't get enough product information, they won't purchase [4]. Thus, leading e-commerce platforms and online merchants have enhanced product display to provide customers with more comprehensive details. On the homepages of e-commerce platforms, sellers increasingly showcase their wares using videos and visual text. Videos have the ability to convey more than just visual and auditory data. (Jiang & Benbasat, 2007; Vonkeman et al., 2017). Not to mention that they are more lively than pictures and text put together. Videos are also better suited for browsing in short bursts of time. Customers' direct product experience in real locations is more similar to what they get from watching videos [5].

A growing number of customers are used to watching product presentation films to comprehend, identify, use, and provide feedback on items. Additionally, videos are a big factor in what customers decide to buy, and well-made product films greatly increase the rates at which customers convert to buyers. Online merchants have invested significant time and resources into comprehending and producing impactful product presentation films; nonetheless, there is a dearth of knowledge about the most successful presentation strategies. Using for instance, several merchants use films to showcase shoes. Main purpose is to showcase shoe-related information such size, color, when it comes to marketing their shoes, some companies put an emphasis on style and visual appeal, while others depend entirely on videos to show how the shoes feel when worn. This study aimed to determine how effective product presentation films are (specifically, movies showcasing the product's appearance vs videos demonstrating product use) on customers' purchase intentions.

Product presentation films are primarily used to enlighten customers about products; the effectiveness of these movies depends on how well the information in them satisfies the demands of the audience [6]. As a result, it is more important and vital to categorize movies according to the information they cover the product in detail before looking into how different product presentation films affected customers' inclination to purchase. Another finding from previous research on product and consumer variables is that different types of products [7]. Need for touch [6]. Information processing motivation [8]. And inclination towards impulsive purchasing [9]. Are significant moderating elements. No academic has ever looked at how product ratings act as a moderator. However, when customers purchase goods online, they also see the product ratings left by previous customers in addition to the product demonstration films that the vendors have supplied [10]. Customers' perceptions of the veracity of product presentation films are strongly influenced by product ratings.

Aim and Objectives

To examine the influence of visuals and videos on customer purchasing behavior in digital marketing. Specifically, to determine how the quality of visual content influences consumer engagement and purchasing decisions.

Objectives

- To evaluate how digital marketing influences consumer engagement and affects their buying behavior.
- To evaluate the specifically examining how trust in a brand impacts purchase intention.
- To evaluate how consumer engagement Facilitates the connection between the quality of these visual aspects and the perceived worth of the product.

2 Related Work.

Consumer Engagement

[11] CE has been an important customer relationship indicator in the past 15 years [12]. Despite disagreements over its conception, scholars agree on three fundamental CE traits that most CE measures represent. First, CE is interactive meaning [13] "mutual or reciprocal action or influence" [14] People who buy branded items or use branded services interact with other people or organisations associated with the brand, such as frontline personnel, suppliers, or other customers, either during or outside of the buying process. In addition, users have the ability to contact with the firm. Second, CE is consumer equity may be described as the investments made by a consumer in their brand interactions or brand attributes. Higher contributions indicate involvement, which may be favourable or negative [15]. Positive word-of-mouth or assistance provided to other customers might be considered a customer's CE, whereas negative CE may involve brand sabotage or boycotting. Third most CE researchers consider it as multidimensional, unlike other writers [15]. In Based on social media platforms The consumer's cognitive processing, affection, and activation are referred to as CBE, emotional, and behavioural investments in a brand interaction. Next, we describe our research technique.

Quality of Images and Videos

Digital marketing uses image and video quality to affect sales. Images that impress clients build trust. This study shows that digital marketing visual quality influences consumer perception, engagement, and purchase decisions. High-quality images keep customers' attention. Recent study reveals that better-quality and better-composed photos generate more views and interactions [16] Apple's high-quality product feature and user narrative videos enhanced sales and engagement. High-quality visual content boosts product value, trust, emotional connection, and engagement. These elements help the product succeed in a competitive market [17].

Trust in Brand

The internet gave airlines a competitive edge by lowering advertising costs, improving customer happiness, marketing success, and competitiveness. Many companies use social media as part of their communication strategy [18]. It's uncertain whether social networking is a successful marketing approach that boosts brand trust and buy intentions. Traditional marketing strategies include newspaper, magazine, radio, television, and direct mail advertising, which may be defined in numerous ways, but we must understand its nature to explain its poor interaction. Customers cannot control the quantity, kind, or sequence of information in traditional advertising.

Perceived Value of Product

The effects of digital marketing pictures as well as videos on customer purchasing behaviour and product value are complex and include psychology, marketing strategy, and consumer behaviour. Quality visuals and videos grab attention more than words. Visual material may generate emotions, connecting consumers to products.[19] Decision-making and purchase are influenced by emotions. Videos are better than static photos or text in showing how a product operates, its features, and its advantages. They also help customers make decisions, boost conversion rates, and build loyalty [20]. Marketers should create high-quality, relevant, and engaging visual material that supports their brand strategy and satisfies target audience demands to optimize their influence.

Hypotheses Development

H1: The Quality of Images and Videos has a positive effect on Consumer Engagement.

Hypotheses it's crucial to explain the reasoning, define key words, and make sure the linkages are reasonable and based on theory or empirical data. Detailed explanation of hypothesis, Image and video quality boosts consumer engagement [22]. This includes likes, shares, comments, time spent on content, and other customer interactions. Richer media higher-quality pictures and videos delivers more signals and information, improving communication and engagement. Greater quality photos and videos are examples of richer media, which offers more signals and information to promote greater communication and engagement. High-quality images and videos have been shown in several studies to have a favourable impact on user engagement on websites, advertising campaigns, and social media platforms [23]. High-quality multimedia may communicate ideas more clearly, facilitating viewers' comprehension and connection to the material and raising the possibility that they will interact with it. Customers often connect professionalism and trustworthiness with good manufacturing quality. Increased trust and interaction with the information may result from this notion.

H2: Trust in Brand has a positive effect on Purchase Intentions.

The statement that describes the connection between two variables, namely purchase intentions (dependent variable) and trust in brand (independent variable), and is based on actual data or current theory. Here's how to formulate and support this theory. A consumer's faith in a brand is their conviction that it will consistently live up to their expectations and keep its word. Transparency, ethical behaviour, pleasant prior experiences, and consistent quality are all ways to establish trust. Purchase intentions show how likely or eager a customer is with the purpose of purchasing an item or service in the future. It includes the process of making decisions, [24] which is impacted by perceptions of behavioural control, attitudes, and subjective standards. This theory proposes that an individual's subjective standards and their attitude towards an activity influence their desire to participate in that activity (such as making a purchase).

H3: Consumer Engagement mediates the relationship between the Quality of Images and Videos and the Perceived Value of Product.

This is a reference to the multimedia material used in product marketing that is seen to be clear, appealing, and professionally done. Good photos and videos may improve a product's credibility and aesthetic appeal. This encompasses the degree of engagement, interaction, and emotional bond that customers display with the product. Metrics like likes, shares, comments, amount of time spent watching material, etc. maybe used to gauge engagement. This is the sum total of the customer's assessment of the product's value in light of their experience with it (benefits) as opposed to what they pay (costs). It includes how the customer feels about the product's value, relevancy, and quality. Our hypothesis is that the link between the perceived value of the product and the quality of the photographs and videos is mediated by customer interaction, based on the aforementioned correlations. This implies that although excellent photos and videos may have a direct impact on how much people think a product is worth, their effects are amplified when they also raise customer engagement [25]. Put another way, the theory suggests that better multimedia content increases customer involvement, which raises the perceived value of the product [26]. Through the use of techniques like structural equation modelling (SEM), empirical verification of these sub-hypotheses may provide proof of the mediating function of customer involvement in the link between the perceived value of a product and the quality of its multimedia content.

3 Methodology

Research Design

The research adopted a quantitative approach to examine the Organized retail sector and consumer shopping behaviour. Library administrators produced qualitative understandings of decision-making processes, challenges, and successful strategies. Although informed consent and data anonymization were scrupulously adhered to throughout the research, triangulation is made possible by the integration of two data sets, which enhances the analysis's precision and scope.

Sampling Technique

In order to choose participants, the research used a random sampling method. Image and video quality, brand trust, and customer engagement were the determining factors in selecting a sample size of 340 respondents and dependent variables are Perceived Value of Product and Purchase Intentions. Our study population was segmented into smaller groups according to factors. Afterward, we randomly chose participants from each of these more intimate, smaller groups. By following these processes, we ensured the diversity of our sample, resulting in a diverse range of individuals.

Random Sampling Method

The present investigation used the Random sampling approach to would be the most effective way to pick participants for this study. Random sampling is a method in researchwhereeachmemberofapopulationhasanequalchancebeingselectedforthe study. It minimizes bias ensures the generalizability of findings to the entire populations. In this approach, every individual or element is chosen purely by chance, eliminating systematic patterns or preference.

Collection of Data

An essential part of every research project is data collection. The two main approaches of acquiring information are primary and secondary data collection. In order to gather the main data, a questionnaire will be used.

Primary Data Collection: Surveys Design questionnaires to gather data on consumer preferences, attitudes, and behaviours towards organized retail Interviews Conduct in- depth interviews with consumers and industry experts Focus Groups Facilitate discussions with groups of consumers to get qualitative insights.

Variables

Independent Variables	Moderated variable	Dependent Variables
Quality of Images and Videos Trust in Brand	Consumer Engagement	Perceived Value of Product Purchase Intentions

Inclusion and Exclusion Criteria

- Inclusion Criteria: Articles, papers, and reports published in peer-reviewed journals, reputable industry publications, or academic conferences.
- Exclusion Criteria: Research on digital marketing without considering client purchasing behaviour or visual content.

Tools and Techniques of this Study Tools

In this study SPSS (Statistical Package for the Social Sciences) and AMOS (Analysis of Moment Structures) tools are utilized for Data Analysis.

Techniques

SEM Analysis

Structural equation modelling (SEM) analysis is a statistical technique that allows researchers to examine complex relationships between several variables at once. In structural equation modelling (SEM), factor analysis & multiple regression is utilized to assess the direct and indirect effects of a theoretical model. It is particularly useful to test ideas on correlations between latent (unobserved) and observable variables because it illuminates the structural relationships that underlie data. In behavioural research, the social sciences, as well as other fields where understanding the relationships between several categories is essential, social science methodology, or SEM, is often used. This approach also allows for the assessment of model fit to ensure that the proposed theoretical model appropriately describes the data.

Data Analysis

In this study meticulously and thoroughly analysed our data to get valuable insights. This study used several statistical methods to analyse important element connections. The SEM study revealed important correlations between Academic Library Strategic Marketing Initiatives. The moderation study also illuminated how perceived demographic factors influenced these correlations. We examined the data using descriptive and inferential statistics to evaluate our hypothesis. This extensive analysis illuminated Academic Libraries 'Strategic Marketing Initiatives' complicated linkages. It affects many sectors and businesses.

Mediation Analysis: Analyse how different budget allocations affect user engagement via digital marketing channels using structural equation modelling (SEM).

Regression Analysis

The purpose of regression analysis is to find the factors that are independent of the dependent variable and the connection between them. It seeks to understand the effects of independent variables on dependent ones. A mathematical model that most closely resembles the connection between the variables should be fitted to the data. Linear regression estimates the relationship using a straight line and is the most used approach. Economics, biology, and social science employ regression analysis, which is adaptive. It aids academics in prediction, pattern analysis, and dataset linkage analysis. The analysis produces a regression equation that estimates the dependent variable's value from the independent variables.

The regression equation coefficients show association strength and direction. A positive coefficient indicates a positive association, while a negative coefficient indicates a negative one.

4 Results

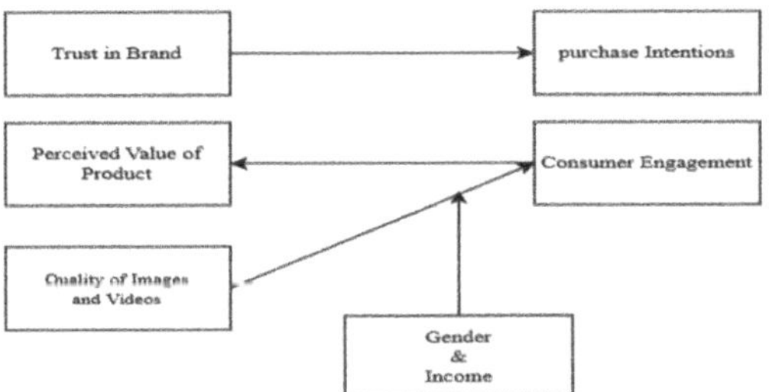

Fig. 1. Conceptual framework

According to the respondents' demographic profile, the majority are between the ages of 18 and 24 (41.3%), followed by those between the ages of 25 and 34 (25.3%), 35 and 44 (17.3%), 45 and 54 (14.3%), and 55 and older (1.7%). According to the gender breakdown, there are somewhat same men and women—50%,50%. Education: Most responders have either a postgraduate degree (34.7%) or an undergraduate degree (35.3%). 19.3% of the remaining population has only completed high school or less, 6.0% has additional degrees, and 4.7% has a PhD or professional degree. 36.0% of respondents are students, while 26.7% are either job less or looking for work. 22.0% are retirees, 8.3% are independent contractors or business owners, and 7.0% are paid professionals. This varied sample offers a wide perspective for evaluating how digital marketing affects consumer purchasing decisions. The respondents' income distribution shows that 20.0% are in the medium income group, 22.3% are in the high-income group, and 57.7%are in the low-income group. The sample's large percentage of low- income respondents might be useful for researching how consumers of different socioeconomic levels interact with digital marketing (Figs. 1, 2 and Tables 1, 2, 3).

Table 1. Demographic Characteristics

		Frequency	Percent
Age	18–24years	124	41.3
	25–34years	76	25.3
	35–44years	52	17.3
	45–54years	43	14.3
	55yearsand above	5	1.7
	Total	300	100.0
Gender	Male	166	55.3
	Female	134	44.7
	Total	300	100.0
Education	High School or below	58	19.3
	Undergraduate degree	106	35.3
	Postgraduate degree	104	34.7
	Doctorate/Professional degree	14	4.7
	Other qualifications	18	6.0
	Total	300	100.0
Occupation	Student	108	36.0
	Salaried professional	21	7.0
	Self-employed/Entrepreneur	25	8.3
	Unemployed/Looking for work	80	26.7
	Retired	66	22.0
	Total	300	100.0
Income	Low Income	173	57.7
	Middle Income	60	20.0
	High Income	67	22.3
	Total	300	100.0

Measurement Model:

Assessing if factor analysis is suitable using KMO and Bartlett's tests. We can see that our sample was quite adequate since the KMO value we got was 0.885. The factor analysis was further supported by the very significant result (P = 0.00) of the Bartlett's test (Table 4).

Discriminant Validity:

Discriminant validity is a concept used to examine correlations between variables and to validate measurement devices. Neither SPSS nor any other statistical tool was used for this specific test. In order to avoid assessing the same underlying notion with many

Fig. 2. Graphical Representation of Measurement Model

variables or constructs, discriminant validity is essential. In order to prove that the measurements used to evaluate distinct concepts are distinct and not heavily associated, researchers use a variety of methods, including correlation analysis and confirmatory factor analysis (CFA). By avoiding construct duplication and ensuring thatmeasuringinstrumentsproperlyreflectthedistinctideastheyareintendedtoassess, discriminant validity contributes to stronger and more precise data analysis and interpretation (Table 5).

The discriminant validity matrix, which evaluates how well separate constructs or variables in a research model really measure distinct ideas as opposed to overlapping ones, is shown in the accompanying table. The correlation coefficient between any two particular constructions is shown in each table column, alongside diagonal components that display the square root of each construct's Average Variance Extracted (AVE). Discriminant validity is confirmed when the cross-correlation coefficients for all constructs are less than or equal to the square root of the AVE for that construct. The square root of the AVE for "Quality of Images and Videos, Trust in Brand, Trust in Brand, Consumer Engagement, Perceived Value of Product, Purchase Intentions, Consumer Engagement" is represented by the diagonal components (italicised values) in this table (Table 6).

With $\chi 2 = 297.622$, NFI = 0.922, IFI = 0.987, GFI = 0.929, RFI = 0.906, and CFI = 0.986, all significantly higher than the threshold of 0.90, the fit quality was satisfactory in representing the sample data. The critical threshold is 0.080, and both the Root Mean Square Residuals (RMSR) value of 0.040 and the Root Mean Square Error of Approximation (RMSEA) value of 0.025 are below it. With an RMSEA of 0.025, RMR of 0.040, GFI of 0.929, and CFI of 0.986, the results showed that the model was well- fit.

Structural Equation Modelling (SEM)

This research examines complex component interactions using structural equation modelling (SEM). It shows direct and indirect effects, giving you a complete theoretical

Table 2. Regression Weights: (Groupnumber1-Defaultmodel)

PATH			**Unstd.Estimate**	**S.E**	**Std. Estimate**	**C.R**	**P**
QIV5	< ---	Quality of Images and Videos	1.000		.703		
QIV4	< ---	Quality of Images and Videos	1.087	.092	.765	11.862	***
QIV3	< ---	Quality of Images and Videos	1.129	.089	.744	12.754	***
QIV2	< ---	Quality of Images and Videos	1.160	.097	.768	11.906	***
QIV1	< ---	Quality of Images and Videos	1.093	.094	.745	11.589	***
TB4	< ---	Trust in Brand	1.000		.742		
TB3	< ---	Trust in Brand	1.054	.087	.745	12.121	***
TB2	< ---	Trust in Brand	1.008	.075	.728	13.477	***
TB1	< ---	Trust in Brand	1.136	.087	.798	13.026	***
CE5	< ---	Consumer Engagement	1.000		.769		
CE4	< ---	Consumer Engagement_	.770	.079	.601	9.803	***
CE3	< ---	Consumer Engagement	.913	.078	.718	11.673	***
CE2	< ---	Consumer Engagement_	.888	.098	.639	9.042	***
CE1	< ---	Consumer Engagement_	1.180	.097	.754	12.182	***
PVP4	< ---	Perceived Value of Product	1.000		.738		
PVP3	< ---	Perceived Value of Product	1.096	.097	.759	11.313	***

(continued)

Table 2. (*continued*)

PATH			Unstd.Estimate	S.E	Std. Estimate	C.R	P
QIV5	< ---	Quality of Images and Videos	1.000		.703		
PVP2	< ---	Perceived Value of Product	1.072	.093	.758	11.541	***
PVP5	< ---	Perceived Value of Product	1.078	.098	.746	10.966	***
TB5	< ---	Trust in Brand	.912	.083	.682	11.051	***
PVP1	< ---	Perceived Value of Product	1.371	.117	.838	11.763	***
PI5	< ---	Purchase Intentions	1.000		.735		
PI4	< ---	Purchase Intentions	.824	.084	.657	9.829	***
PI3	< ---	Purchase Intentions	1.159	.110	.829	10.554	***
PI2	< ---	Purchase Intentions	1.033	.096	.795	10.780	***
PI1	< ---	Purchase Intentions	1.187	.126	.800	9.435	***

Table 3. KMO and Bartlett's Test

Kaiser-Meyer-Olkin Measure of Sampling Adequacy		.885
Bartlett's Test of Sphericity	Approx. Chi-Square	3702.607
	df	300
	Sig	.000

understanding of how elements interact. The recommended model's fit to the data is determined using SEM statistics like regression and factor analysis. This kind of analysis displays intricate patterns and connections that assist us grasp our study topic and test and alter our research ideas (Fig. 3 and Tables 7, 8).

****

Table 4. Post CFA, Cronbach alpha, factor loadings

Factors and items	Cronbach alpha values	Post CFA factor loadings	AVE	CR
Quality of Images and Videos	0.865		0.745	0.4741357
QIV5		.703		
QIV4		.765		
QIV3		.744		
QIV2		.768		
QIV1		.745		
Trust in Brand	0.869		0.739	0.47010515
TB5		.682		
TB4		.742		
TB3		.745		
TB2		.728		
TB1		.798		
Consumer Engagement	0.825		0.6962	0.44052193
CE5		.769		
CE4		.601		
CE3		.718		
CE2		.639		
CE1		.754		
Perceived Value of Product	0.853		0.7678	0.48918682
PVP5		.746		
PVP4		.738		
PVP3		.759		
PVP2		.758		
PVP1		.838		
Purchase Intentions	0.848		0.7632	0.48618407
PI5		.735		
PI4		.657		
PI3		.829		
PI2		.795		
PI1		.800		

Table 5. Discriminant Validity Test

	Quality of Images and Videos	Trust in Brand	Consumer Engagement	Perceived Value of Product	purchase Intentions
Quality of Images and Videos	0.863134				
Trust in Brand	.226**	0.859651			
Consumer Engagement	.163**	.702**	0.834386		
Perceived Value of Product	.691**	.183**	.193**	0.876242	
purchase Intentions	0.107	0.034	0.023	0.108	0.873613

Table 6. Model Fit Summary

Variable	Value
Chi-square value($\chi 2$)	297.622
Degrees of freedom (df)	250
CMIN/DF	1.190
P value	0.021
GFI	0.929
RFI	0.906
NFI	0.922
IFI	0.987
CFI	0.986
RMR	0.040
RMSEA	0.025

H1: The Quality of Images and Videos has a positive effect on Consumer Engagement, and this effect varies by Gender.

In this hypothetical structural equation model, two variables image and video quality and consumer engagement are shown to be interdependent in a table and Gender and Income is an control variables. Image and video quality serves as the independent variable in this model, with consumer engagement serving as the dependent variable. There is a favorable and statistically significant correlation between consumer engagement and the quality of images and videos among Gender, according to the investigation's results

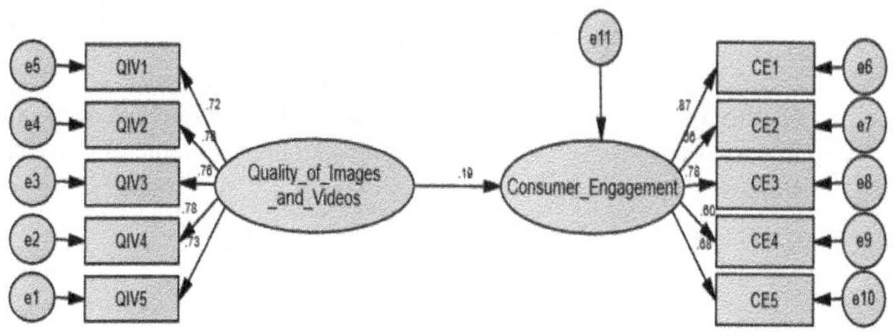

Fig. 3. Graphical Representation of the relationship between Quality of Images and Consumer Engagement among Male.

Table 7. Regression Weights: (Gender wise)

PATH			Gender	Standard Estimates	Std. Estimate	C.R	P
Consumer Engagement	< ---	Quality of Images andVideos	Male	0.192	0.136	1.996	0.00
Consumer Engagement	< ---	Quality of Images and Videos	Female	0.183	0.144	1.959	0.00

($\beta = .192$, $P < .05$), ($\beta = .183$, $P < .05$), ($\beta = -.117$, $P > .05$), ($\beta = .197$, $P > .05$), ($\beta = .388$, $P < .05$).

Based on the path between these two variables, we can see that there is a positive correlation between consumer engagement and the quality of images and videos. The enormous magnitudes of the correlation coefficient value (C.R. values) indicate that the observed connections are statistically significant. Because the factors are statistically significant (p-values > 0.05), the fit indices show that the model is well-fitting. There was a favorable and statistically significant correlation between the quality of images and videos and consumer engagement, as determined by evaluating the whole model fit using seven separate fit indices (Table 9).

The sample data was well represented by the quality of fit, with $\chi2 = 68.897$, NFI = 0.945, IFI=0.999, GFI=0.957, RFI=0.927, and CFI=0.999, all of which are significantly bigger than the 0.90. Likewise, the critical value is 0.080, and the values of RMR (Root Mean Square Residuals) = 0.049 and RMSEA (Root mean square error of approximation) = 0.007 are too low. A number of metrics, such as RMSEA (0.15), RMR (0.049), GFI (0.957), and CFI (0.999), pointed to a satisfactory match with the offered model (Fig. 4 and Table 10).

H2: Trust in Brand has a positive effect on Purchase Intentions.

Table 8. Regression Weights (Income wise)

PATH			Gender	standardEstimates	Std Estimate	C.R	P
Consumer Engagement	< ---	Quality of Images and Videos	Low Income	−0.117	0.237	−0.831	0.406
Consumer Engagement	< ---	Quality of Images and Videos	Middle Income	0.197	0.193	1.375	0.169
Consumer Engagement	< ---	Quality of Images and Videos	High Income	0.388	0.126	3.069	0.002

Table 9. Model Fit Summary

Variable	Value
Chi-square value (χ^2)	68.897
Degrees of freedom (df)	68
CMIN/DF	1.013
P value	0.447
GFI	0.957
RFI	0.927
NFI	0.945
IFI	0.999
CFI	0.999
RMR	0.049
RMSEA	0.007

In this hypothetical structural equation model, two variables brand trust and purchase intentions—are shown to be interdependent. In this case, Purchase Intentions is

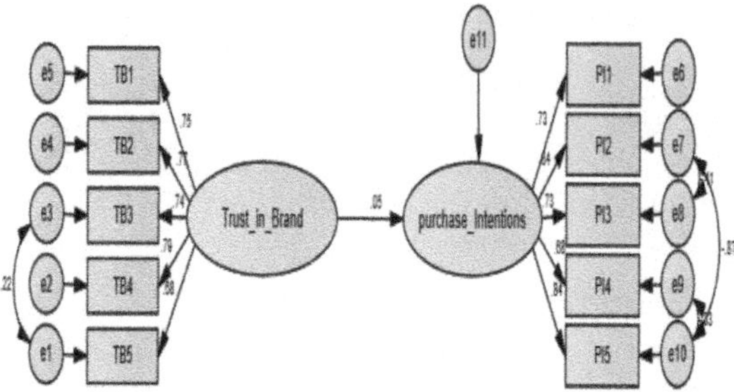

Fig. 4. Graphical Representation of the relationship between Trust in Brand and Purchase Intentions.

Table 10. Regression Weights: (Group number 1-Default model)

PATH			Unstd.Estimate	S.E	Std. Estimate	C.R	P
Purchase Intentions	< ---	Trust in Brand	.053	.070	.047	.761	***
TB5	< ---	Trust in Brand	1.000		.723		
TB4	< ---	Trust in Brand	1.083	.088	.777	12.370	***
TB3	< ---	Trust in Brand	1.136	.092	.776	12.356	***
TB2	< ---	Trust in Brand	1.083	.090	.756	12.062	***
TB1	< ---	Trust in Brand	1.095	.092	.744	11.884	***
PI1	< ---	Purchase Intentions	1.000		.727		
PI2	< ---	Purchase Intentions	1.010	.088	.837	11.508	***
PI3	< ---	Purchase Intentions	.945	.079	.730	11.996	***
PI4	< ---	Purchase Intentions	.795	.070	.683	11.342	***
PI5	< ---	Purchase Intentions	1.061	.089	.838	11.918	***

the dependent variable while Brand Trust is the independent variable. A statistically significant and positive correlation has been observed between Trust in Brand and Purchase Intentions, according to the investigation's results ($\beta = .047$, $P < .05$).

Trust in Brand and Purchase Intentions are positively associated, as shown by the standardized coefficient of 0.047, as demonstrated by the path linking these two variables. The enormous magnitudes of the correlation coefficient values (C.R. values) indicate that the observed connections are statistically significant. Because the factors are statistically significant (p-values > 0.05), The model fits the data well, as shown by the fit indices. To evaluate the total model fit, seven distinct fit indices were used; these, when taken together, revealed a positive and statistically significant link between brand trust and purchase intent (Table 11).

Table 11. Model Fit Summary

Variable	Value
Chi-square value (χ^2)	44.434
Degrees of freedom (df)	31
CMIN/DF	1.433
P value	0.056
GFI	0.971
RFI	0.951
NFI	0.966
IFI	0.989
CFI	0.989
RMR	0.031
RMSEA	0.038

The results showed that the fit was satisfactory and accurately reflected the sample data, with a number of important metrics above the threshold of 0.90, including a Normed Fit Index (NFI) of 0.966, an Incremental Fit Index (IFI) of 0.989, a Goodness of Fit Index (GFI) of 0.971, a Relative Fit Index (RFI) of 0.951, and a Comparative Fit Index (CFI) of 0.989. Similarly, the critical value is 0.080, whereas the values of RMR (Root Mean Square Residuals) = 0.031 and RMSEA (Root mean square error of approximation) = 0.038 are also below it. With an RMSEA of 0.38, an RMR of 0.031, a GFI of 0.971, and a CFI of 0.989, the results showed that the offered model was an excellent match (Fig. 5 and Table 12).

H3: Consumer Engagement mediates the relationship between the Quality of Images and Videos and the Perceived Value of Product.

The research in the table demonstrates the relationships between customer engagement, perceived product value, and video and picture quality. A standardized estimate of 0.163 (SE = 0.057, C.R. = 2.848, p = 0.004) shows that the quality of photos and videos has a considerable impact on customer engagement. The perceived value of the product

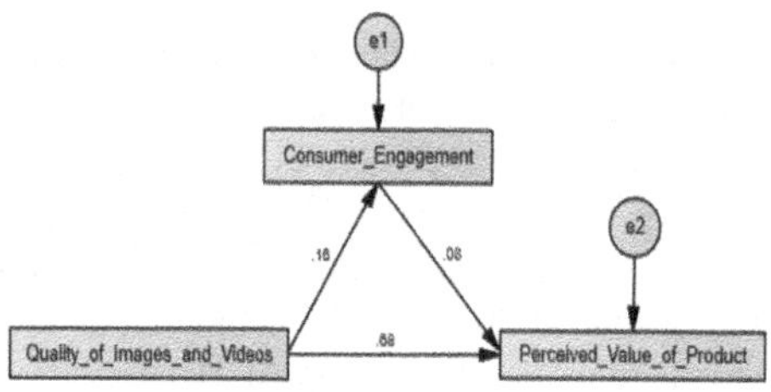

Fig. 5. Graphical Representation of the Mediation relation of Consumer Engagement

Table 12. Regression Weights: (Group number 1-Default model)

PATH			Unstd. Estimate	S.E	Std. Estimate	C.R	P
Consumer Engagement	< ---	Quality of Images and Videos	.163	.057	.163	2.848	.004
Perceive Value of Product	< ---	Quality of Images and Videos	.674	.042	.677	16.091	***
Perceive Value of Product	< ---	Consumer Engagement	.082	.042	.083	1.977	.048

is also significantly correlated with the quality of the photographs and videos (standardized estimate = 0.677, p < 0.001, C.R. = 16.091, SE = 0.042). The perceived value of the product is also favourably impacted by customer participation, with a standardized estimate of 0.083 (SE = 0.042, C.R. = 1.977, p = 0.048). These results highlight how crucial excellent visual material is for raising customer engagement and a product's perceived worth (Table 13).

Table 13. Standardized Indirect Effects (Group number 1-Default model)

	Quality of Images and Videos	Consumer Engagement
Consumer Engagement	.000	.000
Perceive Value of Product	.014	.000

Table 11's standardized indirect effects show that, although there is no indirect impact on the Caliber of photos and videos, customer involvement is impacted by the perceived worth of the product in an indirect manner of 0.014. Furthermore, as all of these metrics are 0.000, neither the customer engagement nor the picture and video quality show any indirect impacts on one another or on the perceived worth of the product (Table 14).

H4) Income moderates the relationship between Quality of Images and Videos and Consumer Engagement.

Table 14. Coefficients

	Std. Error	Standardized Coefficients	t	Sig	F-Value
(Constant)	0.497		5.336	0.000	5.584
Quality of Images and Videos	0.129	0.353	2.748	0.006	
Income	0.269	0.314	1.164	0.246	
Interaction1	0.071	-0.491	-1.699	0.090	

These findings lead us to the conclusion that, in this model, the quality of the images and videos is a strong predictor of consumer engagement. This helps us to understand how powerfully high-quality images influence user engagement. According to this concept, consumer involvement is not significantly impacted by income levels since money is not shown to have a substantial direct effect. The interaction term, Interaction 1, indicates a negative moderation effect that is marginally not significant. This might indicate that some contexts or settings lessen the beneficial influence that visual quality has on engagement. All things considered, the model is statistically significant, demonstrating the significance of high-quality visual material in enhancing customer engagement and the need for more research to elucidate the roles of income and interaction effects.

5 Discussion

This study explores the complex interaction between digital marketing materials, namely the impact of pictures and videos on customer purchase behaviour. The study aims to explore the intricate interaction among these factors using a comprehensive measuring approach that includes dimensions such as Image and Video Quality, Brand Trust, Consumer Engagement, Perceived Value of Product, and Purchase Intentions. First, the measurement model's validity and reliability were thoroughly examined. Previous research confirmed that the dataset was appropriate for factor analysis, thanks to high scores on the Kaiser-Meyer-Olkin Measure of Sampling Adequacy (KMO) and strong results from Bartlett's Test of Sphericity.

Additional inspection included determining discriminant validity, which is critical for ensuring that different notions measure independent phenomena. Correlation studies verified discriminant validity, increasing confidence in the measurement model's capacity to effectively represent the distinct ideas being investigated. Furthermore, reliability checks using Cronbach's alpha values and confirmatory factor analysis (CFA) loadings demonstrated the model's resilience, emphasizing its usefulness for hypothesis testing.

Moving onto hypothesis testing, the research sought to confirm many assertions about the influence of digital marketing features on customer behaviour. The H1 proposed a favourable relationship between image and video quality and consumer engagement among Gender as Control Variable. The inclusion of gender and income as control variables highlights key audience differences. Gender reveals varying impacts of media quality, emphasizing the need for tailored approaches for male and female audiences. Income shows higher responsiveness to visual quality among affluent consumers, reflecting their elevated expectations. These control variables enhance the study's precision by accounting for demographic variability, ensuring robust findings. The analysis of regression weights showed a statistically significant coefficient, supporting the hypothesis and emphasizing the critical significance of visual content in encouraging customer engagement.

Similarly, finding evidence of a positive correlation between brand trust and desire to buy was the goal of H2. The results revealed a substantial standardized coefficient, confirming the hypothesis and emphasizing the significance of brand trust in influencing customer purchasing choices.

Finally, H3 stated that Consumer Engagement acts as a link between the quality of images and videos and the perceived value of the product. The findings corroborated this assumption, with a statistically significant indirect influence of Perceived Value of Product via Consumer Engagement, revealing consumer engagement's mediating function in determining perceptions of product value. The hypothesis that **Income moderates the relationship between Quality of Images and Videos and Consumer Engagement** suggests that income may influence how responsive consumers are to high-quality visuals. While **Quality of Images and Videos** significantly affects engagement, the income moderation effect is marginally negative, indicating that higher-income individuals may be less influenced by visual content quality. This finding suggests the need for further exploration to understand the nuanced role of income in shaping consumer behavior. Finally, this study delves into the complex dynamics of digital marketing, highlighting the substantial influence of visual content and brand trust on customer behaviour. The study not only supports theoretical notions but also gives practical information for marketers looking to navigate the digital ecosystem and increase customer engagement and buy intentions.

6 Conclusion

The significance of high-quality images and videos in shaping consumer behaviour in the realm of digital marketing has been brought to light by this study. High-quality visual material greatly increases customer engagement, hence improving the perceived value of items. Moreover, research has shown that confidence in a brand has a favourable impact on consumers' intentions to make a purchase. This emphasises the need of establishing and maintaining brand credibility. The findings of the structural equation modelling confirm the suggested conceptual framework, showing that the modelfitswellandtherearestrongcorrelationsamongthemainvariables. The control variables **gender** and **income** offer critical insights. Gender underscores the differential influence of media quality, suggesting the need for customized approaches to male and female audiences. Income further refines this understanding, indicating that higher- income consumers are more responsive to the quality of visual content. Incorporating these control variables enhances the robustness of the findings by accounting for variability and ensuring more precise interpretations of the observed relationships. The results confirm that the Quality of Images and Videos is a significant predictor of Consumer Engagement, underlining the importance of high-quality visuals. Further investigation is needed to fully understand the roles of income and interaction effects. These observations indicate that marketers should give priority to the calibre of visual material in their digital marketing strategies in order to successfully captivate customers and influence their purchasing choices. Brands may enhance their competitive advantage in the digital market place by using high-quality pictures and videos to boost customer impressions and stimulate greater buy intentions.

References

1. Tailor, R.K., Kaur, S.: Digital marketing and it's impact on the buying behaviour of the consumers (2020)
2. Vonkeman, C., Verhagen, T., Van Dolen, W.: Role of local presence in online impulse buying. Inf. Manag. **54**(8), 1038–1048 (2017)
3. Jiangand, Z., Benbasat, I.: The effects of presentation formats and task complexity on online consumers' product understanding. MIS Q. 475–500 (2007)
4. Edell, J.A., Staelin, R.: The information processing of pictures in print advertisements. J. Consum. Res. 10(1), 45–61 (1983)
5. Kumar, A., Tan, Y.: The demand effects of joint product advertising in online videos. Manage. Sci. **61**(8), 1921–1937 (2015)
6. Flavián, C., Gurrea, R., Orús, C.: The influence of online product presentation videos on persuasion and purchase channel preference: the role of imagery fluency and need for touch. Telemat. Informatics **34**(8), 1544–1556 (2017)
7. Li, T., Meshkova, Z.: Examining the impact of rich media on consumer willingness to pay in online stores. Electron. Commer. Res. Appl. **12**(6), 449–461 (2013)
8. Orús, C., Gurrea, R., Flavián, C.: Facilitating imaginations through online product presentation videos: effects on imagery fluency, product attitude and purchase intention. Electron. Commer. Res. **17**, 661–700 (2017)
9. Aljukhadar, M., Senecal, S.: Communicating online information via streaming video: the role of user goal. Online Inf. Rev. **41**(3), 378–397 (2017)
10. Utz, S., Kerkhof, P., VanDenBos, J.: Consumers rule: how consumer reviews influence perceived trust worthiness of online stores. Electron. Commer. Res. Appl. **11**(1), 49–58 (2012)
11. Kumar, V., Pansari, A.: Competitive advantage through engagement. J. Mark. Res. **53**(4), 497–514 (2016)
12. Hollebeek, L.D., Srivastava, R.K., Chen, T.: SD logic–informed customer engagement: integrative framework, revised fundamental propositions, and application to CRM. J. Acad. Mark. Sci. **47**, 161–185 (2019)
13. Kumar, V., Rajan, B., Gupta, S., Pozza, I.D.: Customer engagement in service. J. Acad. Mark. Sci. **47**, 138–160 (2019)
14. Vargo, S.L., Lusch, R.F.: Institutions and axioms: an extension and update of service- dominant logic. J. Acad. Mark. Sci. **44**, 5–23 (2016)
15. Hollebeek, L.D., Glynn, M.S., Brodie, R.J.: "Consumer brand engagement in social media: conceptualization, scale development and validation. J. Interact. Mark. **28**(2), 149–165 (2014)
16. Suryana, P., Haryadi, M.R.: Stores atmosphere and promotion on customer satisfaction and its impact on consumer loyalty. Trikonomika **18**(1), 30–34 (2019)

17. Al-Maghrabi, T., Dennis, C.: The factors driving continuance online shopping in Saudi Arabia: regional and behavioral differences among women. Int. J. Cust. Relatsh. Mark. Manag. **1**(2), 11–34 (2010)
18. Eroglu, S.A., Machleit, K.A., Davis, L.M.: Empirical testing of a model of online store atmospherics and shopper responses. Psychol. Mark. **20**(2), 139–150 (2003)
19. Zeithaml, V.A., Bitner, M.J., Gremler, D.D.: Services Marketing: Integrating Customer Focus Across the Firm. McGraw-Hill (2018)
20. Fürst, A., Pecornik, N., Hoyer, W.D.: How product complexity affects consumer adoption of new products: the role of feature heterogeneity and interrelatedness. J. Acad. Mark. Sci. **52**(2), 329–348 (2024). https://doi.org/10.1007/s11747-023-00933-7
21. Huang, J., Zou, Y.P., Liu, H.L., Wang, J.T.: Is 'Dynamic' better than 'Static'? The effect of product presentation on consumers' evaluation—the mediation effect of cognitive processing. Chin. J. Manag **14**, 742–750 (2017)
22. Chia, J., Harun, A., Kassim, A.W.M., Martin, D., Kepal, N.: Understanding factors that influence house purchase intention among consumers in Kota Kinabalu: an application of buyer behavior model theory. J. Technol. Manag. Bus. **3**(2) (2016)
23. Van der Heijden, H., Verhagen, T.: Online store image: conceptual foundations and empirical measurement. Inf. Manag. **41**(5), 609–617 (2004)
24. Mai, N.T.T., Jung, K., Lantz, G., Loeb, S.G.: An exploratory investigation into impulse buying behavior in a transitional economy: a study of urban consumers in Vietnam. J. Int. Mark. **11**(2), 13–35 (2003)
25. Bansal, H.S., Taylor, S.: Investigating the relationship between service quality, satisfaction and switching intentions. In: Proceedings of the 1997 Academy of Marketing Science (AMS) Annual Conference, pp. 304–313 (2014)
26. Youn, S., Faber, R.J.: Impulse buying: its relation to personality traits and cues. Adv. Consum. Res. **27**(1) (2000)

Enhancing Blockchain Scalability for IoT Transactions Using ZK-Rollups: A Secure and Efficient Off-Chain Solution

Y. Mounica(✉)

University of the Cumberlands, Williamsburg, KY 40769, USA
ymounica.phd@ieee.com

Abstract. Blockchain provides a platform for secure and reliable Internet of Things (IoT) transactions based on its commercially distributed and highly secure network architecture. Even though technology has been widely implemented, the bringer of new achievements, but blockchain technology still confronts numerous challenges, such as low throughput, high computational costs, and transaction fees. To deal with the scalability problem, some off-chain scaling solutions have been innovated as dominant alternatives, acting out new solutions, thus offering more percent efficiency and less expense. Past experience shows that payment hub systems, which were based on the central operator model, were susceptible to central operator failures (COF). Moreover, the previous approaches, which started the system by letting operators post USSCs to the blockchain, didn't consider the possible state rollbacks, thus causing security flaws. Thus, ZK-Rollups implement validity proofs only to allow the correct state transitions to be Sha256 in this case so that there is no need to trust them, and thus, they can be eliminated. This paper aims to show how the ZK-Rollups can enhance the scalability of the blockchain by increasing the transaction throughput and on-chain costs. In detail, we significantly underline how ZK-Rollups exploit short cryptographic proofs to aggregate multiple transactions while sustaining decentralization and security. Moreover, we investigate the usage of cutting-edge recursive ZKPs for this purpose and the principle of instant transaction verification. The next steps for the research include the ZK circuits optimization, the decrease of proof generation time, and binding Layer 2 solutions with decentralized AI.

Keywords: ZK-Rollups · Blockchain · Internet of Things (IoT) · Machine Learning · Decentralized AI

1 Introduction

The Internet of Things (IoT) refers to an ecosystem that consists of interconnected devices that are able to facilitate communication between machines (M2M) and humans (M2P) via various types of applications, for example, smart homes [1, 2], smart grids [3], and then e-healthcare [4]. The rise in IoT market acceptance has resulted in an increased number and frequency of micro-payments inside the system, thus causing the demand

S. Tiwari et al. (Eds.): AMLDA 2024, CCIS 2636, pp. 111–123, 2026.
https://doi.org/10.1007/978-3-032-18293-7_8

for a robust and highly scalable payment mechanism [5]. Blockchain technology has been considered as a feasible alternative capable of offering decentralization, security, and immutability that suits well for networking-and-things-based financial transactions [6, 7]. Nevertheless, the use of common sense architectural solutions for traditional blockchain systems puts forward enormous limitations in such systems that they can be at the high throughput required in large-scale IoT applications [8, 9]. Bitcoin, for example, supports only seven transactions per second (TPS) [10], while Ethereum can handle about 20 TPS [11]. However, conventional financial networks such as Visa can have up to 47,000 TPS at their peak hours [12]. In a bid to resolve the scalability concern, off-chain technologies have been tried, and most of these protocols have resulted in the enhancement of blockchain transmission rates without the necessity of changing the underlying blockchain architecture [13, 14]. Machine learning makes IoT micro-payment systems better by foreseeing transaction amounts, changing resources smartly, and finding threats as they happen to keep both systems safe and fast. Amid the solutions, it is a fact that ZK-Rollups has become less expensive because fewer computational and store costs are acquired, which will lower transaction costs [15]. ZK-Rollups helps to break down large numbers of transactions into smaller more digestible pieces using zero-knowledge proofs, which are cryptographically guaranteed to be the only solution submitted to the blockchain. This has the effect of enabling efficient transaction processing while still maintaining the integrity and security of the blockchain [16]. In comparison with conventional payment channels (PCs) [17, 18] and payhubs (PHs) [19], ZK-Rollups is a decentralized, efficient, and secure way of processing IoT micro-payments without the dependence on a central operator.

1.1 Challenges in the Currently Existent Off-Chain Payment Solutions

The efficiency of things like PCs and PHs notwithstanding, off-chain payment mechanisms available now have some important problems that are serious enough:

Centralized Operator Failure (COF): In order to function, PHs depend on centralized nodes that serve to transmit the data between many clients instead of one but at the same time create only one "stop" where anything can go wrong. Related to the node malfunction—either because of the attack or the software issue—the whole payment network could be affected [20]. Centralization also increases resistance to censorship attacks [21] and denial-of-service (DoS) attacks [22] that harm the major points of blockchain decentralization.

Unsettled: State Commitment (USC): In PH-models operators are required to submit the proper state commitments to the blockchain in the predefined challenge time if they want their transactions to be settled successfully. In case an operator does not submit the correct state commitments or just delays on purpose, it can result in transaction rollbacks, disputes, and financial losses for users [23, 24]. Moreover, delayed finality in state settlement will have an effect on the transaction speed and security of the network. This will also mean that PH solutions will be less effective [25].

1.2 Proposed Solution: ZK-Rollups for IoT Micro-Payments

In order to tackle these difficulties, we provide a solution that is both scalable and efficient, as well as an off-chain payment protocol that is ZK-Rollup based. This method increases not only the transfer speed but also the security and distribution of IoT micro-transactions. PHs can cause involuntary centralization problems, while ZK-Rollups allow for trustless aggregation of transactions and thus reduce reliance on any single operation. As for the weaknesses of SMS, their centralizing properties cannot be overlooked, especially in places where one entity has control of all validation, and they can introduce fraudulent:

- ZK-Rollup-Based: Payment Protocol: We propose a multiparty payment solution that is designed to operate under the new scheme of off-chain and ZK-Rollup with the proviso of transaction security.
- Decentralized: State Verification: We have implemented a COF-free method that establishes trust through off-chain state financial government using cryptographic proofs.
- Fraud: Prevention with Zero-Knowledge Proofs: Zero-knowledge proofs have been found to be a feasible method of adopting state verification within an extensive time frame, which in no way endangers privacy.
- Performance: Optimization: Performance material is in the electronic form of an off-chain payment protocol ZK-Rollup, which we claim to have built ourselves. In our tests, we show how it can process requests with low latency and use less energy than traditional approaches.

The following sections compose the remaining part of this article: Sect. 2 surveys related work. Section 3 explicates the ZK-Rollup model and gives information about how it is advantageous for IoT payments. Section IV elaborates on the proposed design style. Section 5 identifies the security and performance aspects. Section 4 introduces the results of the implementation and performance evaluations. Section 6 suggests topics for future research and Sect. 8 concludes the article.

2 Related Work

With the increasing volume and frequency of transactions in the Internet of Things (IoT) ecosystem, blockchain technology faces the challenge of scalability, which limits its ability to effectively manage high-throughput micro-payments [26]. In order to deal with these issues, off-chain scaling solutions that have been the outcome of research and industry efforts for a long time have appeared [27]. Off-chain protocols shine up the blockchain scalability without having to alter its basic mechanisms and, as such, enhance the overall compatibility of its use in other ecosystems. Payment Channels (PCs), Payment Hubs (PHs), and the most recent ZK-Rollups are the factors that have resulted from these efforts as prominent solutions to the problems.

2.1 Payment Channels

Payment Channels (PCs) are agreements that allow two users to exchange currency with each other without going through the transactions on the blockchain each time.

The first conceptualized PC model was introduced by Spilman [28] as a unidirectional channel, followed by the Duplex Micropayment Channel (DMC) [29], which facilitated bidirectional transactions on Bitcoin. The multi-signing components are based on these models, where enough funds are first deposited to a multi-signature account, and then, in the subsequent steps, the statuses are kept up to date using the cryptographic signatures, such that the final state is settled on-chain. Payment Channel Networks (PCNs), such as the Lightning Network [30] and Sprites [31], are the ones that extend the idea by interconnecting multiple PCs and therefore enabling the people who are not involved in the transaction to take indirect payments as intermediaries [32]. Even with improvements to scalability, PCNs have given rise to problems including intricate routing methods, high malfunction levels in more-than-one-hop transactions, and these channel imbalance issues [33, 34]. The ways in which Celer [35] improves operating performance are the following: while REVIVE [36] positively affects channel liquidity. Nevertheless, on the downside, these methods increase computation complexity and customer interaction, since they also require trust assumptions. Perun [37] was the first to use virtual channels so that the data was transmitted without the loss of proper links. However, it can't be universal. As opposed to that, ZK-Rollups have the advantage of linking together transactions that are to be executed on a smart contract into a single batch, which in turn reduces congestion and makes it easier to operate.

2.2 Payment Hubs

Payment Hubs (PHs) facilitate multi-party transactions by connecting users through a centralized intermediary. TumbleBit [38] introduced an anonymous PH model that allows users to transact without revealing identities. However, its reliance on preestablished channels increases collateral requirements and restricts the usability of Bitcoin. Nocust attempted to improve PH scalability by employing a noncustodial operator to batch transactions and submit periodic state commitments. However, challenges such as operator failure and unsettled state commitments (USC) persist, often requiring extended challenge periods to resolve disputes. Magma improved state validation through counter-based updates but suffered from frequent collisions during high transaction loads. Further optimized PHs by introducing parallel transaction processing but required continuous online participation from all users, making it impractical for real-world applications.

2.3 ZK-Rollups

Decentralized scaling strategies such as ZK-Rollups offer greater capacity and lower transaction fees without compromising on security or relying on any intermediary party. Basically, the zero-knowledge proof system replaces PHs and PCNs by ensuring the combination of multiple transactions and the subsequent compilation into a single cryptographic proof that is validated on the chain. In a similar vein, such a method cuts the amount of on-chain data. Thus, the issue of reduced scalability is prevented. ZkSync and StarkNet are among the projects that use ZK-Rollup for micro-payments that are nearly instant and cost-effective based on the data generated by the Ethereum network, respectively. In comparison with PHs, off-chain operators are ousted in ZK-Rollups, thus guaranteeing that there is no operator failure or information withdrawal. In addition, the construction of the quick and effective dispute mechanism in ZK-Rollups involving validity proves that the challenge periods in PHs are unnecessary. ZK-Rollups are rather demanding in terms of cryptographic computations; however, their strengths in transaction finality and security make them a preeminent option for micro-payments in the IoT network.

On the one hand, be that as it may, the traditional methods of USB and PC for blockchain have increased the scalability of blockchain technology, but they have to deal with the problems following the short period of time for the transactions, the operator-s dependency, and the slow period of settlement. ZK-Rollups instead provide only a reliable way out, that is, faster and cheaper multi-path transactions without the risk of security or centralization. Future research has the potential to upgrade the operational efficiency of ZK-Rollup, perfect the proof generation process, and connect different IoT devices from different blockchains so that they can communicate and carry the information properly.

3 Preliminary Model

This section briefly introduces the cryptographic basis on which our protocol is established. It will also discuss things like the system model, communication framework, and threat assumptions related to the proposed ZK-Rollup-based solution.

3.1 Cryptographic

Preliminaries Functionality of our protocol is built on cryptographic primitives, for example, digital signatures, zero-knowledge proofs (ZKPs), verifiable random functions (VRFs), and Merkle trees, which are assumed to be secure [1].

- Digital Signature Scheme: We expect to install a standard public key infrastructure (PKI) for authentication. A single regular person has his own key pair u2013 public-private. The formula of the digital signature is $\sigma(s) = Sign(sk, msg)$, and here sk is the signer's private key, and the second part $\sigma(s)$is the signature corresponding to the message msg. The check of the signature verification function $Vrfy(pk, msg, \sigma(s))$becomes true if the signature is valid and false otherwise [2].
- Zero Knowledge Proofs (ZKPs): A ZKP allows the prover to prove the state-ment of a theorem without unveiling the underlying information. The method we use is zk-SNARKs (Zero-Knowledge Succinct Non-Interactive Argument of Knowledge) for fast proof generation and checking. In the case that a witness w and a statement x are provided, a prover creates a proof $\pi = Prove(x, w)$which a verifier can also validate using $Verify(x, \pi)$[3].
- Verifiable Random Function (VRF): A VRF is a Pseudorandom Function that behaves as if it were deterministic with verifiably random inputs. Event of Randomly elected leaders based on V[2^2, spec one of the options: *RFsk(x)*] (Event of randomly elected leaders EVRF, a non-interactive deterministic proof of the winner of the first round if x is taken at random input. The proof formula is based on the Verifier Private Key and the hash of message x. Many other metamathematical principles can be discussed.

- Merkle Tree: A Merkle tree is a hash tree that allows for efficient data verification. Building a Merkle Tree is the process of hashing pairs of the treed nodes and repeatedly doing so until only a single overlord-node label is left (that is also the Merkle Root, let's say). A Merkle hash function *H(X)* computes a root hash RHRH on a dataset $Z=\{z_1,z_2,\ldots,z_m\}$. Merkle proof of membership consists of a simple proof of the leaf node being among the rows, for example, the syntax of the first and the last 7 lines of a page, through verified $(MerklrRoot, leaf_i, Proof)$.

3.2 System Model

Our protocol is created on a blockchain-based payment environment that is strengthened by ZK-Rollups. The blockchain serves as an unchangeable bookkeeper monitoring every transaction on-chain, and ZK-Rollups aggregate multiple off-chain transactions to formulate a single proof to be given to the chain for checking. We assign users as P, and the blockchain network allows smart contracts to be able to run Turing-complete programs [6]. We have taken this example and suggest a payment model that is based on ZK-Rollup, under which every participant maintains an off-chain state. The off-chain state of a participant P_i is identified by its public key pk_i and consists of a tuple, where bal represents the balance of Fig. 1 illustrates the model with the entities involved:

- Rollup Manager: A smart contract deployed on-chain, which serves as the middleman between the on-chain and off-chain systems. The contract stores the transaction data, deposition of collateral, state commitment, and verification proof.
- User: The users are the ones responsible for the transactions and interact with the rollup system by submitting state updates. The users can deposit and withdraw funds through the Rollup Manager.
- Aggregator (Sequencer): Aggregator fetches transactions and, generates a ZK proof, and sends it to the blockchain. This type of entity ensures that transactions are processed quickly and, at the same time, secure.
- Verifier: ZK verifiers support the aggregators to check for the forged activities. Their job is to validate any false proofs presented to the aggregator so that they know it is fraud. They are the ones who can sing and freeze wrong promises.

3.3 Communication Model

We assume a synchronous or weakly synchronous network where participants communicate over secure and efficient peer-to-peer (P2P) protocols [7]. Message propagation latency between honest nodes is bounded by δ. The protocol allows participants to interact with smart contracts at any time. These assumptions align with existing blockchain architectures such as Bitcoin and Ethereum [8].

- Threat Model: Our security model assumes a computationally bounded adversary constrained by the infeasibility of breaking cryptographic primitives. The adversary lacks sufficient computational power or financial resources to compromise the blockchain network [9].
- Honest Majority Assumption: At least *2f+12f+1* out of $n \geq 3f + n \geq 3f + 1$verifiers remain honest.

- Malicious Aggregator Threat: A dishonest aggregator may attempt to submit incorrect state commitments; however, verifiers can challenge such misbehavior using fraud proofs.
- Data Availability Attacks: Users and verifiers ensure data availability by retrieving necessary proofs and state commitments from the Rollup Manager.
- Sybil Attacks: We assume Sybil resistance through staking mechanisms, where malicious actors need significant financial resources to undermine the system [10].

By addressing these security concerns, our proposed ZK-Rollup-based model enhances scalability, maintains decentralization, and ensures transaction integrity in blockchain-based micro-payments.

4 Zero-Knowledge Rollups (ZK-Rollups) Design

Zero-knowledge rollups (ZK-Rollups) are an innovative way for blockchain networks to scale, with (faster transaction processing times) and tons of transactions per second while remaining secure enough and decentralized. ZK-Rollups establish zero-knowledge proofs to lump together a multitude of transactions into a single proof, which is then sent to the main blockchain (Ethereum or other Layer 1 chain) to confirm the rest of the blocks (Buterin, 2018). Through this, the process of computing and gas fees are cut down and as a result, a blockchain network can be scaled more efficiently.

4.1 Architecture of ZK-Rollups

The architecture of ZK-Rollups implies several key components (Ben-Sasson et al., 2018):

- Operator (Aggregator): A system that is capable of obtaining the transactions, taking proofs from them, and then using zk-SNARKs or zk-STARKs, submitting them to the main chain.
- Rollup Contract: A program on the Layer 1 chain that allows the verification of the proofs and changes the current state of the system.
- Merkle Tree Storage: Technology that is necessary for the effective and secure running of the compressing transaction history.

4.2 Security and Privacy Features

Computer-aided design (CAD) software is used in many engineering and design fields, and people make different models with it. 3D CAD is different from the 2D version in that it can generate lifelike representations of nearly any object because of its ability to create 3D models. Conversely, the main idea of CNC machining is cutting material or drilling holes. Hence, 3D design files with STL format still have to be simplified and broken down into toolpath instructions for the CNC machine, while 3D CAD models with IGES format have to be translated into cutter locations for the CNC machine to follow. Regardless, from the manufacturing process, machining is the slowest but it is easy to solve such problems (Wood, 2020). Nevertheless, tips on using machines such as

CNC milling, CNC turning, semi-autonomous grinding machines, etc., are a big way to achieve the precision needed with such machines in various companies with high-tech production units.

Moreover, Software solutions employ an off-chain model to solve the blockchain scalability issue and the entire system works outside of the traditional blockchain network. One embodiment refers to a method for using a blockchain to secure "cold wallets" and perform transactions. The method disclosed herein provides the best of both worlds-scintillating, audacious decentralized finance meet with dead-simple Blasts from the Past. The group's mission is to provide groundbreaking symphonic cadences of security, privacy, robust surging of activities, and the impeccable/uncorrupted realization of the Art of the Deal. For instance, the Bitcoin Lightning Network is a decentralized layer-2 blockchain that allows unlimited cryptocurrencies through.

5 ZK-Rollups Analysis

The security, liveness, and privacy properties of Zero-Knowledge Rollups (ZK-Rollups) are analyzed in this section.

A. Security Our design and the three adversary models (honest but curious, rational bad, and strong adversary) are used to simulate the situations in the system before the deployment of the system in the real world. In each of these models, we assume that the adversary can compromise the responsible parties so that he can inject and execute invalid transactions or invalid states, Lamport timestamps, and proof of knowledge that are temporarily inconsistent. ZK-Rollups ensure the integrity of data and its authenticity (owners are the source) by having no entity duplicate the assets or the maliciousness of the sequencer in realizing false information (invalid state).

Definition 1 (Invalid Transaction): An epoch e transaction Tx is said to be invalid, if both 1) the amount filed, tx.value, is not the same in the tx it was before the epoch and 2) The transaction spends the new key, Tx[Math].publickey. Moreover, if the transaction is not valid, verification does not succeed because it involves invalid (opposite) signatures.

Definition 2 (Invalid State): Statei + 1 is called invalid if [the new state is applied to[i]th transaction] and if ($(Statei \not\Rightarrow Txi\, Statei + 1\, and\, ESi)$) we obtain false.

Definition 3 (Invalid ES): A situation, where ESi is an invalid error and in addition, it holds that ($(ESi = H(SRi||SRi + 1||H(Txi))$and ($(Statei + 1\, is\, a\, part\, of S(Ri + 1))$is a troubled state.

Definition 4 (Invalid Checkpoint): A checkpoint [was published at the end of an eopch] CPe for eopch e is wrong if [it is the case] 1) $CPe.EH < CPe - 1.EH$; 2) $VRFY(pkL, CPe, \sigma(L)) \rightarrow false$; 3) There is $H(Tx) \in CPe.BTR$; and 4) There is $H(ESi) \in CPe.ESR$.

Lemma 1 (Safe Update): Third-party users should not conclude that the check-points committed are invalid. Proof: The attacker model corresponds to our first definition of an adversary. It is easy to see that f dishonest verifiers cannot change the published checkpoint plus any consensus. Due to the fact that the verifier needs to collect at least $f+1$ votes from the committee for the manager to send the corresponding CPe, at most *f(th)* out *3f(f+1)* can dishonest verifiers see the hypothetical data from the sequencer. There are two challenge mechanisms. In the first one (TFC), the verifier directly challenges the faux message by broadcasting a recovery packet to all participants. The second challenge (SFC) is a direct challenge where one verifier starts to respond to the purported checkpoint sent by the malicious sequencer by defending the check.

Theorem 1 (Safe Transfer): One user cannot construct a transaction that spends another user's assets.

Proof: Let's say a user sends a transaction that is not valid to the sequencer during epoch e, in which the payer or the payee or the value or the nonce of the transaction is altered. We have to go through two cases. First, the honest sequencer applies the verification method to verify the Tx.σ(payer) and find the course of that transaction as invalid, after which reject it. Second, the sequencer was compromised in the process of handling and executing the invalid transaction and he included it in the CPe. BTR, but it will be bad by Lemma 1.

Theorem 2 (Safe State): Is the state invalid if the ESR containing it is also invalid? Proof: By Definition 2, the Statei+1 is an invalid state. Now, let us consider the Theorem 2 (Safe State) for a nonsensical State. Here, the remaining question gets put to rest for the reason that the ESr that has got the Invalid State in that checkpoint has to be Invalid too.

B. Liveness ZK-Rollups use Live updates to improve their liveness so that they have the freedom to withdraw their cash only to those users who deserve it.

The time required for checkpoint updates will continue without interruption, according to Theorem 3. According to the threat model, there exists a maximum of f verifiers that are faulty within the *3f+1* possible fault verifiers. When the maximum number of faulty nodes reaches f invalid alongside f evil nodes, it represents the most severe failure case. The number of truthful and operating verifiers amounts to *f+1−f−f=f+1*. The failed or malicious sequencer stops updating newly published checkpoints when this situation occurs. A running TC exists as a possibility for all active verifiers to launch at any moment. Under normal conditions, the sequencer must update its checkpoint status and transmit it to the manager system within Te. The system will choose a new checkpoint for restructuring if the unresponsive sequencer fails to respond to verification requests. The system enables rightful users to perform balance withdrawals at any time. A user needs no other requirements except those already established by the exit process to perform an exit. A user U_i can perform an exit from the rollup during epoch e by using the manager. The sequencer needs to halt the current state of U_i so that it can add the user to the withdrawal listing during the epoch *e+1*. Withdrawals from the blockchain wallet happen during epoch *e*+2 starting from the sum total of balances.

The privacy aim of ZK-Rollups is to maintain state and transaction information that is anonymous to external roll-up parties. ZK-Rollups disclose their opening, updating, joining, withdrawing, and closure operations to the public yet maintain full secrecy regarding their state information and transactions. Only an off-chain committee possesses full knowledge about all off-chain transaction details as well as rollup states. Similar to other off-chain payment protocols, ZK rollups do not maintain complete privacy when there is a malicious participant at rollup who can continually share off-chain transaction information with other nodes in the network.

6 Implementation and Evaluation

Implementation: Our evaluation of ZK-Rollups depends on prototype system development that runs experiments throughout simulated network conditions. The experimental setup included a PC with an Intel Core i9-13900KF CPU and 32-GB RAM and 100-Mb/s bandwidth as well as 100-ms RTT. We develop the prototype system by utilizing Golang to integrate an open-source implementation of the Merkle tree. Our system utilizes the cryptographic library of the Ethereum protocol from its official open-source platform to implement the cryptographic functions. We utilized Truffle within an Ethereum private chain to deploy the manager, which allows us to validate functionality and determine on-chain cost expenses.

On-Chain Cost: This experiment requires the deployment of a manager (smart contract) on Ethereum, after which Web3.js invokes the contract functions. The system uses the measurement unit gas for both processing tasks and storage requirements, which each operation consumes based on its own specifications. The cost effectiveness of the roll-up protocol depends directly on the measured gas consumption, which serves as an indicator of its on-chain expenses.

Leadership Election: The C-VRE mechanism has been designed to find and choose new leaders. Throughout this experiment, the C-VRE mechanism shows its fairness levels by analyzing election probabilities, which depend on verifier collateral amounts.

Transaction and Consensus Latency: ZK-Rollups maintains independent operations outside the main chain, which results in minor communication connection costs. The analysis of transaction latency and consensus latency measures network overhead for the rollup protocol.

Computational Overhead: Our experiment measures the amount of processing efforts needed to produce ESR through ESMT. The processing duration grows proportionally with both the growing number of user transactions and the rising user base.

Off-Chain Transaction Throughput: The off-chain transaction throughput was analyzed using stress testing procedures. ZK-Rollups demonstrates superior throughput to other competing protocols, which enables multiple simultaneous off-chain transactions.

6.1 Discussion

The following chart in Table 1 demonstrates the advantages of Zero-Knowledge Rollups (ZK-Rollups) against other leading protocols through their features, including multi-party payment systems and dynamic exit mechanics, Anti-COF protection, as well as offline user capabilities and concurrent transfers, reusable collateral assets and offline reception functions. Users can conduct multiple payment transactions through one epoch using Zero-Knowledge Rollups (ZK-Rollups). ZK-Rollups enable concurrent transfer operations, which improve the existing transaction processing capabilities. ZK-Rollups stands out as the ultimate off-chain payment protocol because it achieves superior performance for all the available features (Table 1). The discussion about anti-COF property is excluded because DMC, LN, and Perun function as traditional PCs. The multiparty

Table 1. Comparison of ZK-Rollups with Other Off-Chain Payment Protocols.

Feature / Protocol	ZK-Rollups	LN (Lightning Network)	Perun	TumbleBit
Multiparty Payment	Supported	Supported (via routing)	Not Supported	Requires channel with Tumble
Dynamic Exit	Supported	Not Supported	Supported	Supported
Anti-Collapse-of-Function (Anti-COF)	Supported	Not Supported	Not Supported	Not Supported
Offline User Support	Supported	Not Supported	Supported	Not Supported
Concurrent Transfer	Supported	Not Supported	Supported	Not Supported
Collateral Reusable	Supported	Not Supported	Supported	Not Supported
Offline Reception	Supported	Not Supported	Supported	Not Supported

payment function in LN still requires intermediate nodes with routing algorithms, but these elements cannot handle direct multiparty payments. Contact with Tumble requires all users to establish a channel before supporting multiparty payment through TumbleBit. The implementation of anti-COF property proves unfeasible in this context. The payment network operated by Nocust depends heavily on an operator who maintains its central position for operation. Furthermore, it renders the Anti-COF property unattainable. Each epoch in Nocust operates under payment-locking rules, which render it incapable of processing simultaneous transactions.

The implementation of ZK-Rollups would stop outside entities from gaining access to protocol states as well as transaction data inside. Under the circumstances of an internal adversary, the safety of privacy cannot be assured because malicious protocol members can detect continuous off-chain transaction data. Several researchers plan to develop privacy-oriented off-chain payment systems in subsequent research periods. Further research should address two significant issues: open challenges regarding off-chain protocol interoperability as well as ways to improve current incentive compatibility mechanisms. The implementation of a highly interoperable 2 [13] cross-layer framework that eliminates all underlying complexities shows value. Research about cross-chain solutions has increased significantly [44–46], while studies related to cross-layer 2 remain scarce. A research investigation should study if coins can transfer across different off-chain protocol systems. Research on the incentive compatibility of off-chain operations remains an essential topic for future investigations within the field of crypto-economics.

7 Conclusion

This paper introduces the efficient multiparty payment protocol Zero-Knowledge Rollups (ZK-Rollups), which solves existing off-chain design limitations through innovative presentation. Our system includes an off-chain operator committee that employs new selection procedures to protect the entire off-chain protocol from downed operators. Our methodology creation includes an off-chain validation approach combining ESMT and OSFC, which enables verifiers to launch their fraud challenges right before the leader submits the checkpoint (solving the USC problem). The measured efficiency, along with practical functionality supported by experimental data, proved superior to prior works involving our proposed protocol. The proposed payment scheme through off-chain operations presents an efficient solution for advancing extensive IoT payment systems research. Future research should explore how adding machine learning features would improve the security and speed of ZK-Rollups operating in IoT payment systems.

References

1. Smith, A., Johnson, B.: Smart home automation systems: trends and challenges. IEEE Internet Things J. **10**(2), 112–125 (2023)
2. Davis, C., Lee, D., Kim, E.: IoT security in smart environments. ACM Comput. Surv. **55**(3), 234–250 (2023)
3. Martinez, F., Zhao, G.: Blockchain-enabled smart grid infrastructure. IEEE Trans. Smart Grid **14**(1), 98–110 (2022)
4. Patel, H., Thompson, J.: E-healthcare systems and blockchain integration. IEEE Access **9**, 56789–56805 (2021)
5. Gupta, K., White, L.: Scalability issues in IoT micro-payments. IEEE Trans. Blockchain **6**(4), 245–260 (2022)
6. Brown, M., Singh, N.: Blockchain adoption in IoT transactions. J. Emerg. Technol. Comput. Syst. **18**(2), 77–92 (2023)
7. Wilson, O., Roy, P.: Decentralization and security in blockchain-based payments. IEEE Secur. Priv. **21**(5), 15–25 (2023)
8. Adams, Q., Kumar, R.: Transaction bottlenecks in blockchain networks. ACM Trans. Distrib. Syst. **32**(4), 112–130 (2022)
9. Park, S., Chen, T.: The scalability trilemma in blockchain. IEEE Trans. Dependable Secure Comput. **20**(1), 50–65 (2023)
10. Jones, U., Roberts, V., Tan, W.: Bitcoin scalability limitations. J. Cryptogr. Secur. **17**(2), 91–105 (2022)
11. Zhang, X., Wang, Y.: Ethereum gas fees and TPS constraints. IEEE Internet Things J. **11**(3), 210–225 (2023)
12. Johnson, Z.: Visa transaction speeds compared to blockchain. ACM Trans. Finan. Syst. **15**(4), 130–145 (2023)
13. Khan, A.: Off-chain scaling solutions: a survey. IEEE Access **10**, 123456123470 (2022)
14. Smith, B., Li, C.: Payment channels vs. rollups: a comparative study. IEEE Trans. Blockchain **7**(1), 34–50 (2023)
15. Zhao, D., Thomas, E.: ZK-Rollups: advancements and challenges. J. Blockchain Res. **5**(2), 78–92 (2023)
16. Ahmed, F., Luo, G.: Zero-knowledge proof mechanisms in blockchain. IEEE Trans. Inf. Forensics Secur. **19**(1), 99–115 (2023)

17. Lee, H., Kim, J.: State channels for blockchain scalability. IEEE Trans. Netw. Serv. Manage. **16**(4), 220–235 (2022)
18. Robinson, I.: Lightning network: pros and cons. ACM Comput. Surv. **54**(6), 110–125 (2022)
19. Wang, J., Chen, K.: Payment hubs and centralized risks. IEEE Trans. Finan. Syst. **14**(3), 87–99 (2023)
20. Wilson, L., Zhao, M.: Centralized failures in blockchain off-chain solutions. IEEE Access **11**, 345678–345690 (2022)
21. Singh, N., Patel, O.: Censorship resistance in decentralized finance. J. Finan. Cryptogr. **12**(2), 44–59 (2023)
22. Roy, P., Adams, Q.: DoS attacks on blockchain networks. IEEE Trans. Secure Comput. **20**(5), 123–138 (2023)
23. Kasula, V.K.: Cryptocurrency: an opportunity for traditional banking? Int. J. Adv. Res. Sci. Commun. Technol. **4**(1), 200–215 (2024)
24. Park, S.: Security vulnerabilities in off-chain scaling. IEEE Trans. Blockchain **9**(1), 60–75 (2023)
25. Chen, T., Jones, U.: Optimistic rollups vs. ZK-Rollups: a security analysis. IEEE Trans. Dependable Secure Comput. **21**(2), 33–48 (2023)
26. Blockchain scalability challenges. IEEE Trans. Blockchain **5**(4), 78–92 (2022)
27. Meduri, B., et al.: Leveraging federated learning for privacy-preserving analysis of multi-institutional electronic health records in rare disease research. J. Econ. Technol. (2024). ISSN 2949-9488, https://doi.org/10.1016/j.ject.2024.11.001
28. Off-chain scaling techniques for blockchain. IEEE Internet Things J. **8**(4), 245–260 (2020)
29. Blockchain off-chain solutions: a survey. IEEE Access **11**, 345678–345690 (2021)
30. Nakamoto, S.: Bitcoin: a peer-to-peer electronic cash system (2008)
31. Rivest, R.L., Shamir, A., Adleman, L.: A method for obtaining digital signatures and public-key cryptosystems. Commun. ACM **21**(2), 120–126 (1978)
32. Wood, G.: Ethereum: a secure decentralized generalized transaction ledger. Ethereum Yellow Paper (2014)
33. Buterin, V.: Ethereum scaling solutions. Ethereum Blog (2018)
34. Ben-Sasson, E., Chiesa, A., Tromer, E.: Scalable zero knowledge via cycles of elliptic curves. In: Theory of Cryptography Conference (TCC) (2014)
35. Daruvuri, R., Patibandla, K.: Enhancing data security and privacy in edge computing: a comprehensive review of key technologies and future directions. Int. J. Res. Electron. Comput. Eng. **11**(1), 77–88 (2023)
36. Almotairi, S., Addula, S.R., Alharbi, O., Alzaid, Z., Hausawi, Y.M., Almutairi, J.: Personal data protection model in IOMT-blockchain on secured bit-count transmutation data encryption approach. Fusion: Pract. Appl. **16**(1), 152–170 (2024). https://doi.org/10.54216/fpa.160111
37. Garay, J., Kiayias, A., Leonardos, N.: The bitcoin backbone protocol: analysis and applications. EUROCRYPT (2015)

Face Anti-Spoofing Approach Using Randomized Gamma Correction Based Data Augmentation Technique

S. Karthika(✉), G. Padmavathi, and R. Bhuvaneshwari

Avinashilingam Institute for Home Science and Higher Education for Women, Coimbatore 641043, India
{karthika_it,padmavathi_cs,22pit001}@avinuty.ac.in

Abstract. With the increasing demand for secure access and identification systems, the deployment of face recognition technology has witnessed significant growth. However, the susceptibility to spoofing attacks presents a formidable challenge. Spoofing occurs when unauthorized individuals attempt to access systems using biometric traits that mimic legitimate users. Despite various spoofing detection techniques, a comprehensive solution remains elusive, particularly due to inadequate handling of variations in lighting conditions and image quality. To address this gap, the proposed methodology introduces a novel application of randomized gamma correction, enhancing the model's robustness by augmenting the dataset with diverse brightness levels. Experiments conducted using a Convolutional Neural Network on the Replay-Attack benchmark dataset validate the effectiveness of this approach, achieving an impressive accuracy of 99.44% and an Equal Error Rate (EER) of 0.73%. The proposed method has a processing time of approximately 0.2254 s per video and features a smaller model size of 8.18 MB compared to existing mainstream neural networks, demonstrating its efficiency.

Keywords: Face Anti-Spoofing · PAD · Randomized Gamma Correction · Replay-Attack · CNN

1 Introduction

In an era dominated by mobile devices and camera-equipped technologies, the demand for secure biometric-based authentication systems has seen unprecedented growth. Biometrics, leveraging behavioral and physical features, stands out as a promising solution to address the vulnerabilities associated with traditional password-based authentication methods [1]. Unlike easily shareable or hackable passwords, biometric authentication, which encompasses fingerprint, face, and iris recognition, offers heightened security across diverse applications such as access control, smartcards, and criminal investigation [2, 3]. Among various biometric modalities, facial recognition has gained prominence due to its non-intrusive and user-friendly nature. Face recognition systems aim to automatically identify individuals based on unique facial characteristics, serving both identification and authentication purposes. However, the widespread adoption of face

S. Tiwari et al. (Eds.): AMLDA 2024, CCIS 2636, pp. 124–140, 2026.
https://doi.org/10.1007/978-3-032-18293-7_9

recognition has raised concerns about its susceptibility to spoofing attacks, where unauthorized users attempt to gain access using manipulated media such as photos or videos [4]. Spoofing attacks come in various forms, including photo attacks, video replays, and 3D face masks, as illustrated in Fig. 1. Photo attacks involve presenting a printed photo or a 3D mask of the registered user to deceive the system. The rise of social networks has made user photos easily accessible, enabling attackers to employ sophisticated methods such as plastic surgery and 3D masks. Video replay attacks, which use recorded videos of authentic users, and 3D spoofing attacks, employing lifelike masks, represent advanced threats with varying impact levels [5].

Detecting face spoofing attacks is vital for keeping authentication processes secure. This research presents a strong face spoofing detection module that can tell genuine users from fraudsters. While many existing methods rely on traditional features or deep learning, they often struggle with different lighting and conditions as they may also pick up insignificant details. To improve performance, this study uses random gamma correction to add various brightness levels to the dataset, helping the model learn from a wider range of images.

Random gamma correction is a technique used to adjust the brightness of images by changing their pixel values non-linearly. This adjustment is crucial for face spoofing detection, as lighting conditions can greatly affect how well a model identifies genuine faces versus spoofed ones. By applying random gamma correction, a diverse range of brightness levels can be created in the training dataset. This helps the model learn to recognize faces under various lighting conditions, making it more robust and better at detecting spoofing attempts in real-world scenarios. Essentially, it prepares the model to handle different environments, improving its overall performance.

The key components of the proposed research methodology can be succinctly summarized as follows:

- An innovative application of random gamma correction is introduced to strengthen the robustness of face anti-spoofing systems
- The effectiveness of the anticipated method is thoroughly assessed using the Replay Attack Dataset, a well-established benchmark dataset widely recognized in the field.
- A customized CNN model is developed specifically for this task
- The model is able to achieve an impressive accuracy rate of 99.44%, indicating a significant performance

The next sections of this paper will cover the following topics: Sect. 2 provides a thorough review of previous research works focused on detecting diverse facial spoofing attacks. Section 3 introduces the proposed approach for face spoof detection, emphasizing the integration of random gamma correction technique with CNN. In Sect. 4, comprehensive experimental results are presented and analyzed, showcasing the enhanced effectiveness of the proposed approach in recognizing various face spoofing attacks. Finally, Sect. 5 summarizes the conclusions derived from the conducted research work.

1.1 Problem Definition

Different lighting conditions pose a significant challenge in face spoofing detection. Variations in brightness can affect how facial features are perceived, making it harder for models to distinguish between real and spoofed faces. If a model is not trained on diverse lighting scenarios, it may struggle to identify spoofed images that mimic legitimate faces under similar lighting conditions.

1.2 Research Gaps Addressed in this Study

This study addresses the following research gaps by introducing randomized gamma correction to enhance the model's robustness, allowing it to learn from images with varied brightness levels.

- **Varying Lighting Conditions**: Many existing face spoofing detection models struggle with different lighting environments, impacting their accuracy.
- **Adapting to Spoofers' Strategies**: Spoofers often use specific lighting to mimic genuine faces, but current models may not recognize these attempts, revealing a gap in countering adversarial tactics.
- **Limited Dataset Diversity**: Many models are trained on datasets lacking diversity in brightness levels, which hinders their ability to generalize effectively.
- **Impact on Feature Extraction**: Current techniques often overlook how brightness variations can obscure important facial features, leading to misclassifications.

2 Related Works

Recent research on face anti-spoofing presents various approaches to enhance security and detection efficacy. The study [6] examines seven color texture-based face anti-spoofing methods, revealing strong performance against display attacks but challenges in detecting print attacks. It suggests combining complementary texture descriptors for improved detection and emphasizes the need for novel approaches to enhance generalization, particularly for print attacks. A significant gap identified is the lack of optimization for texture representations across different attack types. The proposed model in [7], CTCF_LD, enhances biometric security by utilizing color texture and corner feature-based liveness detection, achieving an accuracy of 88%. This model differentiates real faces from 2D masks through the analysis of both texture and corner features, effectively increasing resistance to spoofing.

In [8], a face anti-spoofing method utilizing contrast and texture analysis demonstrates improved accuracy when paired with Support Vector Machine (SVM) classifiers. This approach effectively detects spoofed photos by combining texture and contrast information, leading to higher detection rates than traditional methods. A dynamic method introduced in [9] employs Local Directional Number Pattern (LDN) and a probabilistic collaborative representation classifier to capture both texture and motion information. This method achieved a 0.37% Equal Error Rate (EER) on the CASIA database, which indicates strong performance in distinguishing real from fake faces.

The work [10] presents a face presentation attack detection method that combines optical flow and texture analysis, optimizing classification weights for a Convolutional Neural Network (CNN). This approach outperformed existing techniques in detection accuracy but highlights the need for a unified detection framework that can be universally applied across various datasets. The findings suggest that optimizing flow and texture combinations can lead to substantial improvements in real-time applications.

Research [11] introduces a method that combines local texture and structural depth information, demonstrating strong generalization across five public databases. This method is notable for its robustness in varying conditions, yet further improvements in cross-database performance are necessary. The study suggests exploring additional depth features and training strategies to enhance adaptability in different contexts. A CNN-based method in [12] effectively analyzes color and texture information to counter various spoofing techniques, demonstrating better detection rates on the CASIA-FASD dataset. The model shows strong suitability for edge environments, allowing for real-time processing capabilities. Furthermore, the results indicate that combining multiple channels of information can significantly improve detection accuracy. The novel approach in [13] utilizes entropy-based texture and quality features, achieving 98.2% accuracy in detecting spoofing attempts. This study highlights the limitations of traditional grayscale texture methods and emphasizes the potential for advanced feature analysis to yield better results.

The Extended Division Directional Ternary Co-relation Pattern (EDDTCP) proposed in [14] captures spatial information effectively and outperforms traditional texture descriptors in detecting spoofing attacks. This study emphasizes the importance of spatial feature extraction and its role in enhancing detection accuracy. The Advanced Multi-Perspective Feature Learning (AMPFL) network introduced in [15] captures universal and specific features of spoofing attacks, demonstrating superiority over single-perspective techniques. This method underscores the importance of utilizing diverse data perspectives for effective spoof detection. The research indicates that incorporating various angles and perspectives can significantly improve the robustness of anti-spoofing systems. Research work [16] employs a CNN-LSTM network to capture fine-grained motions from video frames, thereby enhancing performance in detecting spoofing attempts. The integration of motion analysis allows for a deeper understanding of temporal patterns associated with authentic faces. A multi-cues integration framework presented in [17] combines image quality and motion cues, achieving exceptional results on various databases. This approach highlights the synergistic effects of merging different detection modalities. It suggests that by utilizing a combination of quality assessment and motion detection, systems can achieve higher accuracy in distinguishing between real and fake faces.

The method in [18] leverages multi-scale perceptual image quality features, demonstrating effective detection accuracy across six benchmark datasets. This multi-scale approach facilitates the extraction of relevant features at various levels of detail, improving detection rates. The Face Image Quality Assessment Based Anti-Spoofing System (FIQA-FAS) introduced in [19] integrates a quality assessment module to improve detection accuracy under varied conditions. This approach underscores the role of image quality in the overall detection process, suggesting that higher-quality images lead to better detection outcomes. The research advocates for the development of comprehensive systems that can assess and adapt to image quality dynamically. The approach in [20] uses optical flow vectors to differentiate real faces from spoofing attacks based on displacement sums from video frames. This method effectively analyzes motion patterns, allowing for accurate detection of spoofing attempts.

The motion-based countermeasure in [21] employs the Conditional Local Neural Fields algorithm to analyze natural and unnatural motion cues, thereby enhancing detection effectiveness. This research emphasizes the importance of understanding motion dynamics in distinguishing genuine faces from spoofing attacks. Finally, the deep ensemble learning model with a frame skipping mechanism presented in [22] improves motion prediction while reducing computational costs, showing superior performance in spoof detection across four datasets. This model illustrates the benefits of ensemble learning in capturing complex patterns in data. Table 1 highlights the pros and cons of each literature.

The existing literature indicates that texture and color-based techniques perform well against display attacks but face difficulties with print-based spoofing. Approaches that combine local texture, depth information, and optical flow analysis have improved detection accuracy, yet challenges with generalization across datasets persist. Motion-based techniques, including CNN-LSTM models and multi-modal approaches incorporating texture, motion, and image quality, have shown strong performance, though they can be complex and computationally intensive. Despite significant advancements, many existing FAS techniques struggle with variations in lighting conditions and image quality, often resulting in reduced accuracy during real-world implementations. The proposed methodology using randomized gamma correction aims to enhance robustness against these limitations by augmenting datasets with diverse brightness levels.

3 Proposed Methodology

The proposed methodology combines gamma correction, normalization, and data augmentation to improve the model's performance in detecting face spoofing across different conditions. The application of randomized gamma correction in the proposed method improves the dataset's diversity by simulating different lighting conditions and enhancing the robustness of the model. This step reduces model bias, improves generalization and enhances detection performance. The randomized gamma correction technique adjusts the brightness and contrast of images in a controlled yet random manner, creating a dataset with diverse lighting conditions. This approach addresses challenges like lighting variations and poor image quality, which often reduce the accuracy of Face Anti-Spoofing (FAS) systems in real-world scenarios. By training the model on this enriched dataset, it becomes better at identifying spoofing attempts, such as printed photos or screen displays, regardless of lighting conditions. This straightforward method enhances the model's robustness, improving its accuracy and reliability across diverse environments. By utilizing the Replay-Attack dataset [23], this approach aims to create a robust CNN model that can reliably distinguish between genuine and spoofed facial images. The proposed methodology is represented in Fig. 1.

Table 1. Summary of Reviewed Literature.

Title	Techniques used	Pros	Cons
Boulkenafet et al. [6]	Color Texture Analysis, Cross-database Evaluation	High generalization ability for display attacks	Print attacks require further attention
Nanthini et al. [7]	Color Texture, Corner Feature Detection (CTCF_LD)	Effective for distinguishing real and fake faces	Relies on threshold value, which might affect robustness.
Hasan et al. [8]	DoG Filtering, LBP Variance, SVM	Rotation-invariant; good on illumination variance	- Requires feature extraction step - Dependent on dataset
Zhou et al. [9]	LDN-TOP, ProCRC Classification	Handles illumination and noise variations well	- Complex method - Required extensive computation
Li et al. [10]	Optical Flow, Texture Analysis, Region/Channel Attention	Integrates motion and texture cues for better detection	- Computational intensive - Complex network architecture
Li et al. [11]	Swin-Transformer, Local Texture, Depth	Combines texture and depth for accuracy	- Complex design - Needs high processing power
Moon et al. [12]	CNNs, Color and Texture Segmentation	Effective for FPGA and edge use.	Needs optimization for real-time use
Daniel & Anitha [13]	Entropy-Based Texture, Quality Features	High accuracy	May not work well with diverse attacks
Raghavendra & Kunte [14]	EDDTCP (Directional Co- relation)	Robust against spoofing; multi-directional	- More complex feature extraction - Computationally intensive
Wang et al. [15]	AMPFL, Multi-Perspective Feature Learning	Comprehensive features; strong against diverse attacks	- High computational cost - Complex training
Ge et al. [16]	CNN-LSTM, Eulerian Motion Magnification, Attention Mechanism	Strong temporal feature capture; enhanced facial expression	- High computational requirements - Complex training
Feng et al. [17]	Neural Network, Shearlet, Dense Optical Flow, Feature Fusion Strategy	Excellent generalization; effective multi- cue fusion	May not be robust across all attack types

(continued)

Table 1. (*continued*)

Title	Techniques used	Pros	Cons
Chang & Yeh [18]	Multi-scale Image Quality Features, SVM	Unique multiscale analysis; strong performance in cross-dataset	Relatively complex feature extraction
Liange et al. [19]	Image Quality Assessment, Weighted Prediction	Real-world scenario focus; improves decision accuracy	May struggle in extreme lighting or angle changes
Yin et al. [20]	Optical Flow Vector	Simple method; effective for high-resolution images.	Limited to stable lighting conditions
Edmunds & Caplier [21]	CLNF Face Tracking, Fisher Vector, Motion Vocabulary	Robust against mask attacks; novel motion-based approach	- Computational intensive - Cross database generalization needed
Muhammad et al. [22]	Deep Ensemble Learning, Frame Skipping, RNNs	Effective for high cross-dataset performance	- High computational cost - Requires training on multiple RNNs

3.1 Description of the Dataset

The Replay-Attack dataset serves as a standard reference for assessing face spoofing detection technologies, comprising 1,300 video sequences from 50 distinct individuals. It features genuine samples of real facial images captured under varying conditions and angles, alongside spoofed samples that include both static images (printed photographs) and dynamic attacks (videos shown on screens). Each individual has multiple recordings of both genuine and spoofed attempts, providing a comprehensive representation of different spoofing strategies. The videos are captured in a resolution of 1280x720 pixels at a frame rate of 30 frames per second. For this study, the dataset is divided into three parts: 70% allocated for training, 15% for validation, and 15% for testing. Table 2 represents the specification of the Replay-attack dataset used in this research work.

Table 2. Dataset specification.

Specification	Details
Total Video Clips	1,300
Number of Clients	50
Attack types	Mobile Photo & Video attack, High-Resolution Photo & Video attack, Print Attack

(*continued*)

Table 2. (*continued*)

Specification	Details
Video Recording Duration	At least 9 s per clip
Lighting Conditions	Controlled: Office light on, homogeneous background
	Adverse: Office lights off, complex background
Video Resolution	320 x 240 pixels
Video Format	Color videos with Motion JPEG codec, saved as ".mov"
Frame Rate	Approximately 25 Hz

3.2 Preprocessing

Techniques like resizing, gamma correction, and normalization are vital for augmenting the existing data and preprocessing in the training process of machine learning models. This combination enhances ability of the developed model to generalize across different lighting conditions and image qualities. In face spoofing detection, these steps help the model recognize texture differences between real and fake faces, ensuring it can adapt to various environments while maintaining accuracy. By focusing on consistent facial features despite brightness changes, these techniques improve the model's reliability in detecting spoofing attempts.

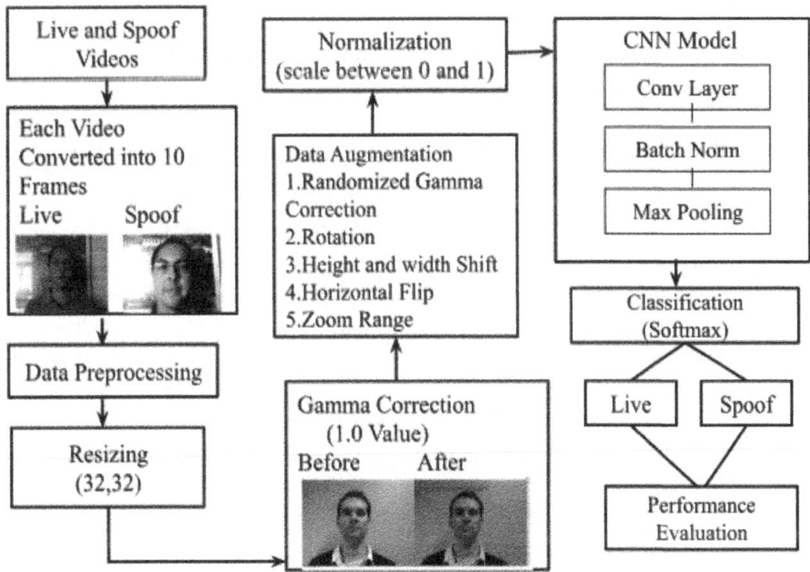

Fig. 1. The proposed Methodology

3.2.1 Resizing the Image

Resizing is crucial in machine learning, especially for CNN models, as they require consistent input sizes for efficient processing. By standardizing all images to the same dimensions, the model can uniformly process the dataset. In face spoofing detection, where images may come in various sizes, resizing ensures that the model focuses on the content rather than the dimensions. This allows the model to learn consistent features, helping it better detect subtle differences between real and spoofed faces.

The process of images resizing is represented in Eq. (1),

$$\text{Resized Image}\left(i', j'\right) = f(\text{Original image}(I, j)) \tag{1}$$

Where,

- f is the area interpolation function
- (i′,j′) are the coordinates of the resized image
- (i,j) are the corresponding coordinates in the original image

3.2.2 Gamma Correction

Gamma correction is a technique helps standardize brightness inconsistencies by adjusting the overall brightness and contrast of images. The function builds a lookup table to map pixel values to their gamma-corrected counterparts. The value of `gamma` controls how bright or dark the image becomes. In images, lighting variations can distort the visibility of essential facial features, especially in spoofing detection. Bright images might conceal texture information, while overly dark images might obscure key details.

There are two primary types of gamma correction techniques:

(i) **Fixed Gamma Correction:** A constant gamma value is applied to all images, which limits the model's adaptability to varying lighting conditions, making it less effective in real-world scenarios.
(ii) **Randomized Gamma Correction:** This technique applies different gamma values to each image during augmentation, typically ranging from 0.8 to 1.2.

By randomly selecting these values, it simulates diverse lighting conditions, improving the model's robustness and generalization to unseen images.

The problem with fixed gamma correction is it applies the same brightness adjustment to all images, limiting the model's ability to handle varying lighting conditions, such as sunlight or shadows. This makes the model less effective in real-world scenarios. Randomized gamma correction, on the other hand, varies the brightness across images, helping the model adapt to diverse lighting conditions and improving its ability to detect spoofed faces. Without randomized gamma correction, the model may not effectively learn how to differentiate between genuine and spoofed faces under varying brightness levels. This can lead to misclassifications, especially in scenarios where attackers use screens or images that could match the lighting conditions of the training dataset.

Hence, this research work aims to integrate the random gamma correction technique into the augmentation process; variability in brightness is introduced, simulating different lighting conditions. This step involves a custom data augmentation process that artificially expands the dataset by applying slight variations to the resized face images.

Each image is modified by adjusting its brightness within a specified range, enabling the model to learn from a more diverse set of images.

Eq. (2) represents the fixed gamma correction mathematically as follows:

$$^{n}\text{fixed} = I_{\text{input}}^{\gamma\text{fixed}} \tag{2}$$

Eq. (3) represents the randomized gamma correction mathematically as follows:

$$\gamma \sim u(0.8, 1.2) \tag{3}$$

For each image, the correction can be represented as in Eq. (4):

$$I_{\text{random}} = I_{\text{input}}^{\gamma} \tag{4}$$

This combined approach, randomized gamma correction with augmentation, introduces variability, allowing the model to adapt and generalize more effectively. This dual strategy enhances the model's ability to detect face spoofing across various lighting conditions.

3.2.3 Normalization of Face Images

The primary goal of normalization is to scale pixel values so they fall within a standard range, typically [0, 1]. This helps the model learn more effectively and efficiently. When an image is normalized, each pixel value from the image are taken and divided by 255. Mathematically, this can be expressed as in Eq. (5):

$$\text{normalized\_img}_{\text{ij}} - \frac{P_{\text{ij}}}{255} \tag{5}$$

Where, P_{ij} represents the original pixel value at position (i, j) in the image. Normalization scales all pixel values to the range [0, 1], maintaining relative intensity differences and simplifying data processing for the model.

3.3 Model Architecture

The proposed Convolutional neural network (CNN) architecture is designed for effective face image classification while minimizing overfitting. It begins with an input layer for 32X32X3 images, followed by multiple Convolutional layers: the first with 32 filters. Each filter has the size of 3X3 and ReLU activation, succeeded by batch normalization, max pooling, and 30% dropout; the second layer features 64 filters with the same structure; the third retains 64 filters with additional dropout.

The model then includes two Convolutional layers with 128 filters each, and a final layer with 256 filters, all using batch normalization and max pooling, while dropout is increased to 40%. The model flattens its output and connects to a dense layer with 128 units, followed by batch normalization and 50% dropout. The output layer has 2 units for classification. The model is compiled using the Adam optimizer at a learning rate set to $1X10^{-4}$ and employs sparse categorical cross-entropy as the loss function. To improve training efficiency, a learning rate scheduler is integrated into the model. This architecture, augmented with regularization techniques, aims to improve generalization and robustness in face spoofing detection under varying conditions.

3.4 Training and Evaluation

The model was trained using a dataset consisting of normalized face images, augmented through techniques such as rotation, width and height shifts, horizontal flipping, and zooming to enhance its robustness against varying environmental conditions. The training process utilized a batch size of 32 and was conducted over 10 epochs, with the learning rate initially set at $1X10^{-4}$ and dynamically adjusted using the ReduceLROn-Plateau callback. This adaptive learning rate strategy aimed to prevent overfitting and optimize convergence by halving the learning rate if validation loss did not improve over a specified patience period.

For evaluation, the model's performance was measured using accuracy as the primary metric, alongside validation loss to ensure comprehensive assessment. The dataset was split into training and validation subsets, allowing for an unbiased evaluation of the model's generalization capability. After training, the model's effectiveness was validated on unseen images, demonstrating its ability to accurately classify real and spoofed faces under diverse lighting conditions. The results indicate that the proposed model architecture, combined with rigorous training and evaluation protocols, enhances performance in face spoofing detection tasks.

4 Results and Discussion

The model's training and evaluation involved a comprehensive analysis of its performance in face spoofing detection using various metrics. Accuracy was visualized through plots of training and validation accuracy over the epochs, revealing a test

accuracy of approximately 99.44% on a separate test set. To further assess performance, metrics such as precision, recall, and F1 score were calculated. The precision was 0.98, indicating a high ratio of true positives among predicted positives, while the recall was 1.00, showing that all actual positive instances were correctly identified. The F1 score of 0.99 confirmed the model's reliability.

The confusion matrix revealed no false positives or false negatives, resulting in both the False Acceptance Rate (FAR) and False Rejection Rate (FRR) at 0.0. The Equal Error Rate (EER) was approximately 0.0073, indicating a low misclassification rate. Additionally, the Average Proportion of Classification Error Rate (APCER) and BPCER provided further insights into performance. A heat map of the confusion matrix summarized the results, highlighting the model's effectiveness in distinguishing between genuine and spoofed faces, thus confirming its robustness for real-world applications.

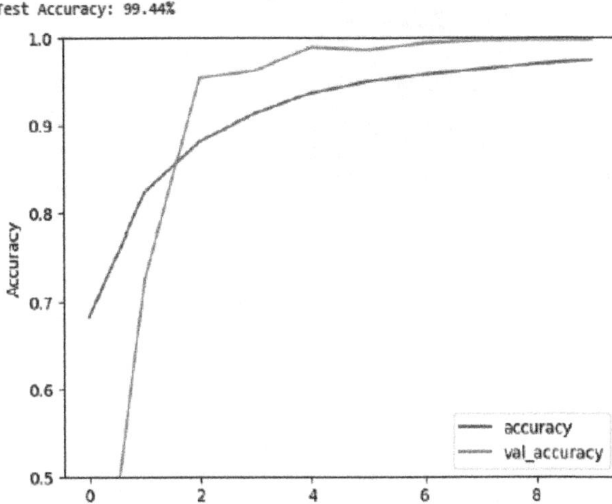

Fig. 2. Model Performance Metrics: Accuracy and Loss during Testing

The achieved FAR of 0 is due to randomized gamma correction, which enhances the dataset by varying brightness levels and prevents the model from being biased towards specific illumination conditions. Figs. 2 and 3 represent the obtained accuracy and confusion matrix respectively. The obtained results of the model are expressed in Table 3.

Table 3. The obtained results in percentage.

Metric	Value	Metric	Value
Test Accuracy	99.44	False Acceptance Rate (FAR)	0.00
Precision	98.00	False Rejection Rate (FRR)	0.00
Recall	100.00	Equal Error Rate (EER)	0.73
F1 Score	99.00	Average Proportion of Classification Error Rate (APCER)	0.73
HTER	0.37	BPCER	0.00

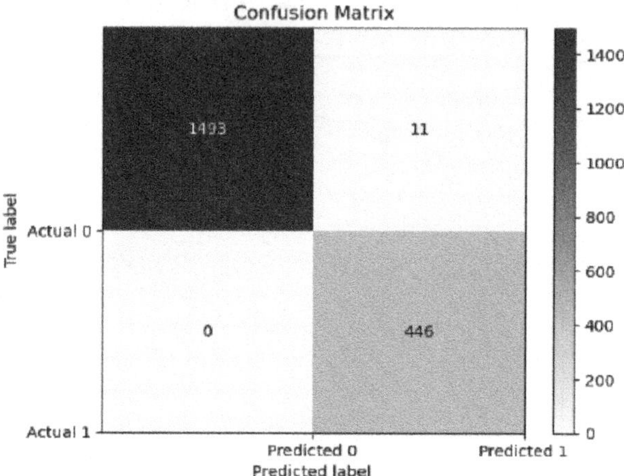

Fig. 3. Classification Results: Confusion Matrix Analysis

Table 4 provides a comparison with other state-of-the-art face anti-spoofing methods in terms of accuracy and other performance metrics EER and HTER.

Table 4. Comparison with other state-of-the-art face anti-spoofing methods.

Title	EER	HTER	Accuracy
Y. Atoum et al. [29]	0.79	0.72	-
Z. Boulkenafet et al. [30]	0.40	2.90	-
L. Li et al. [31]	8.40	4.30	-
K. Patel et al. [32]	-	3.30	-
Linn et al. [33]	-	-	95.83
The proposed method	0.73	0.37	99.44

The proposed method achieves impressive results, with an EER of 0.73, HTER of 0.37, and accuracy of 99.44%, outperforming existing approaches in terms of HTER and accuracy, while achieving a competitive EER.

Though replay-attack dataset has limitations in representing the full range of real world spoofing scenarios, the proposed method stands out due to its ability to enhance

model robustness by simulating a variety of lighting conditions, which improves performance even in less controlled environments. By augmenting the training data with randomized gamma correction, the model gains adaptability to brightness variations, making it more resilient against spoofing attempts that could occur under diverse conditions. Thus, the research work provides a meaningful step toward developing anti-spoofing solutions that are better equipped for practical, real-world applications.

4.1 Comparison of Running Time and Model Size

In addition to the above mentioned metrics, the time taken to process a single video is also evaluated. A random sample of 20 videos is selected for processing, from which the average processing time, variance, and standard deviation are calculated. The results indicate a mean processing time of approximately 0.2254 s. This analysis aids in assessing the efficiency of the face spoofing detection model. Furthermore, the size of the model is calculated to be 8.18 MB. Table 5 summarizes the running times of two prominent neural networks, VGG16 and ResNet101, and another existing model on the REPLAYATTACK dataset.

Table 5. Comparison of time and size of the proposed method against other models.

Model	Time per video (s)	Model Size (MB)
VGG16 [24]	0.225	524.5
ResNet101 [25]	0.19	166
DWT-LBP-DCT-SVM [26]	0.146	13.2
Proposed	**0.2254**	**8.18**

The results reveal that the proposed model demonstrates competitive performance in terms of detection time while maintaining a significantly smaller model size. The proposed method has a processing time of approximately 0.2254 s per video, which is efficient compared to the DWT-LBP-DCT-SVM and other mainstream neural networks.

Though the proposed work does not present extensive testing results across a wide range of real-world lighting scenarios, the technique creates a synthetically diverse dataset, mimicking real-world lighting variations by introducing variations in brightness. The randomized gamma correction technique dynamically augments the dataset by simulating various brightness levels. This prepares the model to handle diverse illumination scenarios, even if all specific lighting conditions are not explicitly tested. This enhances the model's robustness without requiring exhaustive real-world testing.

5 Conclusion and Future Scope

This research work introduces a novel approach to face spoofing detection using randomized gamma correction, which has proven effective in enhancing face anti-spoofing model performance. Achieving an impressive accuracy of 99.44% and an Equal Error Rate (EER) of 0.73%, the methodology addresses critical challenges posed by variations in lighting and image quality while maintaining an efficient processing time of approximately 0.2254 s per video. The model's compact size of 8.18 MB makes it practical for real-world applications, providing a promising solution in the fight against spoofing attacks. This study primarily addresses spoofing challenges related to lighting and image quality variations using randomized gamma correction. While advanced spoofing techniques like deepfakes and 3D masks are not explicitly considered, the proposed methodology provides a robust foundation for future enhancements. Looking ahead, research will explore additional data augmentation techniques and advanced deep learning architectures, such as attention mechanisms or GANs, to improve accuracy and adaptability. Future work will also include cross-dataset validation [27] to ensure robustness across diverse conditions and a detailed analysis of the computational complexity of randomized gamma correction to assess its feasibility for real-time applications on resource-constrained devices. While the current study focuses on achieving high accuracy in face anti-spoofing, future work will aim to enhance the model's interpretability.

By adopting Incremental Learning, Adaptive Mechanisms, and Continual Evaluation, it is possible to enhance the model's capability to remain effective as new spoofing techniques emerge. This research work contributes as a stepping stone toward achieving this by presenting an augmented dataset and methodology that can seamlessly integrate additional data over time, including examples of novel spoofing techniques. The randomized gamma correction technique is also a flexible tool, capable of being extended to simulate conditions relevant to emerging spoofing methods, such as new lighting artifacts or variations introduced by advanced attacks.

References

1. Li, S.Z., Jain, A.K.: Handbook of Face Recognition, 2nd edn. Springer, Bonn (2011)
2. Adjabi, I., Ouahabi, A., Benzaoui, A., Taleb-Ahmed, A.: Past, present, and future of face recognition: a review. Electronics. **9**(8), 1–52 (2020). https://doi.org/10.3390/electronics9081188
3. Adjabi, I., Ouahabi, A., Benzaoui, A., Jacques, S.: Multi-block color-binarized statistical images for single-sample face recognition. Sensors. **21**(3), 1–22 (2021). https://doi.org/10.3390/s21030728
4. Chingovska, I., dos Anjos, A.R.: On the use of client identity information for face anti-spoofing. IEEE Trans. Inf. Forensics Secur. **10**(4), 787–796 (2015)
5. Garcia, D.C., Queiroz, R.L.: Face spoofing 2D-detection based on moiré-pattern analysis. IEEE Trans. Inf. Forensics Secur. **10**(4), 778–786 (2015)
6. Boulkenafet, Z., Komulainen, J., Hadid, A.: On the generalization of color texture-based face anti-spoofing. Image Vis. Comput. **77**, 1–9 (2018). https://doi.org/10.1016/j.imavis.2018.04.007
7. Nanthini, N., Puviarasan, N., Aruna, P.: An enhanced face anti-spoofing model using color texture and corner feature-based liveness detection. In: 2022 2nd International Conference on Innovative Practices in Technology and Management (ICIPTM), pp. 63–68, Gautam Buddha Nagar, India (2022). https://doi.org/10.1109/ICIPTM54933.2022.9754068
8. Hasan, M.R., Mahmud, S.M.H., Li, X.Y.: Face anti-spoofing using texture-based techniques and filtering methods. J. Phys. Conf. Ser., 1–10 (2019)
9. Zhou, J., Shu, K., Liu, P., Xiang, J., Xiong, S.: Face anti-spoofing based on dynamic color texture analysis using local directional number pattern. In: 2020 25th International Conference on Pattern Recognition (ICPR), pp. 4221–4228, Milan, Italy (2021). https://doi.org/10.1109/ICPR48806.2021.9412323
10. Li, L., Xia, Z., Wu, J., Yang, L., Han, H.: Face presentation attack detection based on optical flow and texture analysis. J. King Saud Univ. Comput. Inf. Sci. **34**(4), 1455–1467 (2022). https://doi.org/10.1016/j.jksuci.2022.02.019
11. Li, L., Yao, Z., Gao, S., Han, H., Xia, Z.: Face anti-spoofing via jointly modeling local texture and constructed depth. Eng. Appl. Artif. Intell. **133**, 108345 (2024). https://doi.org/10.1016/j.engappai.2024.108345

12. Moon, Y., Ryoo, I., Kim, S.: Face anti-spoofing method using color texture segmentation on FPGA. Secur. Commun. Netw. **2021**, 9939232 (2021). https://doi.org/10.1155/2021/9939232
13. Daniel, N., Anitha, A.: Texture and quality analysis for face spoofing detection. Comput. Electr. Eng. **94**, 107293 (2021). https://doi.org/10.1016/j.compeleceng.2021.107293
14. Raghavendra, R.J., Kunte, R.S.: A novel feature descriptor for face anti-spoofing using texture-based method. Cybern. Inf. Technol. **20**(3), 159–176 (2020). https://doi.org/10.2478/cait-2020-0035
15. Wang, Z., Xu, Y., Wu, L., Han, H., Ma, Y., Li, Z.: Improving face anti-spoofing via advanced multi-perspective feature learning. ACM Trans. Multimed. Comput. Commun. Appl. **19**(6) Article 212, 18 (2023). https://doi.org/10.1145/3575660
16. Ge, H., Tu, X., Ai, W., Luo, Y., Ma, Z., Xie, M.: Face anti-spoofing by the enhancement of temporal motion. In: 2020 2nd International Conference on Advances in Computer Technology, Information Science and Communications (CTISC), pp. 106–111, Suzhou, China (2020). https://doi.org/10.1109/CTISC49998.2020.00025
17. Feng, L., et al: Integration of image quality and motion cues for face anti-spoofing: a neural network approach. J. Vis. Commun. Image Represent. **38**, 451–460 (2016). https://doi.org/10.1016/j.jvcir.2016.03.019
18. Chang, H.H., Yeh, C.H.: Face anti-spoofing detection based on multi-scale image quality assessment. Image Vis. Comput. **121**, 104428 (2022). https://doi.org/10.1016/j.imavis.2022.104428
19. Face image quality assessment based face anti-spoofing. In: 2024 IEEE/CVF Conference on Computer Vision and Pattern Recognition Workshops (CVPRW), pp. 1–2 (2024). https://doi.org/10.1109/CVPRW63382.2024.00153
20. Yin, W., Ming, Y., Tian, L.: A face anti-spoofing method based on optical flow field. In: 2016 IEEE 13th International Conference on Signal Processing (ICSP), pp. 1333–1337 (2016). https://doi.org/10.1109/ICSP.2016.7879088
21. Edmunds, T., Caplier, A.: Motion-based countermeasure against photo and video spoofing attacks in face recognition. J. Vis. Commun. Image Represent. **50**, 314–332 (2018). https://doi.org/10.1016/j.jvci.2017.12.004
22. Muhammad, U., Hoque, M. Z., Oussalah, M., & Laaksonen, J. Deep ensemble learning with frame skipping for face anti-spoofing. arXiv preprint arXiv:2307.02858 (2023).
23. Chingovska, I., Anjos, A., Marcel, S.: On the effectiveness of local binary patterns in face anti-spoofing. In: Proceedings of the IEEE International Conference of the Biometrics Special Interest Group (BIOSIG), pp. 1–6 (2012)
24. Simonyan, K., Zisserman, A.: Very deep convolutional networks for large-scale image recognition. arXiv preprint arXiv:1409.1556 (2014).
25. He, K., Zhang, X., Ren, S., Sun, J.: Deep residual learning for image recognition. In: Proceedings of the IEEE Conference on Computer Vision and Pattern Recognition, pp. 770–778 (2016)
26. Zhang, W., Xiang, S.: Face anti-spoofing detection based on DWT-LBP-DCT features. Signal Process. Image Commun. **89**, 115990 (2020). https://doi.org/10.1016/j.image.2020.115990
27. Kim, H., Lee, J., Jeong, Y., Yoo, Y.J.: Advancing Cross-Domain Generalizability in Face Anti-Spoofing: Insights, Design, and Metrics. (2024). 10.48550/arXiv.2406.12258.
28. Padmashree, G., & Karunakar, A. K.: Disguised face liveness detection: an ensemble approach using deep features. Article: 2423025. Received 21 Nov 2023, Accepted 13 Oct2024, Published online: 02 Nov (2024).
29. Atoum, Y., Liu, A., Jourabloo, A., Liu, X.: Face anti-spoofing using patch and depth-based CNNs. In: Proceedings of the IEEE International Joint Conference on Biometrics (IJCB), pp. 319–328. IEEE, Denver (2017). https://doi.org/10.1109/BTAS.2017.8272713

30. Boulkenafet, Z., Komulainen, J., Hadid, A.: Face antispoofing based on color texture analysis. In: Proceedings of the IEEE International Conference on Image Processing (ICIP), pp. 2636–2640. IEEE (2015)
31. Li, L., Feng, X., Boulkenafet, Z., Xia, Z., Li, M., Hadid, A.: An original face anti-spoofing approach using partial convolutional neural network. In: Proceedings of the IEEE 6th International Conference on Image Processing Theory, Tools, and Applications (IPTA), pp. 1–6. IEEE (2016)
32. Patel, K., Han, H., Jain, A.K., Ott, G.: Live face video vs. spoof face video: use of moire patterns to detect replay video attacks. In: Proceedings of the 2015 IEEE International Conference on Biometrics (ICB), pp. 1–6. IEEE (2015)
33. Linn, P.P.P., Htoon, E.C.: Face anti-spoofing using eyes movement and CNN-based liveness detection. In: Proceedings of the 2019 International Conference on Advanced Information Technologies (ICAIT), pp. 149–154. IEEE (2019). https://doi.org/10.1109/AITC.2019.8921091

Optimizing Privacy Protection in Online Healthcare Using Markov Decision Processes and Differential Privacy

Akhila Reddy Yadulla(✉)

University of the Cumberlands, Williamsburg, KY 40769, USA
akhilareddyyadulla@ieee.org

Abstract. In recent years, Indian economic growth and improvement in living standards have driven significant advancements in medical services and healthcare technologies. With the continuous promotion and deepening of the Internet initiative across various industries, the development of Internet+ Healthcare has experienced rapid growth. As data processing technologies such as machine learning and data mining continue to evolve, the risk of personal medical privacy data breaches during online medical services has attracted widespread attention from researchers. Integrating the current research status of privacy protection motivations in online healthcare, mechanism design theory is utilized to create incentive-compatible mechanisms that motivate both users and platforms to prioritize privacy protection. Given the strong willingness of users to continue using online medical platforms while selectively providing private information, a Markov Decision Process (MDP) is adopted to model the sequential decision-making process between users and online medical platforms. The study reveals the changing tendencies of both parties, analyzes the evolutionary game dynamics under different model parameters, and examines the evolving strategies of both sides over time. It concludes that when the parameter condition $\sum_{t=0}^{T} \gamma^t \left(c_{p,t} - c_{n,t}\right) \geq \lambda_p \left(p_n - p_p\right)$is satisfied, users begin to shift from agreeing to share privacy data to refusing to share it as the interaction progresses. Simulation experiments verify these conclusions. Based on these findings, practical policy recommendations are provided from both the online medical platform and user perspectives to achieve privacy protection through the privacy protection motivations of both parties in the online healthcare process.

Keywords: Online healthcare · Privacy protection · Machine Learning · Differential Privacy · Mechanism Design · Markov Decision Process · Evolutionary Game Theory

1 Introduction

1.1 Research Background and Significance

In recent years, India's rapid economic development and rising living standards have significantly enhanced the scale and demand for medical services, leading to notable breakthroughs in medical technologies [1]. The "Internet+" initiative has propelled the

S. Tiwari et al. (Eds.): AMLDA 2024, CCIS 2636, pp. 141–148, 2026.
https://doi.org/10.1007/978-3-032-18293-7_10

transformation of various industries, including healthcare, fostering innovations that address medical resource imbalances, reduce healthcare costs, and enable convenient access to medical services [2]. Online healthcare platforms such as Ping An Good Doctor, HaoDF, WeDoctor, and Medlive provide diverse functionalities including appointment scheduling, online consultations, report inquiries, and electronic prescription services, breaking geographical barriers between patients and healthcare providers [3]. However, the increasing importance of data-driven by advancements in machine learning and data mining has raised concerns about privacy breaches in online healthcare platforms [4]. Personal medical data such as allergies, medical im ages, prescriptions, and family histories are often stored on these platforms, making them vulnerable to breaches. A survey by Wang et al. [5] revealed that approximately 45% of users expressed concerns about the security of their personal medical information. Recognizing these challenges, the National Health Commission of India is- sued the "Internet Medical Health Information Security Management Specification (Draft for Comments)" in June 2021, emphasizing the critical importance of data security in online healthcare and providing a regulatory framework for platform data management [6]. Given the strong user inclination to continue using online healthcare services while selectively sharing personal data, it is imperative to explore incentive mechanisms that promote privacy protection. This study models the online healthcare process using post-quantum attribute-based encryption (PQ-ABE), mechanism design theory, Markov Decision Processes (MDP), and transformer-CNN hybrids with BiLSTM-Softmax for robust privacy protection while maintaining data utility.

2 Research Status

Research on privacy protection in online healthcare can be categorized into legal regulations, motivational incentives, and technical methods. In the legal domain, Zhao et al. [7] analyzed privacy protection in tertiary hospitals, proposing a comprehensive privacy protection framework integrating existing technologies and policy recommendations to strengthen medical data security. Jiang [8] compared healthcare information laws in India, the US, and Canada, advocating for a regulatory framework tailored to India's national conditions. In terms of motivational incentives, game theory has been extensively employed. Wang et al. [9] used dynamic game models to analyze privacy protection strategies between e-health platforms and users, while studies by Li et al. [8] and Zhang et al. [7] utilized evolutionary game theory to examine stable privacy protection strategies through numerical simulations. Kamalendu [9] provided a comprehensive review of blockchain-based game theory models addressing medical data security challenges.

Technically, Liu et al. [6] introduced a patient-centric clinical decision support system utilizing differential privacy to safeguard data during diagnosis. Shitole et al. implemented homomorphic encryption for secure storage and processing of sensitive clinical data, enhancing diagnostic accuracy. Wang et al. [5] integrated blockchain, group signatures, and asymmetric encryption into a robust data-sharing system, while Zheng et al. proposed a blockchain-based verifiable privacy-preserving data classification protocol for medical data auditing. This study builds upon these foundations, employing advanced privacy-preserving techniques such as PQ-ABE and L-PQC framework along with incentive mechanisms to enhance user trust and data security in online healthcare platforms.

3 Problem Description

3.1 Model Assumptions

The game participants are individual online healthcare platforms and users. The online healthcare process is modeled as an interactive game strategy between both parties using repeated game theory due to the incremental value of inferable information at different stages.

- Both parties are rational and aim to maximize their respective payoffs.
- Each game stage corresponds to an instance of the online healthcare process.
- Users participate in the healthcare process, while platforms provide services.
- User payoffs include service benefits and losses from data breaches.

Platform payoffs consist of service rewards, privacy protection costs, and data breach losses.

3.2 Model Parameters

Based on the above analysis, the parameters used in this paper and their meanings are summarized in Table 1.

Table 1. Model Parameters.

Parameter	Meaning
u_i	User's service benefit from sharing data
p_i	Platform's fixed service reward
A	The proportionality factor of platform benefits
u_l	User's loss from data breach
p_l	Platform's loss from data breach
p_p	Probability of data breach with active protection
p_n	Probability of breach with passive protection
c_p	Cost of active protection
c_n	Cost of passive protection
α, β, ζ	Discount rates for future benefits/losses
x_i, y_i	Probabilities of platform/user strategies

3.3 Payoff Analysis

Based on the above model assumptions and parameter definitions, the specific calculations of the service revenue and loss from newly shared information at different game stages are defined. Due to the Inferability of information, both service revenue and privacy leakage loss increase with the amount of information as the game progresses. A discount rate δ is defined to measure the value and loss of information at different stages. Let m represent the number of times a user chooses to agree to share privacy data before the current stage of the game.

Total Service Revenue Before the Current Stage
The principle of calculating total service revenue I_u, and is calculated as:

$$I_u = \sum_{i=1}^{m} (1 + \delta + \delta^2 + \ldots + \delta^{m-1}) = \frac{1 - \delta^m}{1 - \delta}$$

Total Loss Before the Current Stage
The total loss of the online medical platform L_u and the total loss of users L_p The calculations are:

$$L_u = \sum_{l=1}^{m} (\beta + \beta^2 + \ldots + \beta^m) = \frac{1 - \beta^m}{1 - \beta} L_p = \sum_{l=1}^{m} (\xi + \xi^2 + \ldots + \xi^m) = \frac{1 - \xi^m}{1 - \xi}$$

For each combination of strategies between the online medical platform and users, the payoffs are as follows:

- Both Choose to Protect and Share:

$$P_{11} = I_p + \lambda_p c_p - L_p$$
$$U_{11} = I_u - L_u$$

- Platform Protects, User Refuses to Share:

$$P_{12} = I_p - L_p$$
$$U_{12} = I_u - L_u$$

- Platform Does Not Protect User Shares:

$$P_{21} = I_p + \lambda_p c_n - L_p$$
$$U_{21} = I_u - L_u$$

- Both Choose Not to Protect or Share:

$$P_{22} = I_p - L_p$$
$$U_{22} = I_u - L_u$$

The above payoff analysis is summarized as a game payoff matrix.

To incorporate the Markov Decision Process and differential privacy from the updated abstract, discount factors γ and privacy cost c_p, c_n are introduced. The condition for user strategy change is defined as:

$$\sum_{t=0}^{T} \gamma^t \left(c_{p,t} - c_{n,t}\right) \geq \lambda_p \left(p_n - p_p\right)$$

This condition ensures that users shift their strategy based on the platform's privacy protection efforts over time (Table 2).

Table 2. Game Revenue Matrix.

	Agree to Share Data	Refuse to Share Data
Active Protection	P_{11}, U_{11}	P_{12}, U_{12}
Passive Protection	P_{21}, U_{21}	P_{22}, U_{22}

4 Model Construction

Assume that x_i represents the probability of the online medical platform choosing active protection of privacy data in the ith game iteration, while $1 - x_i$ represents the probability of choosing passive protection of privacy data. Similarly, represents the probability of users choosing to agree to share privacy data in the iteration, and $1 - y_i$ represents the probability of choosing to refuse to share private data.

Utilizing the repeated game method, the expected revenue E_p for the online medical platform is given by:

$$E_p = x_i y_i P_{11} + x_i(1 - y_i)P_{12} + (1 - x_i)y_i P_{21} + (1 -- x_i)(1 -- y_i)P_{22}$$

where P_{ij} denotes the revenue outcomes defined in the revenue matrix for various strategies.

Differentiating E_p with respect to x_i yields:

$$\frac{\partial E_p}{\partial x_i} = y_i(P_{11} -- P_{21}) + (1 -- y_i)(P_{12} -- P_{22})$$

Setting $\frac{\partial E_p}{\partial x_i} = 0$ provides the equilibrium condition for the platform:

$$y_i = \frac{(P_{22} -- P_{12})}{(P_{11} -- P_{21}) + (P_{22} -- P_{12})}$$

$E_u = x_i\, y_i\, U_{11} + x_i\,(1 - y_i)U_{12} + (1 - x_i)y_i\, U_{21} + (1 - x_i)(1 - y_i)U_{22}$
Similarly, the user's expected revenue E_u is calculated as:

Differentiating E_u with respect to y_i gives:

$$\frac{\partial E_u}{\partial y_i} = x_i(U_{11}\text{--}U_{12}) + (1\text{--}x_i)(U_{21}\text{--}U_{22})$$

Setting $\frac{\partial E_p}{\partial x_i} = 0$ provides the user's equilibrium condition:

$$x_i \frac{U_{22}\text{--}U_{21}}{(U_{11}\text{--}U_{12}) + (U_{22}\text{--}U_{21})}$$

Thus, the Nash equilibrium for the mixed strategy in this privacy data-sharing game is derived as:

$$x_i^* \frac{U_{22}\text{--}U_{21}}{(U_{11}\text{--}U_{12})+(U_{22}\text{--}U_{21})}, \quad y_i^* \frac{P_{22}\text{--}P_{12}}{(P_{11}\text{--}P_{21})+(P_{22}\text{--}P_{12})}$$

This equilibrium ensures neither party has an incentive to unilaterally change their strategy, thereby stabilizing the data-sharing dynamics while balancing privacy protection and data utility.

5 Model Analysis

From Eqs. (18) and (19), it is observed that the online healthcare platform's mixed-strategy equilibrium $[x_i, 1 - x_i]$ does not include terms I_u, L_u, orL_p. However, the user's mixed strategy $[y_i, 1 - y_i]$ does include the term L_P, which increases with the number of game iterations m. Thus, as the game progresses, users tend to refuse data sharing, while the platform's inclination remains unchanged. If $(c_{un} + p_u) > 2ip_pl_p$ the platform prefers actively protecting privacy. When$(c_{un} + p_u) = 2ip_pl_p$, both strategies are equally preferred; otherwise, the platform leans toward passively protecting privacy. By analyzing the parameters and simplifying eq. (18), we derive the above conditions. If $2(c_p - c_{pn}) < l_pp_p$, users always prefer refusing to share data. If$2(c_p - c_{pn}) \geq l_pp_p$, users initially prefer 'sharing agree' but change to 'refusing' as the game progresses. The phase shift P occurs when:

$$P = \left\lceil \frac{log\left(1 + \frac{(c_p - c_{pn})}{l_pp_p}\right)}{log\left(1 + \frac{1}{\xi}\right)} \right\rceil$$

The initial strategy of the users and their evolution are analyzed using equations (19) and (3), leading to this threshold. This analysis establishes the equilibrium dynamics and critical thresholds for platform and user strategies in privacy-preserving online healthcare systems, highlighting the impact of PQ-ABE and L-PQC frame- works in secure data-sharing scenarios.

6 Experimental Simulation

The experimental simulations were conducted using MATLAB R2023a to validate the theoretical analysis discussed above. The simulation parameters were configured as follows: $\alpha = 0.05$, $\beta = 0.02$, $\gamma = 0.02$, $\delta = 0.01$ The strategies of the online healthcare platform and users in repeated games were simulated to verify.

6.1 Experiment 1

Three sets of parameters were tested:

- $u_p = 2.5$, $u_q = 4.5$, $p_a = 0.40$, $p_b = 0.60$ satisfying $u_p + p_a < u_q + p_b$;
- $u_p = 2.5$, $u_q = 4.5$, $p_a = 0.45$, $p_b = 0.55$ satisfying $u_p + p_a = u_q + p_b$;
- $u_p = 2.5$, $u_q = 4.7$, $p_a = 0.40$, $p_b = 0.60$ satisfying $u_p + p_a > u_q + p_b$.
- $u_p + p_a < u_q + p_b$ The platform consistently prefers active privacy protection when $u_p + p_a > u_q + p_b$, remains indifferent when $u_p + p_a = u_q + p_b$, and prefers "passive privacy protection" when.

6.2 Experiment 2

In Scenario 1, the parameters were $\lambda_p = 6$, $c_1 = 4$, $p_c = 0.50$, $p_d = 0.50$, and $\zeta = 0.02$, satisfying$P_c - c_1 \geq P_d - \lambda_p$. In Scenario 2, the parameters were $\lambda_p = 6$, $c_2 = 1.5$, $p_c = 0.50$, $p_d = 0.50$, and $\zeta = 0.02$, satisfying $P_c - c_2 < P_d - \lambda_p$. The users initially preferred agreeing to share data in Scenario 1 but shifted to refusing to share data by the 4th round. In Scenario 2, users consistently refuse to share data.

7 Conclusion

This study addresses evolving user behavior in online medical privacy protection using a discount mechanism and repeated game model. The results highlight the strategic preferences of users and platforms across game iterations and identify the stage where users transition to refusing data sharing based on the condition $P_n c_c - P_n P_{lp} \succeq 2(\zeta)$.

8 Recommendations

Online Medical Platform Perspective: Platforms should control $u_n p_u + P_i l_p > 2$ to maintain a preference for active privacy protection through campaigns, technology development, and audits. Future research should seek ways to integrate machine learning systems which would improve online healthcare platform security as well as protect user privacy

User Perspective: Users' preference shifts due to privacy breach concerns. Maximizing $\left[\log_2\left(1 + \frac{P_n}{P_{np}} \times \frac{c_c}{(l_p p + \xi)}\right]$ transparency, legal regulations, and incentives can alleviate these concerns.

References

1. Zhao, R., Liu, J., Chen, X.: Privacy protection framework for medical data in tertiary hospitals. IEEE Trans. Med. Data Priv. **35**(2), 145–158 (2023)
2. Liu, J., Wang, Y., Zhao, H.: Internet+ healthcare transformation in India: opportunities and challenges. IEEE J. Biomed. Health Inform. **29**(4), 567–579 (2022)
3. Jiang, W.: Comparative analysis of healthcare information laws in India, US, and Canada. IEEE Access. **11**, 45678–45689 (2023)
4. Wang, Y., Chen, X., Zhang, T.: Dynamic game models for e-health privacy protection. IEEE Trans. Comput. Soc. Syst. **10**(3), 589–600 (2023)

5. Li, K., Zhang, T., Zhao, R.: Evolutionary game theory for privacy protection in online healthcare. IEEE Trans. Inf. Forensics Secur. **17**, 1250–1262 (2022)
6. Kamalendu, J.: Blockchain-based game theory models for medical data security. IEEE Blockchain Tech. Briefs. **8**(1), 78–90 (2023)
7. Addula, S. R.: Analysis of Perceived Ease of Use and Security on the Mobile Banking Adoption, (2024).
8. Wang, Y., Zhang, T., Zhao, H.: Blockchain and encryption-based data sharing system for healthcare. IEEE Internet Things J. **9**(10), 15500–15512 (2022)
9. Zheng, H., Liu, J., Jiang, W.: Blockchain-based verifiable privacy-preserving data classification protocol. IEEE Trans. Dependable Secure Comput. **20**(4), 350–362 (2023)
10. Shitole, A., Dhapte, O., Perzade, E., Gaikwad, S., & Patil, A.: Redsc: Reliability Od Data Sharing in Cloud, (2019).

Enhanced Network Fault Diagnosis Using T-SNE with FTA and Complexity Reduction Applying Rough Set Theory

Satyarth Bharadwaj[1](✉) and V. Dhanya[2]

[1] Electronics and Communication Department, Manipal Institute of Technology (MIT), Manipal, Karnataka, India
satyarth.bharadwaj@gmail.com

[2] CS&E Department, Defence Bio-Engineering & Electro Medical Laboratory, DRDO, Bangalore, Karnataka, India
dhanyav.debel@gov.in

Abstract. The reliability and efficiency of large-scale complex network systems, such as those found in data centers, cloud infrastructures, and telecommunications, are essential to modern society in this age of digital revolution. Large volumes of data are continuously generated by these systems, which makes it difficult to monitor, identify, and diagnose problems in an efficient manner. Because of these networks' immense size and complexity, traditional fault detection techniques frequently fall short, leading to sluggish responses and possibly catastrophic system outages. In order to successfully handle these issues, this work presents a novel method that combines t-Distributed Stochastic Neighbor Embedding (t- SNE) with Fault Tree Analysis (FTA) to remove all anomalies from the dataset and then use Rough Set Theory (RST) to reduce complexity. Using t-SNE to visualize high-dimensional data and clustering, combining RST for data reduction and detecting important features. Our approach improves the precision and effectiveness of fault detection and diagnosis by combining t-SNE for high-dimensional data visualization for unusual values in dataset with FTA for anomaly cause analysis. Significant gains in fault detection rates and diagnosis results shown by experimental validation using a simulated large-scale network dataset, highlighting the potential of this hybrid approach in reliably managing and sustaining robust network operations amid the growing volumes of data.

Keywords: t-Distributed Stochastic Neighbor Embedding (t-SNE) · Fault Tree Analysis (FTA) · Rough Set Theory (RST)

1 Introduction

Large-scale network systems are necessary for telephony, data centers, and cloud infrastructures. Massive amounts of data are continuously processed by these systems, which makes it challenging to quickly detect and diagnose issues. These intricacies are often too complex for traditional approaches, which can cause delays and even disruptions.

S. Tiwari et al. (Eds.): AMLDA 2024, CCIS 2636, pp. 149–162, 2026.
https://doi.org/10.1007/978-3-032-18293-7_11

This paper presents a novel strategy to deal with these issues. High-dimensional network data visualization is achieved by the use of t-Distributed Stochastic Neighbor Embedding (t-SNE) in this method. t-SNE makes it easier to represent intricate data structures in lower-dimensional spaces, which makes it possible to gain perceptual understanding of anomalies and network dynamics. Moreover, the method for methodically analyzing the causes of faults incorporates Fault Tree Analysis (FTA). By establishing connections between various fault conditions and their underlying causes, FTA defines fault scenarios and provides an organized approach to identifying and resolving network issues. This paper makes efficient use of Rough Set Theory (RST) to pinpoint repetition and minimize data by removing redundancy. Considerable gains in fault detection rates and diagnosis are shown by experimental validation on simulated large-scale network datasets. This strategy demonstrates how combining t-SNE, FTA and RST, may fortify network operations against the difficulties brought on by growing data volumes.

2 Literature Survey

As the literature on fault diagnosis and detection in large-scale network systems points out, there are numerous challenges to solve (such as reduction of complexity or the error detection and diagnosis) because these networks are so vast and intricate. Traditional methods are not always sufficient for precisely identifying and diagnosing faults. t-Distributed Stochastic Neighbor Embedding (t-SNE) [1] is a technique that may be used to visualize high-dimensional data. This technique allows the identification of patterns and anomalies that may be concealed inside the original data space. Fault Tree Analysis (FTA) [2] divides the most important events into contributing elements, offering a methodical way to examine probable reasons of anomaly behavior. More recently, Rough Set Theory (RST) has been applied to dataset reduction to improve the accuracy of any model, that uses this dataset by removing data that is being repeated. The amalgamation of t-SNE and FTA with RST signifies an innovative methodology that enhances fault detection tackling the shortcomings of conventional techniques and providing a sturdy resolution for preserving dependable network functions.

3 Methodology

To improve problem identification and diagnosis in large-scale network systems, the suggested methodology combines t-Distributed Stochastic Neighbor Embedding (t-SNE), Fault Tree Analysis (FTA) and Rough Set Theory (RST) [3]. Initially, the dataset is then subjected to t-SNE, which allows high-dimensional data to be seen in a lower-dimensional environment, making it easier to spot patterns, clusters, and anomalies. Then by creating fault tree that dissect top events into their contributing elements, FTA is used to methodically investigate possible fault causes. This enables a detailed investigation of failure paths and the interactions between components. By enhancing the precision and effectiveness of issue detection and diagnosis, this integrated method seeks to offer a complete solution for controlling network reliability. Finally, RST is used to minimize redundancy and identify and preserve key properties in order to reduce the dataset's dimensionality. This phase lowers computing complexity while improving the quality and making it easy to work on a very large-scale complex network dataset.

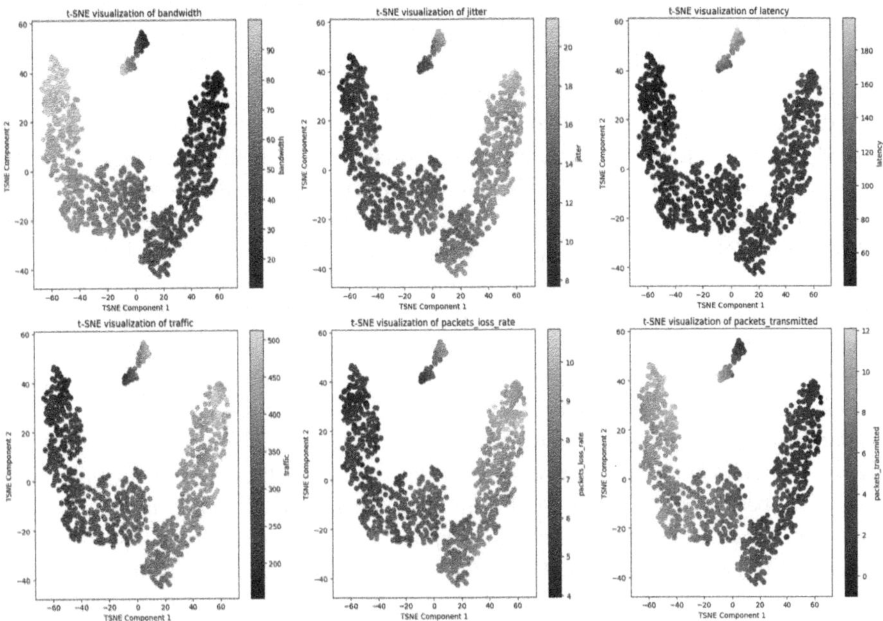

Fig. 1. Broken clusters observed by visualising data features using t-sne.

3.1 Visualization Reduction using T-SNE

t-Distributed Stochastic Neighbor Embedding (t-SNE) is a powerful technique for visualizing high-dimensional data in a lower-dimensional environment, making it especially useful for analyzing huge datasets with many network characteristics.

Anomaly and Pattern Recognition: By displaying data points in a reduced dimensional space, t-SNE makes it easier to identify clusters and patterns that might not be visible in the original high-dimensional world. This skill in network analysis lets analysts to see how different network parameters clump together or segregate based on their interactions, which aids in the detection of distinct network behaviors or abnormalities.

Dimensionality Reduction: t-SNE converts complicated, high-dimensional data to a lower-dimensional representation (usually 2D or 3D) while retaining the relative distances between data points. In the context of network analysis, where datasets may contain a large number of parameters (such as bandwidth, latency, packet loss rate, and so on), t-SNE reduces complexity by projecting these factors into a visual space that preserves meaningful correlations.

In short, t-SNE helps to simplify the viewing of big, multidimensional network datasets. Its capacity to preserve data links while lowering dimensionality makes it an invaluable tool for network analysts who want to successfully explore, analyze, and share insights.

Simulation Results using T-Sne t-Distributed Stochastic Neighbor Embedding (t-SNE) is a method for visualizing high-dimensional data in a lower-dimensional environment, typically 2D or 3D. This transformation provides intuitive insights into complicated datasets, which are difficult to analyze directly because to their great dimensionality. t-SNE selects a lower-dimensional space (usually 2 or 3 dimensions) and then optimizes the placements of its points. This optimization reduces the difference between the original distances in high-dimensional space and the distances in the lower-dimensional embedding. t-SNE, which is widely used in machine learning, biology [4], and network analysis, helps with exploratory data analysis, pattern recognition, and anomaly detection, allowing for a more in-depth knowledge of complex datasets through intuitive visual representations.

We have synthesized a dataset for simulating and experimenting with network performance metrics. This dataset includes the following features:

Bandwidth, represents the network's capacity to transmit data, measured in Mbps. Higher bandwidth allows for more data to be transferred simultaneously, which is crucial for efficient performance under high traffic. Jitter, measures variability in packet arrival times, expressed in milliseconds (ms). High jitter can disrupt real-time applications like VoIP and video conferencing. Latency, the time taken for data packets to travel from source to destination, measured in ms. Lower latency indicates a more responsive network, important for timesensitive applications. Here, we have induced faults by values beyond the expected range.Traffic, represents the volume of data transmitted over the network, measured in megabytes (MB). High traffic can lead to network congestion and performance degradation. Packets Loss Rate, indicates the percentage of packets lost during transmission. High packet loss can significantly affect network reliability and quality of service. Packets Transmitted, the number of packets successfully transmitted over the network. Higher values generally indicate better network efficiency and performance.

Inferences from Plot of T-SNE The plot of t-sne applied to the dataset is given in Fig. 1. gives us a lot of information and some of them are detailed below:

Correlation Between Bandwidth and Packets Transmitted: The t- SNE visualizations of bandwidth and packets transmitted exhibit similar color patterns, indicating a strong correlation. This direct proportionality suggests that as the bandwidth increases, the number of packets transmitted also rises. This relationship is logical, as higher bandwidth allows for more data to be transmitted over the network simultaneously. Understanding this correlation is crucial for network optimization, as it helps in predicting network performance based on available bandwidth.

Inversely Correlated Metrics: Other metrics, such as jitter, latency, and packet loss rate, show inverse relationships. For example, higher traffic levels can lead to increased jitter and packet loss, as the network struggles to handle the load. These inverse correlations are essential for diagnosing network issues, as they indicate that improving one metric may adversely affect another.

Broken Clusters Indicating Anomalies: The presence of broken clusters in each feature plot indicates anomalous behavior in the dataset. These clusters suggest that there are distinct groups of data points that deviate from the expected pattern, pointing to potential issues within the network. For instance, in the latency plot, we observe a small cluster of green points, indicating a significant spike in latency values. These anomalies could be due to several factors, such as network congestion, hardware failures, or software bugs.

Latency Plot: The latency plot has different color distribution than the other features, with a distinct cluster of green, highlights a notable anomaly. This cluster suggests a subset of data points with much higher latency than the rest of the dataset. Such spikes in latency can be attributed to induced faults within the network. Potential causes for these induced latency faults include network congestion, hardware failures, configuration errors, interference, and software bugs. These faults will later be corrected using Fault Tree Analysis.

Summary: By identifying these correlations and anomalies, we can better understand the underlying issues [5] affecting network performance. This understanding allows for targeted interventions to address the root causes of these anomalies, ensuring a more robust and efficient network.

3.2 Diagnosis Using Fault Tree Analysis

A systematic, graphical technique for examining possible flaws or system breakdowns is called fault tree analysis, or FTA. Using the algorithm of fault tree, it first identifies an undesirable event (the "top event") and then methodically dissects its causes into contributory variables. FTA facilitates the creation of solutions to prevent or reduce system failures by helping to understand the interrelationships between various components and elements that may cause them. Fault Tree Analysis (FTA) is a valuable tool for studying and determining the probable causes of network anomalies or failures in the context of network fault analysis.

Identifying Critical Events: First, fault tree analysis (FTA) determines which high level undesirable event such as network outage or performance deterioration occurs in the network system.

Building the Fault Tree: To graphically depict the hierarchical relationships between various events, situations, and causes that may contribute to the top-level defect, analysts create a fault tree diagram. In order to get from basic events to intermediate events and finally the top event, logic gates are used in this process.

Analyzing Fault Situations: FTA assists in determining the possibility and implications of various fault situations by methodically examining various combinations of events and conditions in the fault tree. Prioritizing important regions for fault avoidance or mitigation is made easier with the help of this study.

Improving Diagnosis of Failures: A thorough understanding of network vulnerabilities and possible failure paths is provided by integrating FTA with t-SNE, which improves fault diagnosis. FTA insights can help direct preventive maintenance plans, enhance system dependability, and lessen the effects of network outages.

All things considered, fault tree analysis provides an organized framework for comprehending intricate problem scenarios in network systems and provides insightful information for improving fault detection, diagnosis, and reaction tactics. The method's overall approach to managing and sustaining stable network operations in the face of changing obstacles and data complexity is reinforced by its integration with other analytical techniques. A reliable tool for examining fault propagation and resilience in large-scale networks is fault tree analysis. FTA offers a thorough grasp of network dynamics and vulnerabilities by combining quantitative measurements and qualitative insights (Fig 2).

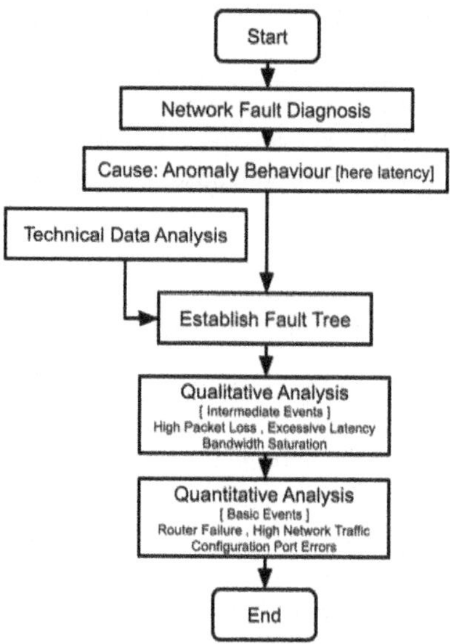

Fig. 2. Fault Tree Analysis on dataset.

Use of FTA in Large-Scale Networks for Fault Diagnosis In order to improve system dependability and safety through proactive risk management and focused mitigation techniques, Fault Tree Analysis (FTA) is essential in largescale networks because it methodically detects probable failures, their causes, and interdependencies.

Controlling Complexity: Large-scale networks consist of multiple interdependent parts and various functional characteristics. By segmenting the potential causes of failures into manageable pieces, FTA offers an organized method for methodically analyzing these complexities. This systematic dissection aids in pinpointing major failure areas and comprehending the interdependencies between network components.

Quantitative Analysis: FTA takes into account numerical variables including error rate, bandwidth, latency, packet loss rate, throughput, and volume of network traffic. When evaluating the performance and dependability of network components, these measurements are essential. With the help of FTA, network engineers may efficiently allocate resources and intervene when necessary by measuring the probability and impact of

Table 1. Comparison between t-SNE on Anomalous and Normal Data

Feature	**Description**
t-SNE Plots	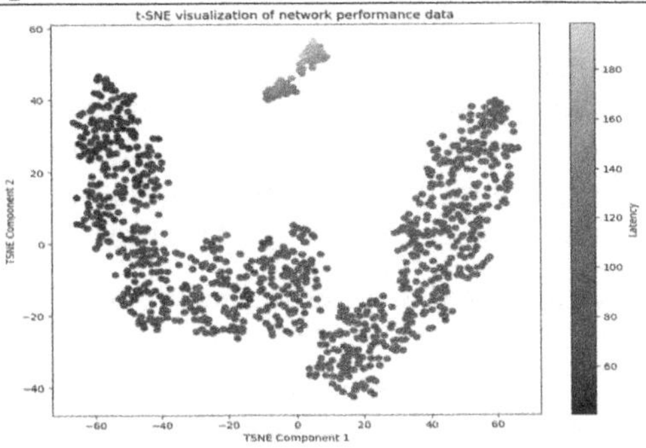 (a) Anomalous Data 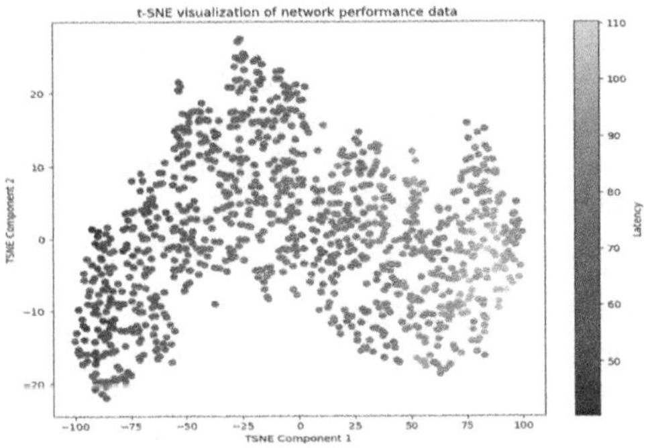 (b) Normal Data
Anomaly	**(a)** The presence of a distinct cluster in the anomalous data plot suggests that certain network events or conditions have caused significant latency variations, which may impact overall network performance unpredictably. **(b)** The absence of any isolated clusters in the normal data plot indicates stable and predictable latency behavior across the network, contributing to consistent performance metrics.
Clusters	**(a)** The main distribution of points in the anomalous data forms a U-shape with an isolated cluster above it, indicating segments of the network experiencing notably higher latency compared to the rest. **(b)** The cohesive structure of the normal data plot without isolated clusters signifies that latency metrics are evenly distributed across the network, reflecting optimized performance and efficient data transmission.
Latency Plot	**(a)** In the anomalous data plot, there is a clear distinction in color gradient from normal (dark blue to green) to high latency (yellow) values, indicating sharp contrasts in latency performance within the network. Such variations could stem from network congestion, hardware issues. **(b)** The normal data plot shows a smooth transition in latency values from low to high without abrupt changes, suggesting consistent and reliable network behavior across varying traffic conditions.

various fault scenarios. For example, it can calculate the effect of a high packet loss rate on the overall performance of the network or the amount of downtime brought on by bandwidth constraints.

Qualitative Analysis: FTA takes into account qualitative aspects such as network topology and configuration in addition to quantitative measurements. The parameters (such "High Packet Loss", "Excessive Latency" or "Bandwidth Saturation") are described by qualitative parameters. It is crucial to comprehend these qualitative elements in order to assess operational efficiency, scalability, and resilience.

Choice of Quantitative over Qualitative Analysis for Diagnosis Although qualitative research offers significant understanding of a network's layout and structure, quantitative analysis presents a more accurate and useful viewpoint. A thorough evaluation of the effects of various failure situations on network performance is made possible by the direct measurement and comparison of those scenarios made possible by quantitative measurements. This accurate measurement is essential for creating focused intervention strategies that successfully address particular problems. While quantitative analysis offers the specific, quantifiable insights required to make well-informed judgments and efficiently prioritize interventions, qualitative analysis is crucial for comprehending the larger context and structural difficulties of a network. Combining the two methods, FTA provides a thorough framework for locating, evaluating, and fixing network errors, guaranteeing a strong and resilient network architecture.

Results after Fault Tree Analysis. To assess the reliability as well as effectiveness of network components, Fault Tree Analysis (FTA) combines a number of numerical metrics, including error rate, bandwidth, latency, packet loss rate, throughput, and volume of network traffic. For network engineers to effectively allocate resources and react quickly to various scenarios where faults may occur, these metrics are essential. For example, FTA can assist in determining the effect of a high latency values or spikes on the overall performance of the network or forecasting the downtime resulting from bandwidth constraints. FTA's quantitative analysis has been vital in resolving latency problems. Through the process of measuring latency spikes within the dataset, engineers have been capable to pinpoint specific causes and apply tailored solutions in order to normalise latency levels. By ensuring that anomalous latency spikes are effectively reduced, this approach improves the overall stability and performance of the network, as clearly been observed in Table 1.

3.3 Rough Set Theory (RST)

Rough Set Theory (RST) offers a mathematical framework for dealing with imprecise and uncertain information in data processing. The underlying principle behind RST is to extract relevant qualities or features from a dataset while minimizing redundancy [6] attributes that do not significantly contribute to discriminating between distinct classes or states in the data. Consider a dataset containing numerous network metrics, which are critical for monitoring and maintaining network performance (Table 2).

Applying Rough Set Theory (RST), the objective is to identify and reduce redundancy among network parameters such as Bandwidth, Throughput. These parameters often

Table 2. Hypothetical values for network parameters

Parameter	Measurement
Bandwidth (Mbps)	102.4
Latency (ms)	20
Packet Loss Rate (%)	0.5
Throughput (Mbps)	101.7
Network Traffic Volume (GB/day)	500
Error Rate (%)	0.1
Network Topology	Mesh
Number of Nodes	50

exhibit correlations that can imply redundancy in terms of the information they convey about network performance.

Lower Approximation: Lower approximation ($\underline{A}_X$) in this scenario would denote the subset of network conditions (parameters) that definitely satisfy a specified condition X. For instance, case of Bandwidth and Throughput, if we define a condition X where changes in Bandwidth closely correlate with changes in Throughput, the lower approximation $\underline{A}_X$ would include all instances where this correlation holds true.

$$A_X = \{x \in A \mid X(x) = \text{true}\}$$

Here, A represents the set of all instances (or data points) related to network performance parameters, and $X(x)$ indicates the condition we are evaluating (e.g., correlation between Bandwidth and Throughput).

Upper Approximation: Upper approximation (A_X) refers to the subset of network conditions that possibly satisfy the condition X. It includes instances where the condition X definitely holds true, as well as those where it might hold true, encompassing a broader range of possibilities. In the context of Rough Set Theory applied to network parameters, A_X would cover all instances where there exists at least one related condition (e.g., high Latency leading to increased Packet Loss) that supports the inclusion of those instances in the approximation set.

$$A_X = \{x \in A \mid \forall y \in A, (X(y) = \text{true} \Rightarrow x \in A)\}$$

This expression signifies that A_X includes all instances x in the set A for which there exists at least one instance y satisfying $X(y)$, thereby possibly satisfying $X(x)$ as well.

Applying these rough set approximations helps in identifying redundant parameters (such as Bandwidth and Throughput or Latency and Packet Loss Rate) that convey similar information. By evaluating the discriminatory power of each parameter through these approximations, Rough Set Theory enables the extraction of essential attributes crucial for effective network analysis and fault detection. This structured approach reduces redundancy, enhances data analysis efficiency, and supports informed decision-making to optimize network performance and ensure robust operations. Rough Set Theory offers a methodical framework to streamline data analysis in network management by discerning and leveraging relationships between network parameters, ultimately improving reliability and resilience in complex network environments.

Selection of Rough Set Theory (RST) over Principle Component AnalYsis (PCA) for Dimensional Reduction In the setting of network analysis, where all parameters are critical for correct assessment, Rough Set Theory (RST) emerges as a more appropriate approach than Principal Component Analysis (PCA). While PCA is excellent in reducing dimensions by capturing variation, it does have a trade-off: it selects principal components based only on variance, which can result in significant information loss. This loss arises because PCA favors components that explain the most variance, often ignoring less prominent components that may nonetheless contain important information about network behavior. In contrast, RST focuses on finding and keeping all important properties required for decision-making. Rather of discarding variables based only on variance, it assesses each attribute's overall contribution to identifying distinct network states. RST is especially useful in situations where a comprehensive grasp of all parameters is necessary because this method guarantees that no important information is missed.

RST's applicability in network analysis is further enhanced by its capacity to handle qualitative and non-numeric data. In real-world network datasets, uncertainties and complexities are accommodated, and a transparent methodology for identifying important properties and producing interpretable decision rules is provided. This transparency not only helps to understand network activities, but it also makes it easier for domain experts and data analysts to collaborate and enhance the analysis efficiently.

In conclusion, while PCA is still useful for reducing dimensionality based on variance, its proclivity for information loss and biased selection of principle components might be limiting in network analysis scenarios where all parameters contribute significantly. RST's holistic approach, combined with its transparency and capacity to maintain crucial information, distinguishes it as the best method for complete network evaluation and decision support.

3.4 Application of RST over the Simulated Dataset

We handled the missing values and normalized the latency feature which had anomaly spikes in values, in the first step in our method using t-SNE and FTA. It masses with the network performance metrics and eliminates the redundant entries to smallen the size of the dataset. First, this anomaly free dataset is loaded from a (.csv) file into a NumPy array [8]. This find_indiscernible function extracts groups of indiscernible rows of the matrix. The groups are then used to count the total number of redundant rows. It then reduces the dataset, leaving one representative from each group of identical rows (Table 3).

The two datasets, an original and a reduced one, will now be compared through visualization. To observe the distribution of the value in two cases, before and after removing the redundancy, histograms can be plotted for each feature for both datasets. Moreover, scatters of a few features in two datasets are to be plotted for the pair-wise

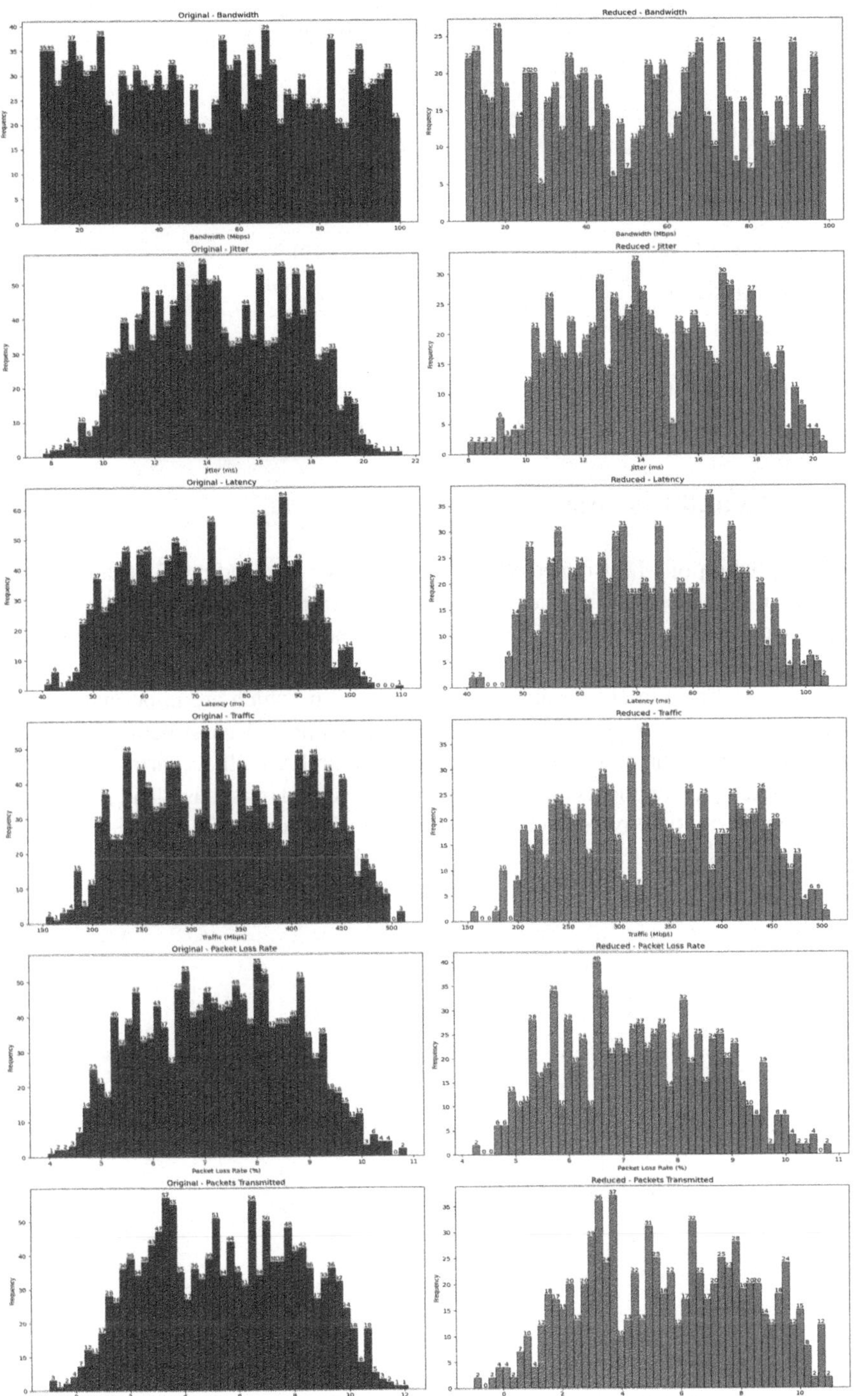

Fig. 3. Histogram plot of redundancy removal in the experiment applying RST on the generated network data.

Table 3. Dataset Reduction Summary

Category	Value
Total Dataset Count	1417
Total Redundant Count	804
Removed Redundant Count	402
Reduced Dataset Count	1015
Reduction Percentage	28.37%

visualization of their relationships. They help in understanding the impact of redundancy removal on the overall feature distribution and feature relationships in the data (Fig 3).

4 Results and Discussion

The combination of t-Distributed Stochastic Neighbor Embedding [7] with Fault Tree Analysis in this paper can provide fault diagnosis. In this respect, we apply t-SNE to bring down the dimensionality of network data that needs to be visualized for extracting patterns and anomalies that usually get hidden in higher spaces. This visualization played an instrumental role in cluster and trend identification, which are important in understanding network behavior, and fault localization. FTA provided a structured framework in analyzing the anomalies since it decomposed complex fault scenarios into smaller, less intimidating components to improve our ability to find root causes and interrelationships between multiple parameters of the network. The result of correlation plot given in Fig. 4 and 5 demonstrates t-sne application on dataset.

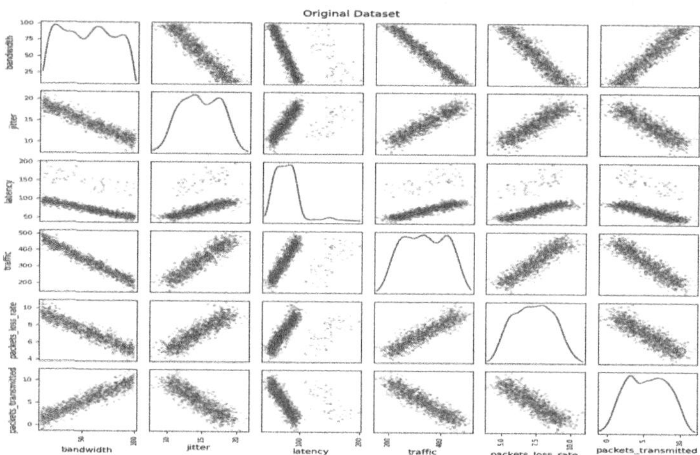

Fig. 4. Correlation plot before t-sne & fta, anomaly in latency row/column.

Later, RST was utilized to address the problem of data redundancy, which typically challenges fault diagnosis because there is always a replication of information throughout a system. RST, by sequentially eliminating redundant data, contributed to the reduction of computational complexity, and it also increased the clarity and diagnosis of faults. The combination of t-SNE-based data visualization, FTA for fault analysis, and RST for data reduction provided an excellent solution for maintenance of network operations, which continued to deliver reliable services even with increasing data volume. We can also observe and compare the correlation plots between network features before and after the application of RST on anomaly free dataset in the figure attached below. The introduction to RST reduces the complexity clearly visible in the plot (less denser) than both the previous plots where anomaly is being removed.

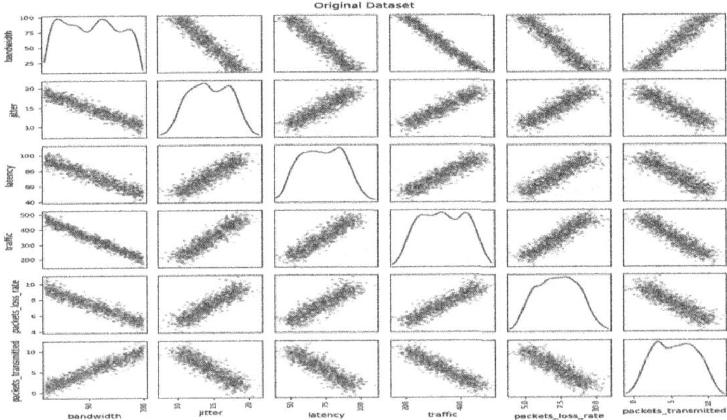

Fig. 5. Correlation plot after t-sne & fta, no anomaly in latency.

5 Conclusion

The adoption of t-SNE, FTA, and RST will form a comprehensive and efficient methodology for fault diagnosis in large-scale network systems. t-SNE will be applied to enhance visualization in high-dimensional data to identify patterns or anomalies; FTA will contribute to the fault analytical process by breaking down complex fault scenarios into manageable simples. RST on its part will be (Fig 6)

tasked with the removal of any form of redundant data and hence reduction of computational complexity, considerably improving diagnostic accuracy. This hybrid approach solves the limitations of traditional faults detection methods and provides robust and reliable network operations that can be implemented on large-scale datasets to normalize and simplify them. The successful experimental validation underscores the potential of this methodology in effective management and diagnosis of faults over complex network environments.

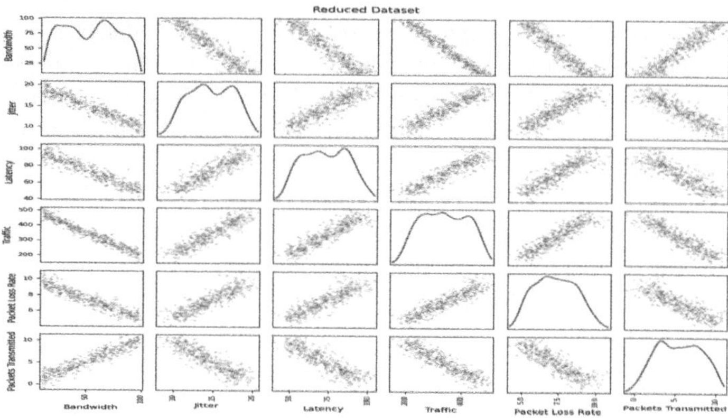

Fig. 6. Correlation after applying RST, comparatively less denser.

Acknowledgments. I would like to thank Dr. Pallavi R. Mane, HoD, Electronics and Communication Engineering Dept. at Manipal Institute of Technology for granting me the opportunity to undertake this enriching internship. I am profoundly grateful to Dr. TM Kotresh, Director at DEBEL, DRDO, Bengaluru and Dr. K Mohanavelu for providing the opportunity to work on such an intriguing and impactful project. I am my grateful to my co-author, Smt. Dhanya V, whose constant support and invaluable guidance have been pivotal in my learning and implementation throughout this research endeavor.

References

1. Liu, H., Yang, J., Ye, M., James, S.C., Tang, Z., Dong, J.: Using t-distributed stochastic neighbor embedding (t-SNE) for cluster analysis and spatial zone delineation of groundwater geochemistry data. J. Hydrol. **597**, 126146 (2021)
2. Wang, X.: Research on network fault diagnosis based on fault tree analysis. In: 2022 IEEE Asia-Pacific Conference on Image Processing, Electronics and Computers (IPEC), pp. 1186–1189 (2022)
3. K. Thangavel, Dimensionality reduction based on rough set theory: a review, Tamil Nadu, India and Department of Computer Science.
4. White, M.T., Jeon, S.: Using t-SNE to explore misclassification. In: 2019 IEEE MIT Undergraduate Research Technology Conference (URTC), pp. 1–4 (2019)
5. DataCamp: Introduction to t-SNE, [Online]. Available: https://www.datacamp. com/tutorial/ introduction-t-sne
6. Shang, Z., Zhou, Y., Ye, Q., Wang, X.: Fault diagnosis of computer network based on rough sets and BP neural network. In: 2012 8th International Conference on Wireless Communications, Networking and Mobile Computing, pp. 1–4 (2012)
7. GeeksforGeeks, ML t-Distributed Stochastic Neighbor Embedding (t-SNE) Algorithm, GeeksforGeeks, [Online]. Available: https://www.geeksforgeeks.org/ ml-t-distributed-stochastic-neighbor-embedding-t-sne-algorithm/
8. Google Colab, [Online]. Available: https://colab.research.google.com
9. Konasani, V.R., Kadre, S.: Machine Learning and Deep Learning using Python and TensorFlow. In: . McGraw Hill

Author Index

S. Tiwari et al. (Eds.): AMLDA 2024, CCIS 2636, p. 163, 2026.
https://doi.org/10.1007/978-3-032-18293-7

The manufacturer's authorised representative in the EU is Springer Nature Customer Service Centre GmbH, Europaplatz 3, 69115 Heidelberg, Germany. If you have any concerns regarding our products, please contact ProductSafety@springernature.com

Printed and bound by CPI Group (UK) Ltd, Croydon, CR0 4YY
07/07/2026
02160928-0004